Song of Freedom

My Journey from the Abyss

Judith K. Moore

Cover art by Rush Cole
Photographs, drawings and poems by Judith K. Moore

ISBN 891824-38-4

Published by
**Light Technology
Publishing**
P.O. Box 3540
Flagstaff, AZ 86003
1-800-450-0985
email: publishing@lighttechnology.net
www.lighttechnology.com

Printed by
SEDONA COLOR GRAPHICS
PRINTING SPECIALISTS
P.O. Box 3540
Flagstaff, AZ 86003

I lovingly dedicate this book
to all souls who have known bondage and
struggled for freedom of their minds, bodies and spirits.
I also dedicate this work to Una Marie
and her journey of healing.

Contents

Acknowledgments

I thank my healers who had the dedication and the courage to make this journey with me. I acknowledge my dear friends who are companion survivors. They are the most courageous people imaginable. We have struggled together for freedom; I have a deep respect for each of these special souls.

And there are those who did not survive this atrocity: the missing children, the ones who have died unnoticed. I wish to acknowledge the wounded, the lost and the fearful. I send prayers and acknowledge all the ones who tried to make the journey and turned back. I honor the pain they live with.

Thank you to the many courageous professionals who risked their professions and reputations to bring these truths to the light. Many have suffered dearly for their convictions of truth.

I wish to honor my parents—courageous, loving people who taught me never to turn my back on my fellow man and to love and honor Mother Earth. I thank my children and grandchildren whose love has filled my life with joy. I single out one brave woman who has suffered from the aftereffects of the abuse she endured before I adopted her. She is my daughter, Denise. I entered recovery because I so desperately wanted to help my wounded child. I have always told her that she is my teacher.

I couldn't have made the journey without my former husband's support. He was my healer, my teacher and my friend. As a Sun dancer, he personally gave so much that made it possible.

I wish to acknowledge two dedicated professionals, the first women ever to read my story: my transcriber and my editor. Thank you for your gifts and the love you gave the project.

I wish to acknowledge my family of origin, those who remembered and those who did not, for their good hearts and dedication to honor and freedom.

Thank you to my housemates, who took care of me while I worked to create this book. Your encouragement and spiritual gifts are real treasures. Thank you to my husband, Randy, for all the times you held me in your arms and encouraged me. You have given me such a precious gift— your love.

I face the four directions and offer my prayers in thanksgiving to the Tunkashilas—my spirit helpers, Quanab, Laiolin, Lantru, St. Michael, the Guardian of the Kingdom of Minerals, Mother Cabrini and White Buffalo

Calf Pipe Woman. Throughout the manuscript I refer to Quanab as my guide and Laiolin as the cosmic being of light or my celestial angel. I thank the angels and archangels as well as my animal guides who have been with me from birth. I stand and honor the Sun dancers and all of the ones who pour water in the sweatlodge purification ceremonies.

Thank you, Wakan Tanka, Great Mystery.
You have made the world beautiful.
I am your daughter. You have brought my feet on the good red road.
You have taught me to pray and honor Earth Mother.
Mitakyue Oyasin (all my relations).

Foreword

Stephen Sachs
September 11, 2002

Ya Nur – Ya Salaam (Invoking Light – Invoking Peace)

> *In these times*
> *even our sacred spaces*
> *are invaded*
> *by negativity.*
> *We have to fight*
> *to clear them,*
> *not by the sword,*
> *but with the heart.*
> *Deep within our own beings,*
> *we have to call*
> *upon the light of peace*
> *to transform ourselves*
> *and the world.*

This book is a story of a journey toward freedom for all of us. It is about being victorious over evil by transforming it in ourselves and in society. It is about transforming fear into love realistically, to deal with people and conditions as they are, for the long-run good of everyone concerned. It is a testament to the principle that we cannot truly be pragmatic without being spiritual, whether we consider we are being so or not, by respecting the sacredness of all people, indeed of all beings.

To me, evil is action that is out of balance, that becomes so narrowly focused in achieving one set of goals that the actor fails to see (or care) that s/he is working contrary to other equally or more important ends. Often evil is undertaken out of greed (for wealth, power, pleasure, etc.). Inevitably, it is pursued out of fear, of which greed is one of many aspects. For it is only out of fear of deprivation that healthy drives to have enough— of food, love, wealth, security—become twisted to become insatiable. This is not to say that fear is not a natural and useful emotion. When we step off a curb and a car is bearing down on us, fear energies us to jump out of the way. But when people are caught up in fear, they magnify dangers out of proportion to their seriousness and see them where they do not exist. This may lead individuals to perpetrate violence on the innocent and citizens to empower governments to implement needless repression. When citizens are overcome with fear, they are in danger of being manipulated by insecure politicians, motivated by their greed for wealth and/or power. When this happens on a large scale, the freedom and well-being of everyone is at risk.

In an imperfect world, it is proper for individuals, communities and governments to have reasonable concerns about security and to take appropriate measures to provide a healthy measure of it. Unfortunately, fear too often drives people, organizations and nations to be so obsessed with security that they do a great deal of unnecessary harm while doing little, if anything, to enhance security. In worst-case scenarios, actions undertaken for the purpose of security end up creating a great deal of insecurity.

A good example of this occurred in the United States during World War I. Although there was no evidence that more than a handful of the country's residents might do anything to interfere with the war effort, even if exhorted to do so, a variety of laws were passed and so loosely interpreted that constructive criticism of the government's handling of the conflict was suppressed. A man skeptical of the efficiency of the Red Cross, seeing a group of women knitting socks for soldiers at the front, was jailed for saying, "No soldier will see those socks." Patriots who argued that it would be fiscally better for the U.S. to finance the war by raising taxes than by borrowing money, lost their jobs and were imprisoned on the grounds that if people believed them, they would not buy Liberty Bonds, although there was no evidence that this might occur. If a significantly large number of people had come to agree, could not Congress have raised taxes?

The worst case was in Minnesota, where committees of bankers required residents to provide statements of their earnings. On the basis of those statements, the bankers required those people to buy so many bonds that they had to borrow from the committee members' banks in order to do so. Moreover, the loans required payment of a higher rate of interest then the bonds paid. Yet when anyone complained or refused to cooperate, they were prosecuted under a Minnesota sedition statute. When banks began foreclosing on people for failure to pay, the atmosphere in the state became explosive. The U.S. Justice Department estimated that if the war had lasted another year, Minnesota's security legislation would have created a rebellion.

Unfortunately, the United States has a long history of overreacting to concerns of national security, often with prejudicial repression that is especially damaging to members of the target group but ultimately costly for the entire population. The World War II "detention" of more than 110,000 people of Japanese ancestry, most of them U.S. citizens and none of whom were ever seriously suspected of any disloyal act, is well-known.

This volume brings to light one of a number of terribly misguided sets of "national security" actions carried out by the government and the military during the Cold War, a particularly dangerous time because it lasted for so many years. Today, a year after the attacks on the World Trade Center and the Pentagon, we are again in a protracted period, where actions taken in the name of "national security" have gotten out of hand. Thus it behooves us to respond to what Judith Moore tells us in these pages, that we as citizens act to keep government security efforts in proper balance, with a broad understanding that in these times national security involves social, economic and environmental security, as well as appropriate action to prevent violent actions.

Perhaps the most important thing that Judith tells us here is that it is even more important *how* we respond—than *that* we respond—if we are to break out of the consciousness of fear that brings about abuse and repression in the name of security. It is good if we are sufficiently outraged to work to stop this kind of abuse. But if we become locked into "getting the perpetrators," we will only continue the cycle of inhumanity. The key to transformation is to focus on the humanity of everyone concerned in seeking a more enlightened approach. We need to learn from our mistakes as individuals, as communities and as a nation, while doing whatever is appropriate to redress injuries and insure better policies in the future. By proceeding always out of mutual respect, we can achieve healing while striving constantly for harmony and balance.

Steven Sachs is Professor Emeritus of Political Science at IUPUI. He has been involved in working for peace and justice for many years, serving as co-editor of Nonviolent Change *and co-coordinator of the Research/Study on Nonviolent Large Systems Change since 1985. He has twice served on the board of the Consortium on Peace Research, Education and Change (COPRED), and is a member of the intern board of the Peace and Justice Studies Association, recently formed by the merger of COPRED and the Peace Studies Association (PSA). With a special focus on justice for American Indians and indigenous people around the planet, he is co-editor of* Native American Policy *and coordinator of the Native American Studies Association.*

Introduction

Welcome to a journey of discovery. I write these words on my fifty-second birthday to fulfill the promise I made to myself years ago: to tell the story of my childhood experiences when I was abducted by the United States covert government and used in a program of human experimentation and mind control. This kind of programming creates a fear wall in the psyche that many people do not get past. But I did. Illuminating my journey to healing and deprogramming are entries from the journals I faithfully recorded over a period of nine years.

Within these pages lie truths untold and rarely believed. The general public has been given little opportunity to explore these truths. We live in a country that permits free speech; many of our ancestors gave their lives for this right. But even though our country acknowledges the right of free speech, wide disclosure of secrets that would shake the foundation of the controlling forces of the covert government is, to put it mildly, not encouraged. I hope my story will help to open your minds and hearts, that it will bring healing for this nation and for the Earth I love so dearly.

To tell you the truth, I found this all hard to believe myself. Until I was forty years old, I had no idea that I was a survivor of human experimentation and mind control. I lived my life completely unconscious of what had happened to me as a child. Later on I will describe for you some of what I knew of my "conscious life."

My journey of discovery has spanned over a decade. I was fortunate to be assisted by many caring professionals who were wise enough not to interfere with the process but gave me the support to make the journey. I recovered the memories through journeywork, a Jungian-type experience in which I meditated, went to a safe place and was sent by my guides to what I needed to know for my higher good. I literally relived every memory. I reexperienced the agony through body memories: incredibly intense sensations accompanied by flashbacks of the experience. I learned to use my breath to open up the blocked energy. I learned that no matter how bad the pain was during the memory, I could breathe through it and it would release. I hadn't realized how much I had always held my breath. I also learned to drink lots of water to flush my cells after a memory.

I do not believe that merely remembering brings healing. There are keys to healing. Remembering was important, but clearing the energy and healing my inner fragmented children were major keys for me. Another key was forgiveness. Jesus Christ said, "Father, forgive them, for they know not what they do." Complete forgiveness is absolutely vital to freedom. Forgiving one's self sets one free from the bondage of guilt. As long as we see ourselves as victims, we *are* victims. Self-forgiveness begins when we accept that we were victimizers as well as victims. We can then forgive ourselves and ask to be forgiven. Guilt is a shackle that binds the soul; self-forgiveness brings freedom from guilt and control.

As I struggled through years of intense recovery, deprogramming and healing from this atrocity, I promised myself that if I could ever contribute to bringing the truth to the light, to exposing it in some credible way, I would do it. This book fulfills the promise I made myself.

When society denies a truth this dark and devastating, it can continue, but when the general public realizes the truth, it really comes home to their hearts. They won't tolerate it; the consciousness of the group will make a change for the better. (Let's qualify the word "dark." All dark is not evil; all light is not good. Life is not that simple. "Dark" is a word used to describe a dense energy vibration based in fear. "Light" is a word that describes a high-vibrational energy that is based in love.)

The brave people in the civil rights movement served to awaken the conscience of society during the fifties and sixties. Through their lives, through their truths, through the way they stood for their freedom, we all started to realize that we could no longer dehumanize other people in that way. The consciousness of a relatively small group of people awakened a nation to the fact that the laws restricting the freedom of our fellow human beings were wrong, and things changed. No, it isn't perfect, but when Rosa Parks had the courage to sit on that bus that day, she changed the world. She helped us to feel what it was like for a tired elderly woman to stand while a "white" seat was empty. She claimed her seat and her place in history. Many courageous people worked to make the change, but in that one moment, the plight of Rosa Parks shifted the psyche of our society.

This is the foundation of social change and the reason I'm writing this book. As long as denial and rationale persist, intolerable acts will continue. The general American public did not oppose the genocide of the Native Americans during the "Indian wars" because they had been told that those people were savages. The general public believed that African people were less than human, born to be slaves. It once was acceptable for a man to have total dominion over his wife and children; what we consider to be child abuse was normal, and women suffered at the hands of abusive husbands with no recourse. Now our sense of social justice has evolved, and much of society finds these attitudes and actions intolerable. We're growing; we're evolving and awakening to a higher state of consciousness.

I believe we are reaching what is called critical mass: the quantum necessary for a leap of consciousness of the entire species. Remember the hundredth monkey syndrome? In this classic study of consciousness, scientists dropped fruit on an island and taught one monkey to wash her fruit. She liked it better washed and began to teach the other monkeys to wash their fruit. They began to teach others. When one hundred monkeys learned to wash their fruit, *all* the monkeys on the island began to wash their fruit. Even more amazing, monkeys on other islands began to wash their fruit also, without ever being taught. This classic experiment demonstrates the power that reaching critical mass has on the collective consciousness.

My prayer is that this book will serve to bring into the clear light of day the long-denied truth of the atrocities committed by our own shadow government I pray that it serves to assist humanity in reaching critical mass. I hope you will feel the pain and power of my journey and the joy of my healing. I hope you realize that we can all be free from mind control. May you gain the conviction that I have, that these secrets must be revealed for our beloved world to heal, for the sake of our children and our children's children.

Don't think for a moment that the only people affected by these programs for human experimentation and mind control were the victims. We were the guinea pigs for a vast program of mind control for the general public. There was indeed an agenda for these experiments. The "conspiracy theory" is no theory but a great threat to humanity. You might wonder what you can do about it. My answer is to seek your own personal freedom. Make your own journey to be free from every aspect of fear programming. Begin right this moment: Make a list of every way fear affects and controls your life; then find the keys to the shackles of your mind and set yourself free. Wake up, before it is too late.

In February of 1995, I had already been working on my recovery for five years when I heard about a committee [the Advisory Committee on Human Radiation Experiments] appointed by President Clinton to hear the stories of people who had been exposed to radiation experimentation. As you will read in this book, I went to Washington, D.C., and testified before that committee. At that time there was no information out about these kinds of programs. But I was to learn much on my journey.

Did the general public hear about this? Did the government act to change policies that permitted such atrocities, never again to allow such violations of the principles of American democracy? Did Congress appropriate funds to compensate the victims? No, they did not. President Clinton did apologize to a group of African-American men who were used in syphilis experiments, and that was about as far as it went. Why was there no vast public outcry? The answer lies in the very root of how mind control works and how our freedoms can be—and are being—lost as we stand by and do nothing.

I am convinced that I will see the day when these deep secrets are brought out, exposed and believed. It's a process, and I'm a very patient person. I pray that this book becomes a vital part of this process. As you read this truth and take it to your heart, you will see that a change must be made. One drop of water is a small thing, but the ripples spread across the entire pond.

I am one of the fortunate ones—I survived, healed and intact. I am free and sound of mind, body and spirit. I have met many survivors who are permanently disabled and deeply fragmented. They live in a world of terror. Most of them would be afraid to write a book like this, too frightened of the pain and repercussions. A friend of mine asked me about that: "What if, because of this book, your safety is jeopardized or your life disrupted?" I replied, "I am able to do this; my story is powerful and it's important. How could I live with myself if I didn't speak up? My silence would contribute to the continued abuse of children in these programs."

I have deliberately omitted some identifying details about my life, but not because I fear discovery. I am certain that after my testifying in Washington, D.C., the dark elements know who I am and where I live. No, I made that choice to protect my family, especially those who are still in denial. I respect the right of every individual to choose. Just because I had a burning need to travel a path of discovery doesn't mean it's the right or healthy choice for everyone.

I do not feel it is necessary to expose personal details about the memories I have recovered that involve my extended family. During the early years of my recovery, I struggled like every other survivor with issues of betrayal and shock. How could these awful things be true about my family? We are good people! I now have redefined the word "good." I believe most people are basically good. My family, like so many others, was a victim of mind control that used terror programming through ritual abuse and betrayal of trust through incest to reach into the core of the psyche and create a split.

When I recovered memories of relatives abusing me, I thought they were conscious of what was going on. I learned that this was not true when I confronted one of my uncles. I took him to a park with a beautiful river and had a good talk. I thanked him for all of the good he brought into my life, the campfire stories and fishing trips, and the good memories. I thanked him for loving me all of my life. Then I forgave him for sexually abusing me and taking me into Satanic rites. He was genuinely shocked. His heart was in a good place; the way I know this is that I learned years later he had entered into therapy to change the cycles of abuse. We made our journey to forgiveness and did our healing work. Our journey is private, and I want to keep it that way.

I used to think that only sick and evil people did these things—this is not true. It is so easy to point our fingers at someone else, saying that's where evil is. But that mindset only furthers the very separation that has held this planet in a mind prison for so long. We must look deeper and move out of judgment and into healing if our planet is ever going to be free.

Christ Jesus said, "It is easy to see the splinter in our neighbor's eye and miss the log in our own." I pray that everyone who reads this book takes these words deep within their hearts and feels compassion for the loving mothers and fathers who have hurt their own children because of mind control, when within their conscious lives, with good intent, they have done everything possible to be good parents. I implore you, my reader, to look beyond all that you have ever believed or thought to be true and seek the truth. "The truth shall set us free."

I've healed my relationships with my family; love is a powerful force. My whole family was torn up when some other family members and I set off on the path of discovery, to heal from the past. For nine years, I was estranged from people I love. There has been much healing and forgiveness in my family; I have no desire to disrupt the peace of those who have chosen not to make this difficult journey. From my perspective, I know the inner peace is worth it . . . for me. Before I found that peace, I had to face terrifying demons. I could never go back to my life as it was then, holding all those terrible secrets inside, but I respect those who chose not to walk my path.

One word of caution: Anyone can be a survivor. Your ability to function in society has little bearing on it. Many survivors are quite functional; they've learned to repress the memories so deeply that they are totally unaware of their history. So please ground yourself before reading this book. Pay attention to what your body is telling you. Observe your

The Awakening

Once we suffered alone,
children isolated in a sea of fear.
No one who cared to protect knew
    of our agony,
shuddering and shaking in the
    silence of our secret torment.
Then the dawn came,
the voice of the awakening,
shattering our shell of isolation.
"Remember,"
the voice echoed with the songs of
    the thunder beings.
"Heal,"
the voice sang to us within our
    souls.
We place our feet upon the
    unknown path,
embarking on our journey
to freedom from fear.

Illusions tried to frighten us
back
to the world of secrecy and
    isolation.
Yet the voice urged us on:
"Remember. Heal. The truth
    will set you free."
The voice shattered our night like
    lightning bolts.
The cleansing rains showered
our souls,
cleansed our spirits,
taught us to breathe,
to trust.
Hope emerged . . .
the dawn came.
Facing our new dawn, we spread
    our wings,
white doves flying free.

reactions. If you experience dizziness, heart palpitations, insomnia, panic attacks, headaches or other bodily symptoms when reading these passages, stop. Consult your intuition. Ask yourself if continuing is for your higher good. Depending upon your answer, proceed with caution. Call a trusted friend for support, or contact a professional. If you choose to seek professional support, work with somebody who is objective and empowering, never with a person who is controlling. Respect your limitations and intuition; your heart is your best guide. Please know that you can succeed in making this journey. Fear is the main obstacle to overcome—and it is a very big obstacle.

Many therapists do not want to work with survivors because of intimidation by the False Memory Syndrome Foundation. Around the same time I was recovering my memories, a lot of other people did, too. I often wonder if maybe some big program broke down, allowing so many people to begin to wake up. That is why people who had a vested interest in keeping the secrets secret formed this foundation. Their big campaign message was that therapists had planted all this stuff in our heads. Of course, these guys know a lot about planting stuff in people's heads, but it isn't done when a therapist asks if you were taken into sacrificial rites. It is done with Satanism, done with fear programming, drugs, electroshock, environmental deprivation and torture. It is done with billions of our tax dollars, at the cost of our nation's soul. Therapists were certainly intimidated by the lawsuits, especially the ones by their own clients who had been reprogrammed. Powerful publicity maintained that all this was a false memory. The gates seemed to close; everything got very quiet. But I believe that freedom is in the wind. It is our nature as humans to seek freedom, and it's also the nature of the times.

Our planet is experiencing an awakening. The prophecies of many nations and religions and keepers of ancient wisdom have foretold these times, the shift of the ages. I see it as the end of the old world of fear and the emergence of a world of freedom, empowerment, peace, healing and what I call heaven on Earth. We are emerging from the age of dichotomy, the age of separation. We see this in myth: the sacred twins, the fall of Lucifer, the war between good and evil. I call this age of separation the long dark night of the soul of humanity. We now are returning to oneness. I believe truly that humanity is on the verge of a great leap in evolution and consciousness. I believe in the cause of freedom, liberty and justice. Mostly I believe in the power of love. Consciousness is evolving, and we are shifting the foundation of our consciousness.

As I travel and speak of my experiences, I refer to my perpetrators as *they*. I often hear the question, "Who are *they*?" I am referring to the victims of mind control who executed these programs, of course, but in a larger sense, my listeners are asking who is responsible for all of this. I cannot point a finger at one evil, demonic person, a Hitler type who can be blamed. I cannot blame the government, for there are many dedicated and honest people serving in the government.

Does this atrocity continue? I believe so. There is nothing to indicate that the programs have ceased. So let's find the bad guys and get this thing cleared up. Right? Wrong. It is not that simple. Social change happens when the consciousness of society heals. I feel that a split has occurred in the psyche of society, that many good people live lives of which they are unaware in their conscious minds. The left hand does not know what the right hand is doing. In his excellent book, *The Nazi Doctors: Medical Killing and the Psychology of Genocide*, Robert Jay Lifton explains the phenomena of doubling, creating a separate persona to deal with difficult issues. It was by means of doubling that doctors, sworn to heal and help, could instead turn to torture, could develop the horrible experiments carried on in the concentration camps. Our society is like Dr. Jekyll and Mr. Hyde: by day, loving, God-fearing citizens, and by night, our own worst nightmares. As the split in the psyche of society is mended, I believe that we as humans will evolve into wholeness. I've come to the understanding that there is no separation, there are no demonic beings who are separate from me, for we are all one part of one creation. The dense energy of the fear vibration exists within the psyche of mankind. When we can reach into that part of ourselves, that lost shadow, with unconditional love, truth, forgiveness and healing, that shadow will be transformed into light: the healing light, the light of Christ, the compassion of the Buddha, the light of Mahatma, the love of the holy mother of life, Mother Gaia, the Earth Mother.

These ideas all come together in a story I heard when I was a little girl. A great prophet came to this Earth as a teacher. Her name was White Buffalo Calf Pipe Woman, and she came to the Lakota Sioux Nation. They say that the Lakota Sioux were originally lake-dwellers. The Lakota were pushed by the Ojibway from the shores of the great lake onto the plains, where they wandered, hungry and lost. This was a very dark time in the history of the people.

Two young men went out to look for buffalo to feed the tribe, and as they came across the prairie, they saw a white buffalo calf approaching them. As it drew closer, they realized it was an incredibly beautiful woman. She appeared on a knoll in front of them, a bundle on her back. As they looked upon her, one of the young men lusted for her, and he wanted to take her power without her consent. The other young man had pure thoughts. She beckoned to the young man who wanted to take her power to come to her, and when he did, a cloud of mist encircled him. When the cloud of mist lifted, there were only bones with worms and snakes. She turned to the other young man and said, "Because you are of pure heart, I have chosen you as my messenger. Go back to your people with my message. Tell them to prepare themselves, for I am coming." The way I heard the story, the village began to prepare for her coming.

Because they were lost people, the village was in disarray. When they went to the river to bathe, they looked in the water and realized that they were beautiful.

The people prepared a great lodge for White Buffalo Calf Pipe Woman. She came and sat in the west, facing east, and brought the seven rites of the Oglala Sioux. She brought respect for the divine union and the teachings of how we can purify ourselves. These sacred teachings are now taught by the Lakota elders to help heal Mother Earth.

In 1998, White Buffalo Calf Pipe Woman came to me in a vision and told me to always think of her. She said to know that all three people in the story are within us, to think of her sitting in our third eye and the two young men, the sacred twins, on each of our shoulders. She told me that she loved the brother lost in fear and confusion with unconditional love; she loved him into healing. When the mist lifted, his soul returned to his twin, the snakes devoured the poison of that great fear and the worms were the fertilizer of the new world of peace. She said that the soul of the sacred twin returned to his brother, and they both met at the heart center. She said to look inside ourselves for that shadow, for both twins, to love our lost dark twin with unconditional love until we can transform the poison and fear into healing and return to oneness, until we can unite with the evolved twin.

"We are the prophet, we are the lost twin and we are the messenger." Please take a moment to meditate on this important sacred teaching and look within for this healing. These are sacred teachings, and when we meditate and pray with sacred stories, we will hear the voice of truth in our hearts. In telling the story of White Buffalo Calf Pipe Woman, I honor my Dakota, Lakota and Nakota brothers and sisters. I honor the elders and the ones who kept these truths from being lost during the genocide of their people. Oh, Mitakyue Oyasin (all my relations)!

This book will find you, if you are meant to read it. A friend will mention it to you, or it will just jump off a shelf in a bookstore. I pray that it opens your heart and helps you to expand your consciousness beyond the limited realm of the past. I pray that it helps you break down the walls that have held humanity in a mind prison, for it is my song of freedom, my journey from the abyss.

CHAPTER ONE

Conscious Memories before Age Forty

I am three years old. I am lying in a small bedroom. It's dark. My body is wracked with fever. I'm too young to understand what is happening to me. I know my parents are worried about me. My mother brings in towels to bathe the fever away. My body convulses and shakes, and I go in and out of a woozy feeling, as if I'm not really there. I'm gone and then I come back. The fever is so high, the pain I'm feeling all over my body is so intense, and I lose consciousness. When I come back, I remember lying there and feeling that I was a wooden person, and that's why my head was so big and heavy and I couldn't lift it from the bed. I know my parents took me to the doctor, and I know they did what the doctor told them to do. We were poor mountain people. They trusted their doctor. He never sent me for further tests or investigated the source of these intense bouts with fevers and convulsions. As I was later to learn, he was most likely the one who had involved me in the experiments in the first place. I know now why I had these spells as a child.

I grew up in the mountains of Colorado. My parents loved me; we were a close family. They were not perfect people, but there was more love than fighting. We had a good life in many ways. We were victims of a cruel and inhumane system that uses people with no regard for the human soul. I know my parents had no conscious knowledge of what happened to me. I do not hold them responsible. They taught me right from wrong, to feed a hungry stranger and to live my life with integrity. They rarely hit me and were not severely abusive. We went camping; we had a very strong connection to nature and Native American teachings and a respect for life. We spent months camping out in the wilderness, away from everybody, in areas inaccessible to automobiles. During these times, I learned to love the Earth. Mother Earth was my healer, my teacher and my guide. As a very young girl, I met my spiritual guide Quanab, who later became my guide through my memories.

My parents were idealists; they fought for the rights of workers through the unions. Early in my childhood, my mother became aware of the plight of the American Indian people. Many of our best friends were

Remember Her Warmth
September 8, 1976, dedicated to my mother.

When I was a little girl
and I woke afraid at night
with the terror only children know,
my mother would rush to me
and envelop me with her sweet warmth.
My head held warmly on her bosom,
her smell so close and familiar,
all terror would go away.
Warm, smooth darkness
would wash away the sands of fear.
In the morning,
I never remembered
what had scared me so,
but the warmth lingered into womanhood.

Somewhere in the Universe Is My Child
September 1973, as I was going through fertility tests,
wanting so badly to have children.

Somewhere in the universe is my child
waiting for birth,
waiting to touch, to be touched.
How long is waiting?
Four years, nine months, three weeks?
For when we shed the tears of want,
there is someone to care,
someone to cry with us,
and when we laugh,
someone to laugh with us,
someone to bake secret surprises,
to let us know we are one.

Lakota and Cheyenne; we learned personally the injustices that were happening to them, and my parents did what they could to help. I was taught that we are all brothers and sisters, regardless of skin color. I know my parents authentically cared deeply for humanity. Those good times and strong teachings helped me stay intact.

I was a happy child and loved life. I remember looking out the window of our home and having a great feeling of the love of God while watching birds, seeing the creation. I was born an optimist and have always seen the good in all things.

I am five years old. My siblings have gone to school. I lie in my bedroom, playing my favorite morning game: I'm a Jewish princess in a concentration camp. In this game, I'm a very brave little girl, and people who are doctors come in and experiment with me. They do very painful things to me, and they violate me sexually, and I'm always afraid. I'm terrified, but I'm strong and brave. I wondered all my life why I played that game. My sister said, "Maybe you were influenced by the publicity about the holocaust after World War II," because I was born in 1949. But I don't think that was it, because we didn't have a television, and I wasn't exposed to a lot of information about World War II. Through my years of healing, I believed that it was partially a past-life memory and partially a way for my psyche to deal with what was happening to me on different levels when I was a very young child.

I had fits of uncontrollable screaming and crying. I was sick a lot— sore throats, ear infections, high fevers. My bones broke easily; I would fall down, and my arm would just snap. My arm was broken four times· when I was a little girl.

I went to a very small school, and I always felt like an outcast. I didn't have a lot of friends; I didn't feel like other kids, didn't feel that I belonged. Later, when my family had to move to a large city and I entered the metropolitan public schools, I was miserable. I have totally forgotten large sections of my life at that point. My whole sixth-grade year is a blank. I know now that this was when some of the most horrible things happened to me. I was easily accessible and lived in a neighborhood that was close to a programming center.

Through the years of recovering my past, a number of memories provided context to my childhood and growing up—memories of friends and family, birthday parties and things like that. When I entered puberty, I started having enormous, incredible pain. At the age of fourteen, I began to experience severe migraine headaches so bad that I'd have to stay in a dark room. I couldn't lift my head up off the pillow without vomiting. And all this time, you might wonder, did my parents take me to a doctor? Yes, they did, but it was the same doctor, from my earliest memory until I was twenty years old. As I look back on my life now, I wonder why, being so ill, I was never hospitalized, why tests

The Voice

*Summer 1976, I was having powerful dreams of
little dark-skinned children. I felt so deeply that they were coming to
me, and they did. I adopted six children, four of whom are dark-skinned.
I wrote this to those children, but now that I read it, I think perhaps
I was writing it to my inner child, to find that inner child, loving
that lost part of myself to healing.*

There is a voice that calls from deep
   within.

I hear it, and it brings tears to my eyes.

My heart quickens,
and I feel it fluttering in my stomach.

The voice calls, and I can see the little
   face.

I can feel the small head rest on my
   chest.

I can hear the laughter.

The voice calls,
and I know there is a child waiting,

waiting alone, without lasting love,

waiting for my arms to chase away
   the loneliness.

At these times I envision the little
   face,

and I wonder, Who? Where?

When will I find my child?

Listen.

Hear me and know,
for you can never feel the voice
that calls from deep within,
telling me I must find my child.

How Do I Thank Thee?

October 1976, in praise to creation.

I look at the star and say, "How do
   I thank thee?"

I touch my child's face and ask,
   "How do I thank thee?"

I harvest the ripe fruit for winter and
   ponder, "How do I thank thee?"

I stand by my sister, hand in hand,
and view the geese going north,
   then south, then north again,
and I cry, "How do I thank thee!"

I smoke my mother's prayer pipe
   and see her eyes so strong
and pray, "How do I thank thee?"

And the faces from the circle fire,
the voices in the night, the songs,
   the laughter—
"How do I thank thee?"

I am living now,
so filled with the warm breath of life,
so thrilled with the creation—
   "How do I thank thee?"

Prayers cannot be enough, for no
   prayer is so great.

"Thank you, Great Mystery" are small,
   hollow words
for what my heart feels.

Each day must be lived to its fullest,
each morsel of food savored,
each sunset ravished,
each love given fully and taken so,
each mysterious gift treasured and
   used.

Then and only then can I say,
"Thank you, Great Mystery, for my life."

were not done. I always explained to myself that it was because my parents were really poor; they didn't have money to do that.

My health deteriorated as I got into high school, with repeated episodes of swollen glands and being so sick I could hardly walk. I'd stay home in bed for days at a time with severe headaches and body pain, and always the feeling that there was something wrong with me. The same doctor diagnosed migraine headaches. No further explanation seemed necessary.

In high school I felt like a champion for the cause of the downtrodden. I had a deep, passionate feeling in my soul for the civil rights movement, for the Vietnam War resistance movement. I went to nursing school and college; I married and wanted to have children. I tried repeatedly, and the fertility tests were terrifying. I had severe endometriosis, and I lived in a world that was filled with pain, but I learned to function, and I learned to be good at functioning. I learned to find freedom in my own way—gardening, camping, hiking and continuing my passion for life in every single way I could.

Journal entry, 1976: Lost I am for words as I sink to the bottom of a pit, unable as it seems to grasp hold of the rope of salvation, let alone the reins of my own life. It is true that as you stumble and fall face first in the mud, the world will but pause a moment to urge you to your knees, then hurry on attending to their own needs. Only one person in the end are you left to live with: yourself. Alone you must wipe the mud from your face, or choose to lie and gurgle in it.

Sterile they say, unable to conceive. They all know I will find the blessing nestled beneath a pile of manure. They expect strength and beauty and therefore take not the time to sit and ache as my heart aches now. Oh! The gift of conception, to feel the growth within my womb, to nurse a child. My eyes are dry; there are no tears suited for my pain. Here I lie, unable to turn for help lest I either degrade myself as a sniffling weakling to my acquaintances, or worse yet, depress those I love who are struggling around me.

So my heart aches, my private hell and empty womb. Yet I smile at the world and try to convince them that they are the ones missing the blessing, for my barrenness reaps a ripe

The Harvest
November 1976.

As the harvest passes and the fruit is stored,
the seed is saved.
Bright leaves darken and fall,
doing their eternal dance in the autumn wind.
Our great tree stands bare against the pale sky.
The garden, once green and full,
withers and browns as the frost touches;
the geese have fled to the warmth of the south.
Our children stood and watched,
with wide and wondrous eyes,
the miracle of their flight.
My eyes turned to the north,
seeing dark, cold winter clouds.
Winter is upon us, our time of endurance.
Will spring come again to our mesa home?
Will winter pass?
It is evening, and I gaze
up from my troubled day with tired eyes
and see the evening star,
there just above the great tree,
offering her special gift, her promise.
The evening star chooses only this season
to appear to our mesa home, to renew our faith.
Spring will come,
as the promise of the return
and the fulfillment of the cycles of creation.

harvest, and yet it does. I want not for motherhood and the love that comes from it. Yet always there was the illusive dream to conceive someday. But it is not for me, not my song to sing. Is it okay, God, if I ache a little in the midst of such an abundant harvest? If I hurt for the child I will never feel growing in my womb?

I adopted children. I am fulfilled as a mother and a grandmother. My children have brought me so many blessings, and I know each one of them was sent to me by God.

I raised my children in an alternative lifestyle. I tried to show them the beauty in life, helped them to choose a good path. I felt so deeply for my children who had been abused. I recall thinking how thankful I was that nothing like that had ever happened to me. I sat with them when they felt the pain of abandonment and abuse; I so desperately wanted to help. One of my foster children, a teenage girl, said to me one day, "You don't even know what it's like; you've never been hurt like I was." It just tore me apart inside. I felt their pain because it truly was my pain; I was goodhearted but very codependent.

I became a child advocate and joined the Citizen's Review Board, advocating for the rights of children in foster care. My anger went beyond a normal anger; it was rage. I was so angry over the abuse of one child I didn't feel the state was protecting that I went to the Secretary of State's office and yelled at him. Well, needless to say, I didn't stay on the Citizen's Review Board very long after that, because it's not exactly a good policy to yell at the Secretary of State. I was so angry at the state's apparent lack of concern about a child who was suffering. Looking back, I realize that it was my own wounded child inside for whom I was angry. I was angry that nobody knew or cared about what had happened to me. I raged through my inner pain, those dark memories that I didn't remember at that time. I was not physically abusive to my children, but my rage was abusive to their gentle spirits. I have apologized and made amends for how I hurt them with my anger. This rage also hurt my marriage. One of the greatest gifts of my recovery is to be free from this burning rage. Peace truly starts within.

I had incidents of hurting myself, accidental burns and cuts. I collapsed with ruptured cysts, endured abdominal surgeries. I had severe panic attacks and night terrors. For years, it seemed, I stayed awake all night praying for morning to come. But the next day I'd be busy canning or feeding the kids or going to work or doing things that made my life work. I was never an alcoholic, never addicted to drugs or prescription medicines—in fact, I refused to use prescription medicines. I never entered a

Fear

In the winter of 1976, my mother died of cancer.
She was my best friend. I wrote this because I felt so much fear
of what she would have to endure before she passed. I know now
it reflected the fear I held deep inside.

Do you know how fear smells,
the bitter taste on your lips?
Have you felt it grab your stomach
    and twist?
You're hollow now, afraid to pray,
afraid to hope, and yet afraid not to.
Have you visited my lonely spot,
here on this lovely winter
    afternoon?
The Sun still shines bright;
the snow lies deep in deep
folds about my winter home.
The children, laughing and giggling,
eyes bright, waiting for their happy
    dreams,
feeling slightly but not knowing

the fear I feel, for her, for us.
I see her face now, so strong,
so patient and lovely,
how she struggles to give love to us.
And I see her pain;
her eyes are filled with quiet tears.
I sit by my kitchen table and life goes
    on,
while she waits for a doctor to tell
    her,
to let her know the outcome of the
    test.
And what will tomorrow bring?
My throat tightens, my eyes burn
    and my
chest is twisted by the fear.

A Prayer of Thanksgiving

March 1979.

Good morning, Father, thank you
    for this day.
I face your brilliant rays,
and a thrill ripples through me,
knowing the joy and privilege
of the gift you have given.
Thank you, Father,
truly today I reach for your warmth.
I know not why a brush
with the emptiness fear brings

has left me rejoicing at your
    creation.
Yet as I sit here in this morning,
my heart is filled
with the splendor of all that
    surrounds me.
May the true meaning of this
    moment
remain with me forever. .
Amen.

mental hospital or had any psychotic episodes. Because of that, I felt my life must be okay, because I could make it work. I had a good credit history, and although I never had very much money, I always kept my bills paid. I continued my deep passion for being close to the Earth—going into the wilderness, practicing prayer and meditation through Earth religions and Native American teachings. These practices helped my soul to heal and strengthened my spirit. I have always been very close to my family. I came into this world and incarnated as a loving person; I came into this world as a strong soul—so strong, in fact, that I could endure this atrocity and emerge capable of healing and emerging into a state of higher consciousness and deep peace. I began writing poetry in the seventies as I was raising my children, and I have included some of those poems in this book. Some were written before my recovery, whereas others trace its course.

It was in January of 1981 that I wrote the following comment on my disillusionment with the world. I believe that I was feeling the ooze of the dark secrets I carried and how they had sabotaged my life. I have noticed that as I healed, my outlook on life has greatly improved. To know me is to know a true optimist. You've heard the joke about the brothers whose parents gave them, for their birthday, a key to a room. When they opened the door, they found the room was filled with horseshit and a shovel. The pessimist began to complain and shovel the manure, saying that this was what his life was like. The optimist went to work with a song, saying to himself, "With all of this horseshit, there has to be a pony somewhere." These words speak to the deep unrest in my soul.

January 1981: The world we are attempting to live in has gone utterly mad. We live far from the insane filth of the cities, and yet it oozes up to our front steps, a world without a cause, a time of violence. Our society lacks the fiber, the fiber that grows within the human soul. I don't buy the paper or listen to the news; instead I walk and look at the stars. And yet, as careful as I might be, as selective as I might be, the filth oozes from the little cracks in the walls. As a people we wonder, "Why it is so difficult to keep our balance?" That is as silly as a person on a tilt-o-whirl wishing not to get dizzy. And yet we struggle for ideals, for beauty, to have and offer our little faces, our children. If I were unable for once to see our Earth, the stars, feel the soil, walk to the river, then I know my struggle for balance would be lost.

I stagger, as it were; I pray for purity. Our words as a society are so degraded by the slime. I pray that I might reach into the heavens and pluck one small star and offer it to my children.

Now at the age of fifty-two, as I begin this manuscript, I can say I *have* reached to the heavens, plucked one small star and offered it to my children. The name of the star is Freedom.

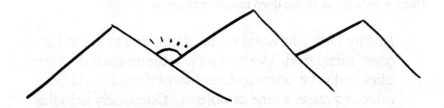

CHAPTER TWO

First Steps on the Journey

M y home became a home for a lot of lost children. Call it codependency, but I think that knowing their pain helped me to touch my own. Sometime in the late 1980s, some of my relatives made allegations of sexual abuse within my extended family on my mother's side. I chose to believe them, and that was a turning point in my life.

I was parenting two abused teenage girls who had entered my home at age thirteen. When one of them was seventeen, she began to recover memories of sexual abuse. But I didn't consciously know anything about that, nothing about flashbacks or body memory or any of that kind of stuff. My daughter, now eighteen years old and living away from home, would call me feeling suicidal. She would be having such intense flashbacks that she thought her perpetrators were in the room with her. I was the only lifeline between her and the abyss.

One very intense episode convinced me that I had to get some professional help. I took her to see a child psychiatrist, whom I'll call Dr. D. He recommended that she read the book, *The Courage to Heal*. Then he turned to me and said, "Well, if your journey continues, you're going to be reading a lot of books. The first one I suggest is *Codependent No More*." I went right out and bought it and started reading it avidly. That book saved my life; it showed me a mirror to self. I began recognizing unhealthy energy patterns, unhealthy fusion, that I was enabling. I was introduced to the idea of boundaries, the kind of boundaries that keep a person healthy inside. As my daughter continued her journey through the terror of her childhood, I decided to join an incest survivor's group, to be a pro-survivor, to help my daughter whom I love so much. So it's really love that brought me home to healing and brought me to join that group. I have always thanked my oldest daughter, who is a very wounded woman, for helping me to wake up.

People ask, "When did you wake up?" Well, I know exactly when I woke up: August 17, 1987. It was the day of the Harmonic Convergence, and one of my foster daughters had just left home. I had gone to South Dakota to a Sun dance (a sacred tradition carried on by Native Americans) and

To My Daughter

*I wrote this after the daughter I adopted at age thirteen
attempted suicide for the seventh time. She was so damaged before I got her.
She is disabled and very wounded from severe child abuse. She is the reason I started
into recovery, to help her. Of course I was codependent; my inner wounded children
were crying out in pain from what I knew she experienced. She has worked on her
healing for years, struggled for her sanity like so many others.*

Struggling through the lost
    fibers of hope
that were strung like broken
    beads
on an old weatherworn
    purse—
a vessel once meant for
    abundance cast aside.
Empty, hopeless dreams
spent like pennies for candy
that cost a quarter,
always coming up at least eight
    cents short.
The life of her dreams at least
    two dollars short,
a childhood ringing in the red.
She kept believing the purse
    held gold coins
to keep her spirits from
    plunging
below the E mark, the place of
    desperation.
After pointless, useless yelling,
    she quietly tells him,
"If the phone rings, don't take
    a message."
Slipping into her dark room
to fill her empty purse and
    stomach
with bottles of pills.
Praying for release from pain,
another string of beads broken,
now rolling about the room.

The purse lying open by her
    side,
open and empty like her heart.
Yet she lives still,
no matter how she tried to
    not.
Oh!
How I wish I could gather up
    those beads
and string them like new,
wash the purse and mend it.
Oh!
How I wish I could fill it with
    gold coins,
move the stones from her path
    of pain,
hand her the mysterious key
    called grace,
this treasure of redemption.
What, oh what, is that
    moment of mystery,
when one lost soul finds the
    grace
to mend her purse and fill it
    full of seeds
that grow a bounty crop?
When with gray hair and eyes
    at peace,
she could hear a young one
    say,
"What a lovely antique purse,"
and reply,
"It served me well."

decided to be on the Rosebud Reservation for the Harmonic Convergence. I was in a lot of pain, both physical and emotional. Part of the Sun dance was a healing ceremony. I stood under the arbor, a shaded area, while two-hundred dancers swirled around us with their feathers and offered healing prayers for us. Toward the end of the circle, an old man came by, and as he blessed me with his feather, I felt bird wings all over my body. Afterward, I asked my friend who he was, and she said he was a uwipi, a healer. When he touched me that day, I know he helped set me free. I remember standing and looking at the sacred tree in the center, often called the Sun pole, praying and asking, "What is this Harmonic Convergence about? And what can I do with my life to do the journey, to be there and be part of what the Harmonic Convergence is about?" A powerful force moved through my life that day and woke me up. But it wasn't until 1989 that I began the incest survivor's group.

I kept detailed journals of my recovery; I have chosen to share these intimate writings with you because I feel it is the most powerful way of telling my story.

October 27, 1989: Seek the truth and the truth will set you free. God grant me the serenity to accept the things I cannot change, the courage to change the things I can, and the wisdom to know the difference. This is my ledger; I will try to write only the truth as I see it. If I perceive the truth inaccurately, I will not do it intentionally. Strength, come to me; beauty I can see; truth removes the veil from my eyes; awareness; wisdom; I seek the truth.

Simple or not, evil or good, the energy that is given them determines their power. Sometimes negative energy enters when we least expect it. That does not make us evil. The only way we become evil is if we give ourselves to evil. We must pray for beauty and strength and love. Once I stood on a mountain; I raised my hands to the universe, to God, and prayed to be an instrument of goodness, prayed to be of service to my people. As I reached the sky, I felt that energy surge through me. I was young, idealistic and hopeful. Within me there was pain, love, terror, strength; I was neither all of one, nor all of the other. Many times evil has tried to consume me; I have held my ground, allowed positive energy to focus on beauty. Yet I have touched evil at a time when I denied its existence. Thereby I gave evil power. I gave away some of my strength. To deny evil will give that evil strength. I touched evil; I allowed evil people in my home. I could not see them for who they were. As a woman, I lift my hands to the universe and I pray to God. I ask humbly for strength, love, power, beauty, that I may walk always in the light. The veil has been removed from my eyes; help me to have the courage to seek the truth.

I was in very poor health, my symptoms including a severe sensitivity to light. I had begun working with Chinese medicine in my mid-thirties because of severe endometriosis, ruptured cysts and the trauma of fertility testing. One of the tests is a fallopian tube x-ray, where they send dye up in your fallopian tubes. I had that a couple of times, and every time I would go into white pain. I would experience heart palpitations and extreme trauma. It seemed odd to me that the doctors and nurses had no clue to the agony I was going through. I thought, My gosh, how come I'm not getting more emotional support through this? But now I realize that most people don't have that kind of trauma, because they didn't experience what I experienced as a child. This terror actually blocked me from going on with fertility tests and played a big part in my decision to adopt children.

As I began to heal my physical body, I started doing exercises to bring light into my body, visualizing the healing of my abdomen and doing other visualization exercises. I'd also begun working with herbs and vitamins in Chinese medicine. By the end of the 1980s, my physical body was already starting to get stronger. It's a good thing too, because I needed that physical strength to endure the trip I was about to make.

I remember when I first went to the incest survivor's group, which was a twelve-step program. The meetings were some distance from my home, and at that point I was so afraid that I couldn't drive at night. I was always afraid of who might be in the back seat when I returned to my car at shopping centers. Week after week, I forced myself to attend every meeting. Someone had to come out and pick me up, because I was too afraid to drive. The twelve steps took hold and became a vital tool for my journey to wholeness.

I joined the group to be a pro-survivor for my daughter, but as I sat there and listened to story after story, I began to experience physical sensations: terror, panic attacks. These meetings were bringing up feelings I had long ago buried. I learned the list of symptoms of posttraumatic stress and realized that I had most of those symptoms. I identified myself as a survivor of trauma.

One night, coming home, my friend and I were talking about the possibility of incest in our childhoods. As we parked for a few minutes to continue our conversation, something horrifying happened: a big, dark figure loomed up at the car window, then disappeared. We screamed and drove away. I know that was an apparition from the darkest side of life, a visitor from the other side, the world where demons wander in search of their lost souls. I cannot remember being so frightened in my life as I was those first days of identifying myself as a survivor. I didn't dare write; I didn't dare journal. I did mention to a relative that I was attending a survivor's group, and she said that was disturbing. She asked, "How would you feel if your sister joined a mind-control group?" I thought that was kind of a funny reaction. I said, "No! I'm trying to get free; it's not about that!" My relatives really flipped out; all at once an iron curtain seemed to rise between me and the relatives in denial. I did not realize that my actions were triggering huge amounts of fear with my relatives. I lived in a neighborhood with family members, and that very existence was threatened. I wrote the following to a relative in denial:

> November 1, 1989: We stand on different points of a circle, a lake perhaps; between us there is a sea of confusion. We are trying to swim across the water, but we can't seem to reach each other. We are afraid we will never stand close together in our circle as once we did. How foolish we are. The lake is too deep; the wind is too strong. If we could walk toward each other or even look over the lake, we would know we stand in the same circle and always have. I pray for patience; I pray for trust. We have never failed each other; perhaps the lake will calm, or one or both of us will be able to walk to a closer point where we can see each other clear. But know this, my sister: The truths we found will not fail us. We respect each other; we are strong. We are good people; we are doing what we must. This, too, is not an answer, merely a prayer.

It took nine years before the strength that existed in my family got us through that torrential lake. Now we are once more a close family.

As some of my relatives and I began to awaken and go into recovery, the whole family was turned upside down and backward. Shortly after I wrote that last journal entry, I moved my home and my children away, to work on my recovery in privacy. During that move, we learned a lot about psychic attack and psychic protection. In my numb state of denial, I couldn't feel the demonic energies. Prior to waking up, I couldn't really experience those energies that were around me all the time, that were sabotaging my health and happiness, and as I awoke, it felt as though I were being attacked. Indeed, I think there *was* a lot of psychic attack as I energetically pulled away from the old patterns and started on my path of healing and breaking through the initial fear barriers. I learned to protect my home and family, to clear objects and spaces with sage, to work with the light of Christ. It wasn't easy. I would clear the house, and it would feel better for a little while; then I'd forget, lose focus and get hit with a panic attack, or my kids would have nightmares. I'd go through the process again. A friend had been doing psychic protection for me, and one day I told her, "You know, you don't need to do that anymore." She asked, "Are you sure?" I said, "I'm a big girl; I can handle this myself." "Okay," she said, "I'm removing my protection." I was immediately struck by a blast of negative psychic energy that almost knocked me to the floor. That taught me in a big way that there was a lot more to protecting our homes and ourselves with the Christ light, prayer and clearing our energy fields than I had ever imagined. Of course, because I never understood the power of the dark energies, I couldn't possibly understand how important it was to protect myself.

January 17, 1990: I am angry beyond belief. Feelings of frustration. Tired of seeing people I love hurt. I feel betrayed. I hate what is happening. Why does it have to be so hard? I have a fear of moving; hope for peace, serenity; searching for truth; trying to hold things together; trying to understand; not wanting to believe. I have a fear of what the truth will reveal. Why? It already happened; I can't control it. Let it go! Help me, God, to find the way back to serenity. Help me to break this depression, to find the light, to find the light, to bring the light in truth, beauty, trust and patience.

They say I need to write. How? What? Bullshit fills my mind. Free me from my compulsion; let me out of this box. Open my heart; open my energy; return to a path of positive energy. We are what we are; we are what we are; we are what we are. Leave me alone; get out of my life; leave me alone. I can write; I can be free; I am strong; I am clear. I can be beautiful, free. Let it go. God, it's yours. Who was my mother? A woman struggling for her sanity, for beauty, for dignity. Angry, hurt. A hurt child, abused, used, not knowing, trying to find out what happened to the little girl who screamed for help. Angry child, loving beauty, feeling fear, loving life, forgetting pain. Who is telling the truth?

January 21, 1990: The Sun is shining; it is a warm winter day. I've broken most of my depression from a week ago. I have regressed these last two weeks; I don't understand. Sugar cravings, rage and migraine headaches. I started to read *Codependent No More*; it makes sense. If I have memories, I want to know. I must have, or else these symptoms wouldn't recur. When I go into denial and backslide into depression, so much eludes me. How can this be, that our family has such a dark secret? The other night I had a dream of a little girl in pink being carried up wooden stairs by a man. The walls were wooden slats; the little girl was laughing. I feel a tightness or spasm near my bladder when I think of the dream, and I am ready, or feel I am ready, to remember my dreams. God, help me to know.

January 26, 1990: Felt I broke through a barrier that was stopping me from forward motion, recognizing and accepting that there are forces, internal and external, bombarding me. The golden light does make a difference; it is God's light. So much I don't understand, yet I realize the value of what I'm learning. Why is the dream of the little girl in pink hounding me? I want to know, to unblock. I smell something very sweet. I am nauseated; my lower back feels tight. Whew! Every day so much happens. I am going too fast; things are too intense. Now that I've realized and come out of denial, there is a sickness where once I believed things were okay. I had no idea how sick; how could I be so naive at forty? Naive? No. Blind? Yes.

What I don't understand is, once I get all the truth, what am I going to do with it? Ignorance is bliss, they say, but is there another way? I pray so: Creator of all, help me find a way to truth and serenity.

I can't believe how ignorant I've been. What I wonder is, once I sort it all out, what will be left to believe in? Who will be untouched? No one. What is the world? One big mess of abuse and illusion? Where is reality? I have friends who are so beautiful, yet so wounded. Is this what my mother meant about the two-faced woman? I know it is. I need a rest from it all, yet it is swirling around me.

About this time in my life, I began writing with my left (nondominant) hand and continued going to the incest survivor's group. During the time of transition, when I was getting ready to move out of my neighborhood, I wrote in my journal:

February 1990: A little girl watching; she can't run. She is frozen with fear. She watched in horror; no one noticed her. She is quiet; she is alone. She has blonde hair. She is afraid. She is quiet. She is terrified. She is helpless, alone. She runs; he chases her. He knows she saw. He knows she will tell. But don't worry, ma'am; everyone thinks she is a liar. No one will listen to her; she is a bad little girl. She makes up nasty stories. This is just a story, not a fact.

On the night of February 15, there were disturbances in our house. We awoke to find the air thick and heavy. We cleared it and felt better. Around that time, people who work with light energy began to come into my life. I would work a little while with the light energy and feel better, then I would backslide and be filled with agony and fear again. I began working with a massage therapist who helped me with light exercises, and I made a big breakthrough.

March 2, 1990: Last week I felt like I was up against a brick wall, working on unblocking it. My massage therapist asked me to be in touch with the pain in my back. I told her how it was when I was five, how I screamed a lot, and about my convulsive-type spells. No one could understand my speech until I was in first or second grade. My doctor said I would grow out of it; it was because my mind moved faster than my ability to communicate my thoughts. My handwriting was illegible, and I had a great deal of difficulty in reading, because the lines went into each other. This gave me a lot of trouble in school.

She asked me to go back to two years old. I have no memory before three, when I broke my arm. I talked about the red spot on my neck, and how it relates to rage and fear. I started remembering early memories as a child, about a person who hurt me and locked me in a cellar. At two years old I saw myself, all at once, in a dark place with cold walls, alone and terrified, where I had been locked in a cellar, and I was calling for my mother for help, and no one came. Time lost all meaning; there was just darkness and fear. When finally he let me out, I remember him laughing at me and thinking it was funny that I was upset. (This was one of my early memories of fear programming.)

I remember coming out of that dark building and that the Sun was very bright. I felt the light of the oneness; in that moment, I chose the light of God. I chose the light that day, when I came out of that cellar as a two-year-old.

During that session, I almost passed out when I tried to sit up. I was just swarming with dizziness and emotion. But I felt relieved; the massage therapist got me some tea, and I felt wonderful. I felt relief. A burden had been lifted; I felt free. I realized all at once that when I moved these memories, I got relief. That was a major key to my healing.

CHAPTER THREE

Piercing the Wall of Terror

March 2, 1990, written with my left hand: The witch people in the fringe of life, in the darkness, when they walk amongst us, they wear a mask. We can't see them. We will remove the mask. The light will flow upon their witches' souls. They don't want us to know who they are. I flood my life with golden light.

I continued with sessions where I would be in touch with my deep pain. I started realizing how much pain I was really in. I didn't have anything to compare it to; having been in severe pain all my life, it seemed normal. As I experienced those first little spaces of relief, I started realizing that there was another way to feel. That gave me incentive to move on.

I began the next phase of my journey. I had moved to a new neighborhood, and now I sought the help of a caring professional. I went to Dr. D., who had helped me with my children who were adopted at an older age. I was shaking in fear the day of the appointment. I liked and trusted him because he had already helped me a lot with my kids and he was a kind, gentle person. I told him, "I've got something really dark in my past, and I want to know what it is, and I want to know safely." Then the most incredible thing happened. He said, "Come back next week with a safe place and a guide." I asked, "A guide? What do you mean, a guide?" "Well," he explained, "you need to think of some place where you feel safe and think of a guide for this journey, so you can safely discover what it is you have in your past." I went away thinking that my guide might be Archangel Michael, because I'm really close to him.

Then I remembered those wonderful times when my mother and father packed up the family and moved to Bald Mountain to live in tents all summer. The road went only part of the way in, so we had to pack in our provisions the rest of the way. Memories flooded back: the taste of beans cooked over a campfire with fresh salsa and homemade tortillas, rainy afternoons in the tent as my mother told stories of High Horse and Red Deer. She told me that Quanab was the spirit of Bald Mountain, that he would always protect me. She said that when I was afraid, I should close my eyes and repeat the phrase, "Quanab will protect me." These magical summers were a powerful part of how I managed to survive the atrocities intact. The next week I went back, and I said, "Dr. D., the safe place I have, and I have the guide."

He taught me to go into deep states of meditation, to journey to Bald Mountain and ask Quanab to take me only to those places I needed to go for my highest good. He was immaculately professional from the beginning. He never led me with questions or asked whether this or that had happened. He agreed to help me at a very reasonable rate. I began seeing him once a week, with occasional breaks when I went out of town. It was a routine that would continue for five years. I would go into his office and connect with my safe place and my guide, and I would take a journey to discover the inner sanctum of the lost part of my soul, the lost part of my childhood. During the journey, the walls of terror began to crumble. I could process the feelings, release them and move them to get physical relief.

I was also blessed to work with some very gifted practitioners in acupuncture and massage. I learned that one of the most important things that could happen in my healing journey was to move body memory. I started learning what a body memory felt like; I learned to go to different areas of my body and ask why it hurt, why I felt pain here or there. I learned to ask my body to tell me what my conscious mind had forgotten. The information I recovered became increasingly bizarre. I began to recover information about Satanic rituals.

I continued working in the incest survivor's group and began to wrestle with the concepts of mind control and terror programming. The memories that began surfacing were increasingly strange and disturbing. I do not know how I survived these horrible things, or for that matter, how I survived remembering them. Ritual abuse, psychic and sexual abuse, Satanist ceremonies, human sacrifice . . . the memories were horrifying. On one particular night after I had just recovered some very dark memories, I awoke around midnight. I lay trembling in my bed and thought I'd go out and sit on the porch to calm down a little bit. Then, suddenly, a very even, cold voice spoke in my head: "Why don't you just go kill yourself?" I was able to answer. "What? I'm not suicidal! I have no intention of killing myself!" With that, I began to be able to identify programmed messages. I might be driving, for instance, and a message would say, "It would be better for your family if you just turn the car in front of a truck and kill yourself." Or a voice in my head would say, "Um, you're telling secrets; you know the punishment is when you get home, your house is going to be burned." When I got home, the house would be fine, but we learned to work with a lot of psychic protection. We had plenty of help from the angelic realm, especially from Archangel Michael, who stands on my right side. He came to protect my family, clear the energy and keep our land safe and protected. I entered into a contract with my family that anyone around whom my children (inner and outer) didn't feel safe was not allowed on our property. I created a safe place, and we kept the energy in that place clean and healthy. This helped me through the worst of some of the memories. Around that time, I wrote the poem, "Unseen Monsters."

September 1990: When I got home from shopping, my stomach was sick. I took baking soda and went to bed, but there was no rest. I threw up. Nothing was digesting. I thought I could sleep but just drifted into a half-sleep state; then I was arguing with someone or myself. I told something evil to leave; I was angry and yelling, half conscious and half asleep. I was aware of the room; then I screamed in my mind. In my mind is my perpetrator, I guess, because my perpetrator controlled me so much of my life. Then, at warp speed, I burst into another dimension. I thought my head and arms and legs would explode. It was very real and terrifying. I was little. Hands held me down while someone held a sharp, shiny instrument with a sharp hook on the end. They were going to cut me with a scalpel. I have never felt or remembered such terror. And there was an angel there, protecting me, by the way. I remembered consciously knowing to call for help; I moaned and called my husband. I knew if he touched me, it would stop, and it did. But when I came out of it, I was hysterical and shaking all over. It was 11:40 P.M.

It took me until 12:30 A.M. to calm down. I got up and drank a cup of tea; I remembered when I was little, when I was afraid, my mom would get me up and give me some cereal or tea. I went back to bed at 1:00 in the morning. My husband and I worked on telling the evil to leave and bringing in the light. I had a sharp pain in my left abdomen, and we made it leave. I was relaxed and wanted to sleep, but

Unseen Monsters

Evil men and women walking
　　amongst us,
calling us friends.
Two-faced woman smiling at us,
an evil curse on a family.
The dark side unrevealed,
except when the nightmares
　　scream
and women tremble and shake
　　with fear.
Hidden in the dark,
safe, forgotten memories of
　　children, now adults.
Hidden in alcohol and drugs and
　　broken lives.
Hidden in myths of dark lords.
The secrets,
the lies,
the untold horror of dead cats
　　and infant mortality.

Secrets of children no longer
　　virgins,
of basements and dark secrets
　　hidden.
For anyone who looks will not
　　see who they are, for who
　　they are really.
Hidden in fat women and
　　drunken death,
lost to the light.
Forgotten but for a whisper in
　　the wind.
Forgotten but for a distant song
　　of freedom.
Chasing away the darkness,
speaking the truth,
the courage to heal.
Open the box; the light will
　　flood its dark corners.
God's truth will free our souls.

I couldn't. I thought, calmly, that I should go sit on the porch. Then, just as calmly, I thought, "Why don't you go and get a knife and cut yourself instead?" I thought, "That's stupid," and then again, "Just get a knife and cut yourself." I told my husband, and I got up and called a friend for support and help. Finally I got to sleep around 2:00 in the morning and felt okay the next day.

September 29, 1990: I am a beloved child of God. At last I have seen the sense of pure light and brought the light within me. Much has happened since my last entry. I contacted a woman in New Orleans whose child had been Satanically abused at a daycare center. (This incident had occurred nine years before our conversations, when the child was two years old.) Unaware of the abuse and for unrelated reasons, she began keeping her child at home. The child began to tell about what had happened at the daycare center. Six months later, another case of abuse surfaced from the center, and the woman took her daughter to a therapist. I asked, "Were there any extreme symptoms?" "No," she said. "She had trouble with fear of sleeping and going to bed. One day there was a little drop of blood on her underwear." She told me she had become cautious about her child's friends because abused children automatically make friends with other victims. She avoided the Scouts because Scout leaders sometimes use the organization to find victims. There are also sensitive times during the year; she has a calendar she gives to parents of victims, because it helps them identify when their children are depressed or have behavior problems by the times of the rituals. She confirmed some of the information I had already been working with through my recovery group, involving things that were being done to people to make them forget. It all matched up, and it also helped me understand my fear of autumn, because there are a lot of Satanic rituals in the fall.

Slowly I put the pieces together. It seemed that people who had information just came to me when I needed them the most. As I struggled with different pieces, information and spiritual assistance came to me. I met a wonderful woman who talked to me about the miracles of the Holy Mother and the apparitions of her in Medjugorje. She gave me a medal from Medjugorje from which I drew a lot of strength.

October 24, 1990: I've started to work with Dr. D. We are doing inner voyages to my inner self. I have met some of my inner children and have found Quanab to be very helpful. He will tell me where to go and to know what I need to know. Last Thursday he took me to a relative's basement.

I was hiding from that person and found something I wasn't supposed to see. I triggered into a black hole, swimming and swirling; I had to stop. I came back through my safe place and empowered myself but felt disconnected and disoriented. That night I became violently ill and vomited bitter stuff. I grieved and released something. I drew a picture of the dark-cloaked figure and myself as a little girl, cold. She is huddled at his feet; she is in a box of snakes. I remember that I liked the snakes better than the people. I was exhausted the next day and over the weekend. A lot has come into focus for me to feel.

As I have stated, I am making an effort not to embarrass my family in denial. On my mother's side of the family, seven of us have recovered memories of ritual abuse. This uncle, my mother's older brother, and his wife were deeply tied to this experience. A Catholic couple, they had eleven children, a significant number of whom have recovered memories of abuse. I remember I stayed at their house a lot in the summer. I liked my cousins, but even as a child, I feared their father. His daughters have attempted to expose him as a pedophile, but he seems to have some kind of political protection in his area. One of his daughters believes that he profited from selling us in some way. I have no proof of this, but I find it significant that I recalled Satanic memories in their basement and in the Catholic church and hospital in their neighborhood. One of my cousins lives in another state. We have not seen each other or spoken for over twenty years. During the early stages of my recovery, I spoke to her therapist and told her what I was recalling. She said she couldn't discuss details, but our memories were significantly similar. I feel it is important to mention that my cousins even tried to bring a lawsuit against their father. There are dark secrets in the family that I feel need to come to the light for the healing of all involved. One of the mysteries is the death of babies. I feel that my uncle and his wife have no recollection of what happened. I know that he worked two jobs to provide for his family. He was not all evil—merely split like the Nazi doctors in Lifton's book.

At the same time, I began doing chakra work, learning to clear my chakras, working with crystals, working a lot more with bringing in the Christ light and dissolving dark energy with the light of Christ.

October 25, 1990: On my journey at Dr. D's office, I returned to the basement. The floor was covered with dark, black stuff. I brought in the light. A dark-cloaked figure met me with a smirk. He said, "So you want to know? When I've shown you what you're going to see, you'll never come back." Then there was a slide of a ritual with the dark-cloaked figure holding up a chalice for a moment as he drank. I told him I would return to know; I didn't fear him. That evening I tried to sleep and threw up. I was so sick. I lay on the floor moaning. Together my husband and I faced that dark-cloaked figure and made him leave.

November 1, 1990: I talked to Dr. D. about Halloween and lots of other stuff. I felt so much like I was not talking about real things; none of it seemed real to me. But he promised me that if I ever got too far out in left field, he'd tell me. We talked about freedom. I went to visit my inner children at my safe place. I had already met some of them; they were very brave children. That day I met Kathy. She was sitting in my path, holding her knees and screaming. She wouldn't let me pass. She is tall, thin, with brown hair, and wears black. She remembers. I asked her what she needed. She started screaming at me and calling me a stupid bitch. I asked her to tell me; she said, "You talk of freedom? I've been trapped inside Pollyanna all these years. You forgot; I never have. I remember everything and have lived with the hell." I asked her to trust me, that now I am healing and want to know. I promised her I would listen to her. Then she calmed down, and I went back through my safe place. I remembered that Dr. D. said, "Clarity is a state of grace."

The work progressed and became more intense, bringing up memories of sexual abuse. And every time I'd go through one of the memories, I'd have full feeling of the sexual perpetration. I would have episodes of convulsive shaking and panic attacks in the middle of the night; my husband really went through a lot during those years. Sometimes I'd become so paranoid that I thought somebody was going to come and kill me or my children.

January 1991: Just for the record, I don't believe all this crap. If anyone ever read this, my ledger, they would know that I've gone mad. I've been warned, and I guess I should have listened. Now I have two lives—inner kids and Kathy—and I don't know what I'm going to do with it. I feel like a freak in a circus or sideshow—"Come see the snake lady, fifty cents; she's not worth much." I've gotten great at carrying on a dual existence: Mom one moment, and a withering, vomiting madwoman the next. I guess that last piece of memory was one too many; I just was hysterical. Who am I anyway? I don't know what to believe. I feel like killing myself. It would be nice to cut my skin and see the blood trickle. Then I say, "Bullshit, it would not." If anyone ever reads this, it is an experiment in creative writing. It's pretty bad when movies about past lives and time travel get me down. I think I'd better call someone for help.

Boy, that's going through the long, dark night of the soul, isn't it? Don't think I didn't doubt myself, but even in the moments of self-doubt, I had a deep desire to continue the journey until I knew the whole truth. I could stop with nothing less.

Other memories continued to surface.

Mid-January 1991: Last night I woke up vomiting red-brown and bitter stuff, like before when the memories surfaced. A message/command came to me to kill myself, before I remembered. I went to lie down, with no intention of suicide, and asked for protection and brought in the light, and I went through my safe place. I couldn't stop the screaming inside for a long time and finally contacted one of my inner children I could feel or hear. I wrote, "Karey is dead." Then I had flashbacks of a hooded figure with both hands on a sacrificial knife, paused to plunge—not just to plunge, but to cut open a victim from the chest to the abdomen and then hold the intestines up, lift the heart and drink the blood. I had very intense sexual body memories. I couldn't see or know what was happening around me. Then I was confined in a dark space—a coffin or a box or a closet—with another kid . . . a boy, I think. More sexual body memories; I couldn't figure out who it was, but there was something about an erection. I came back shook up and spent most of the night up, awake and trembling. Finally, I fell asleep about 4:00 in the morning.

I began an intense quest to find and nourish these inner children. I began to use a form of journeywork that I found out later to be soul retrieval. My spiritual guide taught me how to do this. I'd go in and find the little wounded children, hear their stories and feel their pain; then I would bring them home to my sacred mountain to heal. What's important is that

The Well of Terror

Screaming in the bottomless well of terror,
hanging by a rope above the abyss.
Screaming,
transcending time and space,
shattering the black void of empty feelings.
Shut up terror!
Terror, resonating from the depth of my soul.
Screaming, the voice of my mother, myself, all
of the children of pain,
the screams unscreamt, locked up in the
darkness.
A little girl standing helpless, hearing her
mother scream,
running to the aspens, hiding from him, lest he
make me scream, too.
Mommy, mommy, come back to tell of the day
he made you scream, too.

I kept going and nothing stopped me. I kept remembering, kept strug-
gling, kept going from day to day. I got more help. One very wonderful,
gifted professional did Hakomi therapy and acupuncture with me. I
couldn't afford to pay for sessions; she volunteered her time for years.
After our sessions, she would take me out for lunch or coffee. She was
kind and compassionate and professional. I began reaching out to my in-
ner wounded children, helping them to be loved, holding and nourishing
them, bringing them back to a safe place. One at a time, I'd meet these lit-
tle kids who had been through these horrendous experiences, and I loved
them. Gradually, I started noticing that my anger with my own children
was diminishing, and we set up contracts around the house that helped us
have better boundaries. We talked, and we actually set up contracts about
me not yelling at them so much. We talked about how I had changed, and
I was encouraged because I saw positive things happening in my life.

> April 10, 1991: "Lift every voice and sing till Earth and
> heaven ring, ring with the harmonies of Liberty; let our
> rejoicing rise high as the listening skies, let it resound loud
> as the rolling sea. Sing a song full of the faith that the dark
> past has taught us, sing a song full of the hope that the
> present has brought us, facing the rising sun of our new day
> begun, let us march on till victory is won." I do not know
> where I found this quote, but it is called the "Negro
> National Anthem."

> April 1991: A list of effects on my life: migraines, sugar
> cravings, foot pain, back pain, neck pain, electric energy
> inside, controlling personality, dominant, overcompliant,
> blind to perpetrators, fear, terror, fear of parking lots, unable
> to conceive, sexually blocked, shut out, erases things I don't
> want to know. As a teenager: severe cramps, night terrors,
> nightmares, fear of driving, insomnia, insecurity, unable to
> take care of or nurture myself, taking care, taking, rage,
> feeling unwanted, compulsive, overeating.

That same month, there came a powerful image: I was hanging on a
rope down a deep hole over an abyss, screaming, and everywhere there
were echoes. Every cell of my body was screaming; I was terrified, pan-
icky. And I recovered my first memory of being in the doctor's office in

Golden, Colorado. I'm maybe four or five years old, sitting in a chair and feeling very woozy and wondering why. I believe that was because I was drugged. I am in the examining room; I'm sitting there, waiting for the doctor. I know that I am little because I am swinging my feet and they do not touch the floor. I don't know if it's morning or afternoon; I'm very disoriented. Two people come in with big headdresses and masks on. They come in the door my doctor is supposed to come through. That seems funny to me. They go through the door that I think is a closet, and it's really connected to a room. There are candles in there and a whole bunch of people gathering. Later I'm taken into the room, into some ritual. That was the doctor I went to throughout my childhood.

Later I remembered being taken from my home to that doctor's office. A woman I called Hilga took my clothes off and gave me a brown sack dress. Her voice was rough with a strong German accent. I was a bad girl, she said, and I was going to be punished, which was something that always happened, because you never knew what you were being punished for. I was taken down a set of steps; a dark door opened, and I was put in a vault. It was completely dark in there. I remember crawling around and smelling something really awful. I crawled to the end of this little, tiny chamber that I was locked in and found a pile of dead cats. I was terrified. I didn't know why I was there; I didn't know what was happening to me. It was dark, moist and filthy; it smelled bad. I didn't even have my clothes, and I wanted my mommy and I wanted to go home. I remembered wanting to go home more than anything on Earth, and I was shaking and crying.

Then I lost time, and the next thing I remembered was that I didn't think I could take it anymore and I wanted to die. I didn't want to be in that awful room another minute, so I left my body and went to a beautiful place. I was in a tree, looking down on this little girl's figure, lying in the darkness in that little gunnysack cloth dress. I was really happy in the tree; I knew I had died, and I was really glad that I had died. I had no intentions of going back. Just then, an angel of light appeared and said I had to live, because I had something very important to do. He told me I had to go back into my body, that I had agreed to live. He said that once I got back in my body, I should crawl away from the dead cats to the other end of the room and run my finger along the base of the wall, where I would find a crack. I was to run my finger back and forth across that crack until the door opened, because if there's a crack, the door will eventually open. And that's really true. That's what this is all about: finding that crack and waiting for the door to open.

April 1991: The German woman came; she scolded me for being a mess. She said, "Little girls make such a mess when they play; we wouldn't want your mother to get mad." She was brusque and harsh. She had big farm hands and a broad face and brown hair in a bun. She cleaned me up and braided my hair and put on my dress. We left in a brown two-door coupe, and I was taken home.

I spoke to a relative about this memory. She recalled being worried as a child because I had not come home from the trip to get ice cream. She remembers asking where I was, and nobody seemed to connect to the fact that I hadn't just gone for an ice-cream cone; then I was carried in and was in bed, very sick. I believe this was the time when I had convulsions and high fevers and my head felt swollen. I felt like a wooden person. My temperature got up to 106 degrees. Again, my parents took me to the same doctor in Golden.

A couple of years after this, I took an investigative trip to Golden. I discovered that my old doctor's office connected to an Odd Fellows Hall. By then I had discovered that Masonic groups have been known to deviate into Satanic rituals. Of course, not all Masons are Satanic. I used to think so, though, because I met so many survivors with Masonic memories linking to Satanism. Like so many other parts of society, the Masons are subject to falling into dichotomy. The local people told me that it was a very strange order of Odd Fellows. I also learned about the underground chambers in Golden and that my doctor was retired from the military. He died long ago. It is important to note that although I was at his office a lot, I have no conscious memory of his mistreating me. He was always kind. I believe that his mind, also, was split.

Throughout the summer of 1991, I continued to struggle through these difficult memories. But I was no longer alone. Dr. D. had put me in touch with two other survivors of ritual abuse. We formed a group and met every week. We had guidelines and set good boundaries—so vital to survivors of abuse. This was such a beneficial experience. I could speak of these terrifying memories with people who were also working to transcend fear and deprogram the terror. We could talk about these bizarre things and realize that we weren't the only ones who had experienced them. We were careful not to feed one another's memories, but rather to approach it from a higher perspective. The group continued in one form or another for five years, and I personally made great progress through the work we did, transcending fear and struggling to unravel the beads and tangled knots of our lost memories.

CHAPTER FOUR

Bricks in the Wall

August 29, 1991: I had acupuncture today. During a flashback, I experienced many flashing lights—bright, strobelike, but at different frequencies. Needles put in my vagina; intense pain, white pain, vaginal and abdominal. Then flashing lights, clicking on and flashing, then off. When they were off, I'd go inside my abdomen and sit with the pain; then switch, flashing lights. On the way home from the session, I had intense sexual body feelings. I kept having flashbacks of robotlike responses, the needles, the flashing and the manual stimulation, climaxes until I think I'm turning inside out, and still hands continuing to manipulate me like a puppet. Then the flashing lights, needles, pain, sexual stimulation and the piano playing, over and over, the theme from *The Bad Seed*, over and over and over. As I write this journal entry, the pain in the top left brain is intense.

Around this time I read *The Nazi Doctors*, with its explanation of the phenomenon of doubling in the concentration camps. According to the author, Robert Jay Lifton, the people who worked in the concentration camps actually had two lives. It wasn't like multiple or split personalities—they actually were doubled. There was the person who would go into the concentration camp and work, and then the person who would be part of the family and have a "normal life." This book helped me to cope with my memories, because that's exactly what my life was like. I had one life when I was a kid growing up, going to school and all the normal things, and then there was this other totally bizarre life—with no context of reality to connect the two. I also began researching how to deprogram mind control, how to identify programs, how they affect people and the way they control through programming.

At this point in my recovery, I had some contact with some of my relatives who were recovering memories, and I even spoke with one of their therapists. In our conversation, I talked about the dark forces and how their power is an illusion. Isolation and fear are their weapons. I shared some of my memories and learned that my cousin was having similar memories. We didn't talk about any of the details, and my cousin and I have never shared our stories. I began to see that survivors are afraid to talk to one another. They are isolated; they don't feel safe reaching out to contact others. That very fact keeps them enslaved. I realized that the more I reached out and networked, the stronger I got.

October 22, 1991: I woke up last night with the most intense brain sensation I've had yet. It was incredible. This morning I am in a very bad way: my neck is tight, my head hurts and my brain is exploding. Fear, hysterics. Can't meditate; can't be safe; can't be private. Just feeling lost and stuck, lots of pain. Stomach queasy. Lost in the agony of pain—red, red pain.

October 23, 1991: Needed to process a memory all day; finally broke through this afternoon. First, the bad seed was screaming, my inner child was screaming. Then, her chatter about them getting us and hurting us. When I was able to calm her down and go to my safe place, the memory came. I was in a little black room on a hard bed. I felt the shot; my body went numb. Then he came—tall, heavy-built, in a doctor's coat. His bald, shiny head had a ring of short hair. A woman helped. They put tubes in my ears and nose. They put something hard and cold in my vagina and inserted medicine, then tied my feet together. It was excruciating. Now I know why the dye hurt so bad when they x-rayed my fallopian tubes during fertility testing and I went into shock. I remembered saying, "No, you can't have my children." There were papers; if I signed, they would stop.

It seems strange, but my symptoms were greatly relieved after the memory surfaced. I had been in agony—body pain, exploding head, starting into rage. After I recovered the memory, I felt a deep sense of peace. I did a meditation and went to my safe place. I told Quanab the story. It was very emotional; I cried. I relived being a child, free and safe, on that mountain. Then we brought all my inner children together and gave them spring water. He sent them to the forest to be safe and know their freedom. Then he spoke to me about not getting lost in the details. The wall I had to go through is filled with incidents (just like bricks in a wall). A few must come out for me to heal, but I must go through them always. Then I said, "I had been thinking this was a delusion." He said it was the truth. To help me know this, he would let me feel just a little of the pain in my womb, to stay with it as long as I could. The pain was intense and incredible. I stayed with it as long as I could until I passed out; then there was complete, floating peace.

November 6, 1991: At forty-two I have discovered the lie. I have discovered so many lies that reality is very difficult to define. Where does the lie begin? Where does the truth begin? Where does it all affect my perception of right or wrong? Where have I believed the lie (for example, that I was a virgin when I got married)? Who of my role models can I trust? How far? Where is the boundary between my daytime life and the lie-time life as a child? I know that somehow I learned not to use sex as a weapon for control, I know the importance of truth in intimacy, but how did I learn this? I learned it from my mother. She had a positive influence on my life from the beginning. I always believed that people who were severely abused in turn abuse their children. That is a pattern, but not the rule. How, then, did I develop reasonable parenting skills? It must have been because my mother and father provided a role model as loving parents. Where is there a malignancy in my approach to parenting my children?

I listed things: I was overly dominant; I was controlling; I interrogated instead of listening supportively; I had rage; I intimidated my children; I had poor contact with myself and my intent and the reality of my projection. But I had assets: I was basically honest; I had a need to trust and an intense ability and need to love and be loved; I had good intent and a desire to be free; I loved beauty and life and adventure; *and* I really loved my children.

Another fallacy I had believed is that children who were severely sexually abused would be promiscuous as adults. This is not true. I was sexually repressed, didn't connect to myself as a passionate woman, but I wasn't promiscuous. And because I wasn't promiscuous, I thought maybe I had not been sexually abused. I started unraveling these things and asking myself the question: "Who didn't betray me as a child?" I knew my father hadn't betrayed me, that my mother had taught me decent standards. These teachings were validated by the way they cared about people, about the homeless, about civil rights. Those things in my life gave me the strength to be the person I am. But I grew up with a deficiency: I could see evil only to a point. Things that were too close and threatening, I couldn't see. I needed to control everything and everyone in my life, because to lose control for a minute would be to give my power to those dark shadows that were lurking inside.

November 11, 1991: Awoke after midnight with a memory. I was terrified. I reached for my journal. It was hell. The memory was in the darkness. I was straddled around a pole. Something kept getting tighter. Initially, I experienced sexual body feelings, then just the pain. My shoulders felt like they would leave their sockets; my feet were crushed and bound tightly. The main pressure tightened on my arms; sometimes my feet were bound with something tight, but not being stretched like my arms. No medicine to dull the pain. I became a wild beast; my voice changed. I vowed to kill my captors when they came, snarling and growling. Then finally I whimpered, saying, "I'm sorry," over and over, pleading and begging, calling to my mommy, praying that she would come and get me. Finally, I tried to dissociate and float like a white light in the dark, almost getting to my sacred place but being pulled back as the bonds on my arms tightened and stretched on my tiny shoulders. Then convulsions, and they cut me free. They must have been watching from the darkness. I went to my safe place and came back into consciousness.

Hours went by, days, weeks and months, as I struggled to process memories, to find my wounded children, to contact inside altered parts of myself who had believed the programming, to help them reprogram and get free. Freedom was the light that guided me as I struggled through those months, and I was encouraged by the fact that I grew stronger, my health was improving and I continued to go forward.

CHAPTER FIVE

The Light Shines Through

March 27, 1992: I meditated and went to my safe place. There I found my guide. He told me that just because I need other survivors, they are not necessarily like me. He reminded me that my soul and spirit were connected to the spirit of that sacred mountain. He showed me how, at one point, the trees on the mountain got blight, but the mountain was still free and safe. There was still pure water there. He showed me the medicine of the sacred hawk and lightning butterfly. Then he took me to the sacred spring and told me to drink. He said, "This sacred water fills all your cells with purity. When they poisoned you, it was diluted by the purity of the spring water the Native Americans call 'first medicine.' Feel the spring water in your cells."

Then he took me to a cave in behind my sternum, by my heart, where I have always protected my soul. He told me to place a crystal geode around my soul, warning me that the next part of the journey would be very difficult and dangerous. He took me to a cliff and showed me how I had scampered up and down in safety as a child. Then he stood me on the edge and gave me height sickness; I teetered, ready to fall. He said if I fell, I would fall to my death, but that I had the power to maneuver in safety.

I thought the journey was over, and I started to come back, but then I closed my eyes again and she came to me—a beautiful celestial being of light, radiant blue. She told me her name was Laiolin. She dressed me in a beautiful blue dress and said she was always watching me. She hadn't come until I needed her the most. She told me I had been chosen to help the cause of freedom on Mother Earth. She gave me three gifts: strength without power, battle without war, protection without defense. Then she placed me in a light chamber; it was like being inside the Sun. My body was irradiated with the light, with Christ light. When I emerged, she gave me a shield (very lightweight, like aluminum foil, but impenetrable), a sword with a silver Druid blade to help me find truth and a headband with a silver ribbon down the back. She said that my journey was important, but that there was a lot more going on than just my personal freedom, that I was part of a bigger plan. She asked me if I wanted to work with her and if I would help heal Mother Earth.

When I was fourteen years old, I had stood on my sacred mountain and vowed to Creator God that someday I would find a way to be of true service to my people. That has always been my goal in life; everything I did was focused toward that goal. So when she said that, I knew deep in my heart that it was the right thing for me. But I didn't just go blindly into the agreement of working with her; I established some boundaries and made some agreements with her. I said, "I will work with you, providing that this is for the highest good." I had already seen that she was of the Christ consciousness; if any entity comes to you and is bringing the illusion that they are of the Christ light and they're really not, and you say, "In the name of Christ Jesus, declare yourself," they have to do so. She was of the Christ light. But I still respected my boundaries and was cautious. We agreed that if at any time I didn't want to work with her, that was that. It was entirely of my own free will that I chose to work with her. We also agreed that it would be for the highest good for me, my children and my family, and that my health would improve. I knew that last part was major, because I had known people who had depleted their health working with spiritual beings. I said I wouldn't be part of anything that wasn't good for me. We made an agreement to work together temporarily, based on how I felt about being with her. She explained that to work with me, she needed to enter my heart chakra, and I agreed. At that time, when she entered my heart chakra, I had the most powerful light experience I could ever imagine. I've had a lot of light experiences since then, but this was truly phenomenal. In the following weeks and months, she would speak through me, but it wasn't until six months later that I realized that I was doing what they call channeling. Much later I would learn that I am a conscious-merge channel; I never leave my body.

Now, I'd always been suspicious of channels and channeling, because I would not step aside and let something take over my body. I didn't feel safe doing that. But this felt completely safe. She is a higher-dimensional part of myself; we are coexistent. When she would come and talk to me in the sessions, she would use my voice, but I was entirely co-conscious. I knew everything that was going on, and I was healthy enough to be able to monitor my body and know it was for my highest good. That began a two-year period in which my healing was accelerated. She began to teach me about the awakening of what she called the House of David and the plan to liberate the planet and assist humanity in awakening into a higher state of consciousness. She was connected to a mothership, which I later learned was Arcturian. There were times when, in sessions with my acupuncturist, Dr. K., energy would be transmitted from the ship through her to help balance the right and left hemispheres of my brain, to heal the neural synapses of the damage done during my childhood experiences. She taught me some phenomenally powerful exercises: how to clear my energy field and activate my chakras. She became my main healer, but I also continued to work with a gifted massage therapist, my acupuncturist and Dr. D. Every Wednesday, from 8:30 in the morning to 3:30 in the afternoon, I went to therapy and worked all day on my healing. I did this for several years. It was hard work. I feel that the main body of my healing was complete by 1998.

With the assistance of my angel, my sword and my shield, my work accelerated. I feel I had to go through the first part of the terror wall to attain my own empowerment and connect to my reality at a certain level before I was ready for her to come—before I was ready to start claiming my spiritual gifts, which quickened and accelerated my path. I began to learn that the tools for protection and safety were right there inside of me, and that they could be used in a very powerful way.

Almost immediately—within two weeks—I stumbled upon a major piece of brainwashing and mind control. I discovered that I had been programmed with Blackjack chewing gum. I had been put through programming sessions where I was shown Blackjack gum and given commands and pain cycles. They also tied this in with playing cards—either of the black jacks was a death card. That was my trigger. [This is described at more length in Chapter Six.] Once I discovered this trigger and realized that I had been subjected to mind-control programming, I began to understand how mind-control programmers often use common, everyday things for their own purposes. It is not the item that's dangerous or evil, but the association in your mind.

Once you discover the triggers, you can spot attempts to program you. I set up safety systems inside my psyche to set off alarm systems in my body if a program was brought out. Even if my conscious mind didn't get it, my deep conscious would. This was a very powerful part of my healing and recovery. I learned to brush myself to clear the energy, to clear my aura field. I learned that a lot of negative energy is held in our hair. Sometimes just brushing my hair in the sunlight would make me feel so much better. As I discovered these things and worked more with the energetics of wholeness, I began to have more good days. I began to appreciate a sweetness in life that had been numbed by the pain and agony of my years of confinement in the mind prison.

Once again, a helpful person appeared in my path—a therapist at a center in Colorado who works with people who are trying to get free. He consulted with me on the telephone. Around this time, I was wrestling with notions like, "Hey, I'm functional; how could this be true about me?" I'd always been capable of manifesting things in my life—doing things, working hard, making things happen. He compared me to a football player who had played the game with a broken leg.

Dr. D. also helped me to understand; he said, "Most of the people in the world who have contributed the greatest gifts have done so out of great pain." At some place, our soul, our psyche, makes the choice to destroy or create. Those of us who really want to make social change and to reach out to humanity in a caring way, frequently do so out of the depths of our own pain. He also gave me a graphic analogy, that to match the deep, low curve of my life's pain, I had developed an ability to create a corresponding curve to reflect the ecstasy and joy in life on a higher plane. This made sense. I thought of sunsets, how they have always been a passion, a beautiful experience. I'd stand there going, "Omigosh, look at these colors! They're so beautiful!" And other people would say, "Yeah, that's a nice sunset." I'd think, *Wow, we must not be seeing the same sunset.* I've always had this passion for beauty, for music, for the wonderful experience of being by myself in a cool canyon on a hot day and finding a petroglyph. Understanding this helped a lot as I struggled through these excruciating memories. I realized that I am not the trauma I experienced.

During this part of my awakening, I went through some of the worst memories. I remembered rites of passage at a mortuary in Denver. I later located the mortuary and made a visit. I had no conscious memory of ever being inside this place. My husband was shocked because I had accurately described the floor plan from memory. I believe that a lot of effort had been invested in creating a depiction of the underworld, like a Hollywood set. People were dressed in demonic costumes to conduct the sacrifices. In these rites, I was made to believe that I was married to Satan. After I recovered this memory, I had what is called a "satori"—an awakening or profound realization. I realized that I was not being filled with darkness, that I was there to fill the darkness with light. For the first time, I felt as if I were an angel of light who had agreed to bring the love of God to inaccessible places of the deepest fear. At first it was a little glimmer of knowing, but through the years that knowledge has grown. I now understand that I consciously agreed, before I incarnated, to do this piece of work. I consciously agreed to enter what I call the belly of the beast, like Jonah in the story of the whale. I agreed to go into the dark caverns of the uncharted area and crack the paradigm.

I remember a deep emotional reaction when in 1989 the Berlin Wall was taken down. As I began breaking down the walls of secrecy, the crumbling of the Berlin Wall was a guidepost for me. I believe that wall's destruction had a powerful impact on the psyche of humanity. It had divided families. People took dramatic chances to escape, to get to their families on the other side. On one side of the wall was freedom; on the other side was oppression. I feel as though our psyches—as a race, as a society—have been divided just in that way, that we as human beings on this planet have lived on both sides of that wall. But there was a part of us throughout history that always tried to go toward freedom, always knew there was a better world. When the Berlin Wall fell, it was as if our psyches opened to the knowledge that the worlds would return to oneness, families would be reunited, freedom was in the wind. Freedom was imminent for our souls, for the souls of humanity trapped in dichotomy. I knew deep in my heart that I was to play a part in this quest for freedom. I also knew that there was no darkness, no evil element capable of filling my golden soul with their poison. I had come to bring the light.

CHAPTER SIX

I Discover the Black Hole

April 10, 1992: I had a massage and connected with my vision of empowerment—the angel of light who manifested two weeks ago. I also connected to the potential effects of subliminal programming by the cult. I did a meditation and went to my safe place. I saw a black hole. I picked up my sword, shield and headband, and started to explore. It is a cave where the wolf child lives. I was pulled back by a stern voice telling me I was crazy, lying, disobedient, destructive, insane. I checked it out; it was the German woman. The German woman was the source. I allowed her to speak through me to my practitioner. She had a hoarse voice; it was very deep. As she spoke, my face twitched violently. Then all was still. I felt myself empowered with my tools to face her, and I commanded her to leave. I spoke to her in my voice. When she spoke, my voice changed. I told her I was no longer a helpless child, that my body, mind and soul belong to me. She tried to hold her ground, but I made her leave. As she left, the pain in the left side of my head went away. I believe that at the age of three or four years old, when I met this German programmer-woman, she was an implanted alter (a fragmented personality intentionally implanted for programming and mind control). I confronted her, that she was somehow implanted to control me because she was the one who had put me in the vault with the dead cats as a little girl.

This was a major piece in the opening up of my freedom. The same journal entry continues.

> April 10, 1992 (continued): As I left her, my guide told me to go and do a ceremonial bathing in my safe place, on my sacred mountain, and I bathed and washed myself. I felt all of her ugliness wash away. Then my guides told me that if I was ready, we would voyage to the wolf child. I floated in a void for a while; then I saw a cage, a box about four feet by four feet, metal, with a cage door. I felt a lot of pain in my right ear. I realized that the wolf child was inside the box, chained by a collar on its neck. They beat on the outside of the box to cause the metal to boom and bang inside. Then I was inside with the wolf child. I *became* the wolf child, growling, angry, fierce, lapping water, clawing the walls. I asked how old I was; my guide said I was eight years old. My practitioner held me. Then I entered as myself, with my sword and shield and ribbon, and soothed the child. At first, it did not respond. Then I told it that it had suffered long enough; I had come to free it. "That's okay, my darling," I said. "I'm here now." There was a strength I had never felt before. It was empowering, and eventually the wolf child calmed and slept. I found myself sunbathing on a rock in cosmic light.

That same day at Dr. D.'s office, during a journey, I went to my safe place, to the beautiful waterfall where I had washed myself. My guide told me that if I chose to go past the box, I could go on with the gifts that my tools brought. Behind the waterfall, I entered a cave; it was a long, dark tunnel. Deeper and deeper I went. I struggled to go on. At last my guide said that if I chose to enter the next dimension, there would be a door. But the warning came again: I would have to see horrible things, but only to heal. I chose to open the door. I opened one door after another, and at last I came to a heavy vault door. I pulled and pulled. When it moved, beyond was a blue void; that is all. I had a very hard time afterward; I felt like I was in a state of shock. Taking my kids to the dentist, I almost passed out. It was terrifying to feel so traumatized. I got to bed early. My brain and my whole head were sore. I had a bad night, but I finally fell asleep and had a nightmare about being chased by a monster.

April 16, 1992: My mind is building up pressure; I feel like running away. I feel out of control, self-destructive. I am afraid. I want to die. I want to leave my family. I want to be left alone. I want to hurt myself. I feel trapped. I feel crazy. I feel helpless. I feel like bursting. I feel terrified. I am afraid. I want to get free; maybe death will free me. I feel like a failure. I feel like a lump of shit. I feel like there is no way out. I feel they are closing in around me. I feel like I could hurt myself. I must be strong. Where are my sword and shield? Where is my protection? I call to my guides; I ask for help. I need my higher power to lift me up and carry me, as I am unable to go a step further. All is lost in blackness and confusion. I want to hurt myself. I don't need to act; I feel crazy.

I believe that as I grew closer to discovering the innermost part of the mind control, these programs were put in place to make me think I was crazy and stop me from further discovery. After I got to the bottom of these memories, I did not have such self-destructive thoughts.

April 1992: With this agreement, I call the attention of all my inner children and alters, even those I have not met yet. I ask for a committee of inner people to help me reach all of my parts, for a complete agreement with self. I do this as an act of self-love and nurturing. I enter into this agreement of my own free will, for my best interest. The terms of this agreement are as follows:

1. I will not attend any ceremony that is not of the highest interest of the one Wakan [Lakota name for sacred] God.

2. I will not welcome perpetrators into my home or my life.

3. I will not allow anyone to hypnotize me.

4. I will be appropriate in public with the information revealed to me by others and always respectful of my own safety and privacy.

5. I will not share my memories with people who are not

safe or who will not be acting in a protective way for my higher good.

6. I will not permit anyone to use old triggers or control mechanisms installed by the evil ones.

7. I will dedicate my life to freedom, self-love, inner light, the sacred path and truth.

8. I will not permit anyone to use evil energy to harm my family or myself.

9. I will clear my house of all entities that are not for my highest good and of a sacred spirit, and I will not permit them to intervene in my space and my sanctity.

On April 25, I went back and tried to go through that doorway I had opened, but something was stopping me. When I asked what or who it was, I met Charlene, an alter. She was twelve years old, heavyset; she wore black clothing and lots of makeup. Charlene became a fragmented part of me when I was forced to have an abortion by the nuns. I went back to the basement of the hospital. I know I had two abortions when I was around eleven or twelve years old. This particular one was very difficult. I recovered a memory of another early abortion that was not so traumatic. Nobody knew that I was pregnant; in fact, I never knew until I recovered this memory.

This was not the only memory I had regarding Satanism and the Catholic Church. Because of the "doubling" phenomenon already described and the deep dichotomy permeating our society, it is not so surprising that certain divisions of the Church deviated into Satanism and served as an instrument of terror programming by the covert government for the purposes of mind control. The television series *20/20* produced a program on Operation Paperclip, the code name for the project that sponsored bringing the Nazi doctors from the concentration camps to America to continue the programs of human experimentation. The documentary listed the Church as an organization that funded the project. Please understand: I am not saying that all Catholic churches are involved. Just as some groups of Masons were involved, so were some parts of the Church. These are merely two manifestations of the split in the psyche of our society. Laiolin used the analogy of a spider on a mirror: For every force of light and love on our planet, there has been a counterforce of darkness and fear. This affects all facets of society in some way.

The abortion memory was excruciating. My acupuncturist was a compassionate woman who held me as I physically went through the birth of this child who was taken from me. I remember them showing him to me—a tiny fetus, but you could tell he was a boy. They told me that they were taking him to use him in ceremonies. I went through a lot of grief at that time, because I never could conceive children. I had so much wanted to have children, to feel a baby grow, to nurse it. And my only son was taken from me. I grieve for all the women who don't re-member. Maybe they don't have to. Maybe in some way my soul was strong enough to experience these things and remember, to grieve not only for myself and that lost part of my childhood, but for all the young women who were forced through experiences like this. Perhaps I helped to heal this wound, this deep scar of women who have experienced this atrocity.

In that room where the abortion had happened, I let Charlene speak. I mentioned before that a playing card and Blackjack chewing gum had been used to program me. The following journal entry relates a memory of how that was done and how I unraveled and deprogrammed it.

April 25, 1992: She spoke in her own husky voice. She came after the abortion. I was exhausted and thirsty, strapped to the table. They were injecting something up my vagina; there were wires on my head. They showed me a picture of my brother as a baby, then a package of Blackjack chewing gum, while bright lights flashed in my eyes. At the same time, I was given alternating pain induction and sexual stimulation. The message was repeated that I must obey, I must do what I was told, or I would hurt my brother. They said that when I was shown a package of the gum or the black jack playing card, I would not remember seeing them, but I would follow the instructions that had been given me. I had not signed the second contract; it lay on the table. Charlene came and signed my name to the contract. She told me she agreed to cooperate, to participate, to forget all that happened after age twelve and to be a "good girl." If not, if I violated the contract on the table, I would hurt my brother. He was very precious to me. This is how the cult works to control people, because they program us to hurt each other. I knew at that time that if I didn't sign, they'd make me hurt my brother, and I didn't want to do that. So

I made that agreement that day, through Charlene, to cooperate, to participate and to forget.

I asked Charlene to see the contract; she had a box she kept it in. I explained that the paper was probably lost years ago. At first she didn't want me to see it, as she had promised not to destroy it. One of my spiritual animal guides, Lame Cat, came to help me, and my guides came to give me support. They told us that we could erase it [the contract]. Charlene let me see it. We erased it—not to destroy, as she had promised, but now it was blank. We took it and the black jack card and her to my sacred safe place. On that sacred mountain, we built her a fortress and gave her a new job, where she could build the fortress to protect the contract. But now it was blank, and the power of the black jack card was no longer controlling me. I put the card with the blank contract and Charlene. She has built her fortress to protect it. We explained to Charlene that they have lied, they had no such power, but all she understands is to protect the contract and not let it be destroyed. Now the jack is a joker; the contract is safe in the fortress, but blank—powerless over me. I believe the contract is undone in my own mind; Charlene is free and so am I, and I have the freedom to remember after age twelve. I am free of the rule that said, "Violate this contract and you will hurt your brother." I will never have to feel that terror again.

April 1992: The blind never awaken to the screams of the innocent. I need to prepare for a battle by strengthening my center. Then, yesterday morning, I had a memory. I went back to the room at the hospital. A nun and the German woman were with me; they had me undress. I remember my twelve-year-old nakedness, my small breasts. The nun molested me while the woman waited. It was very erotic, like an orgy. She took off her clothes too, and we danced. Later they put me on the table and put the seeds of

Satan in my vagina. Finally, the woman brought a baby, dead already, and I showed them that I could do gross things with it. It was a very disgusting memory. I performed well and passed the test. They put me on the table with the dead baby on my abdomen and told me it was my son, the one who was aborted. Then, again, they placed Satan's seed in my vagina.

I realized, through this memory, how a person's mind can be twisted to do things he or she would otherwise never do. In seeing how this could happen, I found a major gateway to freedom.

The following week was incredibly difficult. I was dissociating and really feeling out of it. Luckily, Dr. D. had an appointment time open, and I went in for an emergency visit. I went to my safe place.

May 3, 1992: I was feeling all the children suffer; to heal, I must feel my inner children's pain. They said that for me to heal, I had to have the determination of the coal miner who viewed his family at Ludlow [a town in southern Colorado where there was a massacre during the Coal Mining Wars] and then went to the mountains to fight, or the Sioux warrior who kept his soul strong after seeing his massacred family and was undefeatable, or the slave who defied all logic to be free.

I had the courage to feel the pain of those inner children and to love them. Knowing their agony gave me the strength for the battle that lay ahead. I ask you, the reader, to open your heart to a twelve-year-old who experienced this atrocity.

May 4, 1992: It has been a very peaceful day. The rain is gentle, and the essence of spring is in the air. I took a ride and experienced the beautiful apple blossoms. The blossoms were so beautiful. I stopped and picked lilacs. My land is safe; my home is safe. I am free here. I am so very thankful to be here in this beautiful valley; it's wonderful beyond imagination. I felt I would die at times through this journey, but finally I have found freedom and peace. I pray that I am able to protect my family and help my children heal. I wonder what this all will lead to. So much I feel like I'm wandering through an unknown forest, on a twisty, hidden path that I have never seen before. Where once I knew my way, in the same territory all the landmarks have changed. My direction is different, and I must find a way with courage.

May 5, 1992: Yesterday, the gates opened, and I cried until I couldn't cry any longer. I felt the grief for that twelve-year-old; I felt degraded and humiliated and crushed. It was so mortifying to remember my act as a participant; it was just another trick, just another way of working my mind.

May 12, 1992: I went to my safe place and asked for understanding about what was happening. My guide showed me my meditation of May 3: feeling the pain of the children, awakening the warrior spirit as a Sioux who sees his village massacred. Then my guide showed me a tunnel, a hall under a city, like the hall leading to where they split my brain: concrete water pipes along the corners of the ceilings, cold, semidark. He showed me a nursery with more than ten hospital bassinets. He said that these children are not on birth records; they were born and bred to the cult and raised institutionally without parents—no home, no school, no record of their existence. Then he showed me the classroom where they are trained and educated. They are the people of the underworld. They have a completely controlled environment. He showed me summer camps where kids suffer ritual abuse. But beyond where the normal children go is the special training for the children of the underworld. He showed me the uniforms of all key public positions where these people are planted, particularly a judge who left his judge's stand and entered the underworld through his chambers. He is not who people think he is; he is replaced. He has perverted sex as part of a daily routine. He returns to the underworld for instructions. He is very powerful.

I believe my guide brought me to this information with a form of remote viewing. I have had other remote-viewing experiences since this initial one. This kind of thing is going on in our society, unbeknownst to the people who go to these officials expecting justice. Not all judges are contaminated; not all public officials are contaminated. Our government has a lot of good people working in it, people who really love freedom and work to do what's right. But this showed me that key people were put in places of power and were carefully trained so they could be used in whatever way the covert government might want to use them at critical times. This knowledge strengthened my conviction to explore my own journey, to find out how this evolved in my own life. I knew that in some way the covert government had used me to do things that were not conscious choices.

According to Native American teachings, elk medicine has a lot to do with sexuality. In one of my journeys, I saw what happens when a man uses contrary elk medicine. Often men are not even conscious that they carry this power, but it happens anyway. Within the realm of spirit are many allies as well as entities who drain our power and keep us in a victim's role. I saw spiritually that a fiery elk rises out of a man with burning nostrils and pulls the power out of a woman. After that happens, she feels suicidal and empty and drained. I remember teachings from the Native Americans about a beautiful young woman who was crazy in love with this ugly old man. I wondered how a beautiful young woman could give her power to such a man. The elder said that was contrary elk medicine. I began to understand that the spiritual forces that control people in fear exist among all cultures of humanity. The dark shamans use power animals to manipulate the spiritual realms to take power. What I realized is that many men unknowingly carry this energy, even if they have no training in dark shamanism. However, once we claim our spiritual empowerment, once we learn protection and change the energy of being a victim, we are no longer pawns of these negative spiritual forces—whether they are intentional or not. I also learned through my journeys that the covert government had sent people from the CIA out to Native American shamans to steal their power. Their objective was to misuse and contort the power into a tool they could manipulate for evil. Many of my Native American brothers and sisters are aware of this and are working to bring a healing to these ancient ways that are so sacred. This demonstrates once again how the psyche of humanity has been split. Regardless of culture, all of humanity is affected.

Later that month, I recovered one of the most important memories in the entire process. I went back to a childhood home, in a small canyon high in the mountains of Colorado. We had no close neighbors. I was a baby, standing in my crib.

> May 25, 1992: I enter through a red stone in my womb and an enormous amount of pain. I was standing in my crib and saw fires outside; people were yelling and screaming. I must have been one or almost two. They came in and carried me from the crib. My siblings were locked in the shed. They placed me on a high table; I saw two men hold my mommy. She was screaming, "Not my baby!" Then they hurt me sexually. They killed my pet ducks and dripped the blood on me while they hurt me. I was tied down. The object was to get my mom to sign, to cooperate. They had fires built around. Then they got a hot poker—it was white hot—and were going to kill me with it. My mother agreed to sign. This memory was accompanied by shaking of my arms and convulsions. She signed the paper, and they left. I know my dad wasn't home. My mother got my sisters out of the storm cellar, and she took us to bed and cried and held us and apologized. She said she thought we would be safe in this canyon. She held my face and the tears ran from her eyes and streamed over my cheeks, and she said to me, "Baby, someday you'll be free." She promised me then to find secret ways to resist, and she did. Then my guide showed me the way my mother had worked to deprogram me, how she had taught me to defy fear, how she had taught me to love the Earth and how even though she never consciously remembered this, she was a freedom fighter all her life.

I have no proof of the paper that was signed. I know that my mother had no conscious memory of this event. My sister confirmed that she recalls being put in the shed; she recalls that my father was arrested on a parking ticket. She has no other memory of the event. I have, however, inventoried all the ways my mother served as my deprogrammer. She told me, "Let not death or fear of death stop you from doing what is right for your people." Her words are my code of honor. She taught me not to let fear stop me, told me stories of brave Indians, took me on hikes where we played a game called courage: making believe that monsters would test my ability to stay centered in a fearful situation. I can't possibly relate how many things she did to help me prepare for this journey. Now I am no longer controlled by my inner fears, and these childhood experiences helped me have the courage to break through the fear barriers.

In June of 1992, I recovered some extensive memories of my doctor's office in Golden and being taken into Satanic rites. The memories were very detailed about the building and the connection of the examination room to the chamber that had the rites in them. Within the year, I had an opportunity to go back to Golden, as I related previously. The doctor is no longer living; his office is closed. But I went to the building and compared the architecture with my memories. They were the same. I had learned one of the ways I had been inducted into the experiments.

Shortly after that, I discovered an alter inside me, a little princess who, through psychic perpetration, had a bomb strapped to her. If I ever woke up and started telling the truth, the bomb would detonate and destroy me. There was a part of my psyche that really believed that the bomb could be detonated. That belief kept me from knowing the truth. I deprogrammed the bomb; I deactivated it, and I moved on. I took care of that princess, loved her, taught her to be safe. I taught her that children don't have to be used that way any longer.

CHAPTER SEVEN

Reclaiming the Sacred

In July of 1992, I had a memory that took me back to rites of passage. I've mentioned this previously. I want to share the last part of the narrative in my journal, because it demonstrates taking power and breaking the bondage of the death fear. The details about the rites need not be recounted here for the meaning to be understood, but I will say that they were held at a mortuary.

> July 1992: I entered the underworld. It would have made any movie producer proud—Stephen King, step aside! Flames danced from cauldrons, and torches hung from walls, creating an evil fire-flicker effect. Demons cloaked in black with skeleton faces danced forth from a door to the left, then a lot of super-orgy stuff. The idea was that by entering the underworld and communing with the demons, we were permanently linking a ceremony of the dead, bonded with the underworld. Puke! Which I did a lot of, in the memory. I got very fed up with the bullshit. I took up my sword and my shield, and beckoned to my helpers. With the help of Archangel Michael, Lame Cat and my guides, I cracked the walls of their temple. Light streamed in. Then I brought water from my sacred spring and poured it into the chamber. From the ceiling, light beamed down, and I was lifted up to heaven and Christ appeared to me. I asked to be forgiven for what I had unwillingly participated in as a child. He lifted me up from my childhood bondage, saying, "Go forth and sin no more." I explained that I wasn't used to being taken up to

heaven and meeting Christ. He said I'd get used to it. It was really wonderful to be with Jesus. I don't know what to make of it. I still feel the shock when I try to think of it.

Now, this was strange. I wasn't a Christian. I didn't believe in heaven. But that summer, a dear friend had given me a Bible. I'd read about how Jesus ordered demons out and helped people to heal. I'd read the story where the woman washes Christ's feet. And in that moment, in being lifted up by Christ, my soul was set free. I knew I had broken the bonds. I also knew there would be psychic repercussions, and I called friends for support, to help me batten down the hatches for psychic attack.

One of the most powerful teachings I read in the Bible that summer was the parable of the sower. When someone sows seeds, some of them fall onto rocks, in places where they can't grow. Other seeds land in fertile soil and flourish. I knew in my heart that this was about truth and that I was one of those seeds that had been dropped in fertile soil—to "grow" the truth. My only association with the Catholic Church had been negative; I feel that it was through my Catholic uncle that I experienced much of the Satanic ritual abuse. I always avoided churches. When I was a child, my mother taught me to love Jesus, but I never trusted organized religion. I didn't have a personal relationship with Jesus until that day when he lifted me up from this pit of despair. This began a series of visions of Christ that were very powerful in my life. In time I had such intense personal experiences with Christ Jesus that I did indeed get used to it.

A part of me resisted this experience. On July 10, 1992, I recorded that my guides told me to trust these sacred visions; they reassured me that I could have faith in this process, that I would not be misled. They taught me that I could accept the blessing of the sacred ones, be they Native American or Christian or cosmic. They are all part of the one God force of what the Lakota call the Wakan energy, the sacred energy. Quanab said just to accept that some of my parts were experiencing extreme doubt. The voices inside my head said, "Boy, now you're seeing Jesus! You're really flipping out!" We located the voice of doubt and confusion; it turned out to be an alter (an inner person) who had been planted by the cult so that if I ever reached a point of connecting to Christ, that alter would create doubt and tell me that only crazy people had such visions. She was beautiful but twisted. I used soul-retrieval techniques to help her to heal. I took her home to my sacred mountain and created a safe place for her. I learned not to be afraid of what lies inside me. I know that the only thing that keeps us in bondage is fear and the only way fear can control us is if it's anchored somewhere in our psyche. Once I could reach deep into my own psyche and set these children free, then the fear no longer controlled me. I can relate to the Negro spiritual song that has always been so dear to me. The lyrics are, "Go down Moses, 'way down in Egypt land. Tell ol' Pharaoh, to let my people go."

> July 15, 1992: Today is a beginning for me. It is a milestone of enormous size. I am free, free at last; my God, I'm free at last. When I shattered the temple, I shattered all the holds the people of the lie ever had on me. There is more work to do, more resolution, but I walk forth as a free human being. I feel an enormous blessing from the Wakan one, the elders and Christ. I no longer live in the shadow of the Dark Lord; I fear him not. I am free.

I questioned every part of myself: my own integrity, the very core of my existence.

> Journal entry from around July 1992: Do I love sunsets because I've known this hell and sought beauty? I know that in the very core of my being, there are traits that are part of my essence-self. I love life; I am optimistic. I love the Earth; I love gardening and growing things. I love my fellow man. I am an idealist. I am a human rights activist. I love adventure. I strive for higher ideals. I love intense, explorative conversations. I love hard work. I'm an intense person. I'm highly energetic, doing lots at once—too often, much too much. All this is me, not what they tried to make me into. This is what I can own as a person, as a human—not choose to compensate with, but the reality of my identity. What a relief! What a freedom! I have made a huge breakthrough.

That summer we learned that my mother-in-law was dying of cancer, and I left some of my children with my husband and took a couple of the kids with me to Colorado to care for her. She was a dearly loved soul, and I knew I could make her journey easier. That occupied most of my time. I began reading the Bible every day to my mother-in-law, and I became excited about what Jesus was talking about, about casting out demons. I read parts in the Bible where other people had had visions of him. In my own vision, when Jesus lifted me up, I had been dressed in a white gown.

The Bible speaks of that. I realized that I wasn't the only person to be dressed in a white gown, taken to Christ and absolved of demons. One day I said to my mother-in-law that I was there for a bigger purpose than helping the family out, and this very precious person said to me, "You came to read me the Bible."

I was terrified of Holy Communion because of what they say about it being the body and blood of Jesus. I could never bring myself to take Communion, and now I understood why. The words about the body and blood triggered the old memories. I overcame the fear and participated in one of the most sacred rites in my life. I took the holy sacrament just a few days before this precious person crossed over, and I learned that something powerful happens in the ceremony of the Holy Eucharist. That sacrament is a way for us to ingest the spirit of Christ, the spirit of God, in a special ceremony. I also believe that through the alter side of the church—not the "altar," but the alter—the body and blood part is like a trigger, like a little dark part popping up from the forgotten side of humanity. I learned to go beyond the words, to go beyond what the church said. I learned to have a personal relationship with Christ.

My church is Mother Earth. I pray wherever my brothers and sisters gather together in praise of creation, in praise of God, whatever name they might use in the name of love. I call myself a Universalist. I have taken Christ within my soul, and I serve him with my very life. I do, however, believe he walked among all children of Mother Earth. Elements within organized religion have used his teachings, distorted sacred truths and manipulated these sacred ways for power. This distortion is found within all religions. It is for us, the children of the light, to find our own pathway to God through the gateway that is within our hearts. In the past, we had a priest between our Creator and us. Now we are to enter into a personal communion with the Creator through the power of unconditional love.

CHAPTER EIGHT

The Journey Continues

I began working with a therapist in the metropolitan Denver area who helped me to deal with some of my alters. I met Flower Blossom, a little one who believed she was a bad seed. I also met Lolita, my pent-up passion. She scolded me for never allowing my passion to come out. I did some deep work with my wounded inner children and became comfortable talking to them.

I continued on my path of recovery, even though I was under a great deal of duress personally. I continued my fight for personal freedom. There was an advantage to being in that area for the three months I stayed there: I got to go to some of the places I remembered. I went to Golden and to Colorado Springs. Through the therapist, I met some other survivors, and we went on investigative trips. I had gone to Colorado Springs initially because I remembered a story about a relative of mine there, and I had conscious memories of going to Manitou Springs in my childhood. During the fall of 1992, I went to Manitou Springs and discovered, with another survivor, the deep roots of Satanic activity in that area. I also joined a survivor's group in Denver. It would seem that moving two of my five children to Denver to take care of a dying relative would slow me down, but it didn't—it actually quickened my recovery. Of course, my workload was lighter, so I had more time to contemplate. Compared to managing my own business and raising five children—including four teenagers—it was a vacation. I also was living once more in a neighborhood where I had lived as a teenager. I found that I felt quite safe, which I believe opened the door to deeper discoveries.

During my recovery-group meetings, I wrote some poetry that speaks to the terror that dwelt deep within my secret mind. One was "Childhood Ways." Another, "Denial," has been published in *Safe Passage to Healing*, by Chrystine Oksana. Susan Toney, a California-based artist, has incorporated that poem into a song, which appears on her CD, *Strange Child*.

Childhood Ways

Long hallways, doorways to hell.
Chambers of horror behind
*   locked doors.*
In secrecy, beneath normal floors,
*   wrenching pain and violence,*
splitting off parts of me needed to
*   survive the ordeal*
of pain beyond white death.
Forgotten, sitting in the chambers of my mind,
cells that scream with agony in memory of betrayal.

My Terror

Repressed terrors screaming in my mind.
Eyes wide open, heart pounding wildly
*   in the darkness.*
Alert to every sound, to motion, to fear,
reeling in my head.
In the very cell of my body,
*   the memory of pain*
*   denied me as a child.*

Breaking the Silence

Karey shivering, cold, naked, the
*   blackness of night chill,*
wondering who will come to
*   bring me to the center,*
wondering what agony awaits
*   me, the terror of the night.*
Beneath brilliant stars,
little body shivering in
*   anticipation.*

My time in Colorado was finished, and I returned home. On November 17, I had quite a powerful experience.

November 17, 1992: The cosmic being of light took me up a golden stairway. I felt an access, an alignment star to Earth's core, an awakening in my womb, a vital stirring of life energy. Then I felt an opening, a blossoming, spiraling, whirlpooling energy entering the center, to plant the cosmic seed. I felt elated and holy and whole; it took me awhile to return. As I walked out of Dr D.'s, it was evening time. I looked at the horizon and saw the bright and shining face of the evening star. I felt a deep sacred connection to Venus—I always have. I said a silent prayer in thanksgiving for this special gift.

In another session, I went to my safe place, and Quanab gave me the power of the lightning butterfly. He told me never to use it to intimidate anyone, but only for protection. During this vision, I had an unusual and intense sensation in my body, the awakening of sensations long numbed. It was hard to stay with it. I was in a very deep trance.

Earlier in that week, I had dreamed of going to a shop in the back of a marketplace, where blankets, bowls and Indian artifacts were sold. As I walked down the street, I was guided to find the shop. I was told that I would find a valuable crystal that would help me heal. Amazingly, in "real life," I did find the shop, just as in my dream, and I found the dark purple fluorite crystal, beautiful, with three peaks circling the central one. I bought it and cleared it, and later I looked up the properties of fluorite. I learned that it opens the door of illusion, permitting vision of the reality behind it. Its properties include advancing the mind as well as balancing positive and negative mental aspects. This crystal has been referred to as a third-eye stone. It helps in understanding and integrating nonphysical aspects of the fourth, fifth and sixth dimensions.

For years after that, I used that powerful crystal. I held it to my third eye and slept with it. Later I learned that purple fluorite helps to harmonize brain frequencies. Finally, in 1996, in a sweat lodge, it exploded into many pieces. I think that the crystal was anchoring the energy of powerful healing assistance in my process of finding freedom. I began to experience a depth of spirituality I had never known. I always thought I was a deeply spiritual person, but it is something different to feel the light of God surge through you and open up communication to the higher realms.

Denial

Tonight I saw the news and
heard my family gasp
at the sight of a small,
battered boy.
Yet, if I spoke of what
    happened to my body as
    a child,
they would gaze blankly and
change the channel and
silently deny.

Prayer for Freedom for My People

Wakan Tanka,
I pray for freedom for my people, for myself.
I pray for healing of the mind, body and spirit,
for my people, for myself.
I pray for the strength to do what is right,
for my people, for myself.
I pray for the light of truth to shine and spread
to all the dark places,
for my people, for myself.
I pray for a path of beauty and peace,
for my people, for myself.

My journal for 1993 begins with this quote from Patrick Henry, one of my childhood heroes: "Is life so dear, or peace so sweet, as to be purchased at the price of chains and slavery? Forbid it, Almighty God! I know not what course others may take; but as for me, give me liberty or give me death."

Over the next two years, I faced what I believe was a cult attack on my husband's integrity and healing practice. As with many other people who were trying to break ties with the cult and mind control, the legal system was used to persecute us. The situation taught me a lot about protecting myself from cult attack. It gave me a great opportunity to declare my freedom, to learn about psychic protection and to call upon the allies to protect my family. If anything ever taught me not to be a victim, it was that situation. After a two-year battle with the Attorney General's office and the local licensing board in the state where we lived, we were awarded a settlement. The conspiracy was exposed. I told them to keep their dirty money and just to clear my husband's name. What a way to get a lesson! By the end of that time, though, I had learned more about the gifts my cosmic angel had given me: battle without war, strength without power and protection without defense. This physical battle helped me strengthen my inner core for my inner battle, and I continued to move forward.

CHAPTER NINE

Spin Programming

It was in January of 1993 that I experienced what I call the whirlpool of memory. My journal tells the story better than I could explain it now.

> January 8, 1993: I was paralyzed, my arms hurt and my entire right side was a mass of excruciating pain. A child was being led away. I was in agony. I called to my guides. I summoned the power to break the paralysis, and I grabbed the crystal rock, vowing never again to be paralyzed while a child was hurt. I returned to the source of the programming to paralyze me. I empowered myself with my crystal, with my guides. I entered the chamber, unstuck the door. There was a circular platform, like a disk. Overhead, a light was very bright. I was spinning. First pain in my right arm; a metal cast was on my shoulder. Arm pain, then spinning. Sometimes I was lying down, sometimes tied to a chair, sometimes to a post. All at once the spinning would abruptly halt, and the word was, "Freeze! Frozen!" Then the action was repeated. I was too disoriented to walk. I returned with my sword and destroyed the platform. I took the energy and called upon Archangel Michael to purify this memory.

In mid-January, I uncovered a memory of my high school and a counselor I really liked a lot. I began remembering being taken down into the basement of my high school for government indoctrination. This is when my memories began to be associated with government programming. I recall being in a room, and an alter named Carolyn was created. She thought she was enlisted in the military. They played all kinds of videos like the ones that come over TV, where the airplanes are flying over and guns are booming and the national anthem's playing, and there were all kinds of "serve your country" programmings—"You'll be proud to serve your country"—all different kinds of indoctrinations. Now, this is odd, because in my high school years, I wasn't attracted to the military at all; in fact, I didn't trust people who were in the military. So this shows a battle in my psyche. There was a part of me who really believed she was serving the government. Carolyn really bought the program. When I met her in sessions, she saluted. She was quite the flag-waver. Thank heavens I did get to know her, so that we could help her understand that service to our country is service to the cause of freedom. Our flag does not represent the people who misuse it; it does not represent the covert aspects of the government. They just *used* the flag; they used democracy and service to our country as a tool to twist my psyche. True service to our people, to our country and to what this nation of ours stands for is serving the cause of freedom and truth. During those sessions, she got reeducated.

I also met Laura.

January 10, 1993: At Dr. D.'s office, Laura came out and told him that no one was safe. She told him that my high school counselor betrayed us. She made a phone call, and we were taken at night. The year is 1967. Laura started by telling Dr. D. that she would shatter me like a glass to stop me from remembering. She is totally submissive to terror. During the journey, I found a key. It is the key to programming, a visual tool that I used to unlock a program, allowing access to a memory. I remember hearing my counselor's name. I know that I am in the basement of my high school. I know that it is a secret place with a secret door. I am in a long, narrow cell. I remember being naked except for a small gown and taken down a long hallway to a cell with a metal door. The room is bare except for a chamber pot. The door shuts. I am in total brightness. The ceiling is a light panel. There is no day or night. A woman comes and knocks me around. She tells me that I am not to be trusted, but she could give me a chance to prove myself. Then she leaves me in isolation with the bright lights. I am thirsty and hungry; time is lost. I try to hide from the light, but she returns. I beg forgiveness; I beg and plead. I am thirsty; I feel pain in my heart and my head. The lights are constant. I cry and tell her I will never lie again. I promise to forget that I was ever there. I beg to be forgiven. Again I am accused of lying. I will do anything just to stop the pain.

At this point I enter as my hero-self, with my sword, shield and guides. We confront the perpetrators and tell them they have no power over me. We soul-retrieve Laura to my sacred mountain, and I protect her with the power of the lightning butterfly. I know Laura knows more about the programming. I called a survivor friend I'd met in Denver. She too had recovered memories of spin programming and torture. We reasoned that laboratories had to have been set up for this kind of mind-control programming. I started to feel that I had also been taken to a college campus.

January 16, 1993: Dr. D. said that the power to be free is within my mind. There is no external source stronger than my own mind. Within my mind is the knowledge of the programming; once I undo it, no one will have any power over me. None of their tricks or illusions will work. The only power they have over me is in my mind, and that is reversible.

I notice, in reviewing my journal, that by January of 1993, my handwriting is legible. Throughout my life, no matter how I tried, I could not write straight. My grade school teachers always complained about my penmanship. One of the things I could look at every day, as a benefit of my recovery, is that I began to be able to write legibly. I also could read better, because the lines didn't run into one another.

January 22, 1993: I read a paper on spin programming; it send me into irritable rage. All week I've had to control it. I am functioning well, but it has been hard. An alter came out—his name is Kahn, the destroyer. He has a ravenous killing energy.

On my journey to my safe place, I met one of my strongest alters, Suzzanne. My guide had told me that I needed to deal with Kahn. He was hiding, because he thought that he would be locked up if he ever came forward. Suzzanne told us that Kahn was programmed to kill me. We promised him that if he came out and spoke, nobody would lock him up. Kahn came out and spoke in a booming voice, calling himself Lord Kahn, the destroyer—his power, the power of death. He told Dr. D. he should hide, for Kahn kills. Dr. D. wasn't afraid and told him that he had been lied to by evil people. I remember Kahn as a twelve-year-old boy. Maybe we could find him something else to do; I could be his friend. He boomed, "I am Lord Kahn. No friends—only power and death." I asked him if he just happened or was made, and I went into a convulsion. It took me awhile to slow it down.

After it stopped, I went to my acupuncturist's office. We called Archangel Michael to help us. I got a good image of Archangel Michael—strong, medium-long blond hair, with wings and all. He sent a golden red light from his sword into the top of my head. The light met resistance; I had located Kahn in my stomach. It was like fire. My practitioner said, "Fire in the stomach stops the mind and kidneys from communicating and blocks the vital energy to the tantien, the energy source below the navel in your body." So we worked on opening a pathway through the fire; then I arrived in my abdomen. I found vast amounts of pain in waves like contractions: bad, then better, then bad. It hurt so much; I had to breathe. I started to try to intellectualize, but my practitioner reminded me to let my mind go and just work on the energy flow. We found the color of the pain; it was deep black-purple with flashing lights, programming lights.

Then I went through a birth experience, as if I were having a baby. Labor: painful, breathing, pushing, birth position, lots and lots of pain. I told my practitioner I was sixteen years old and around four months pregnant. I experienced the birth of my second child, a boy. I looked between my bent knees and saw the Dark Lord's cape and hood; he was like Satan personified. I thought I heard the baby whimper or cry or squeak; he was tiny, but definitely a boy. The Dark Lord held him up by his feet and named him Kahn, son of Satan. Other people were chanting and repeating oaths. Then came the awful part. He proclaimed him our son— his, the Dark Lord, Satan's, and mine. Then they proclaimed the growth of Kahn within me, to rule as lord of death. I don't know how, but they made him grow to twelve years old fast, so he was old enough to be a boy, a man, and do their bidding. I was told Satan was his father, and boys always obey their fathers.

As soon as I became aware of this, I also knew that I had rebirthed his soul just then when I experienced the labor. I renamed him Eagle Song. We called the eagle to carry his soul, now free, to be born to Earth once more, transmuted and healed. An incredible eagle cry came from within me as I watched him fly to freedom. I was filled with hope, and tears streamed down my face as I became aware that once free, his soul would return as a free man, a gifted child. I knew he would love the Earth, and I was full of the feeling of his tiny feet, free to run on the warm sand, to be in the Sun. Archangel Michael and my guides called a blessing, and as I stood at my sacred place, a gentle female rain came. I blessed my son: "Hold precious to freedom, and love the Earth, the Sun, the water." I didn't care that I'd never see him; I know even now that he has entered a body to be born free. Finally, his soul is free.

The cosmic angel appeared. She reminded me of my vision of the conception, when the nuns put the bad seed inside me and told me I was conceiving Satan's seed. She said that this is the conclusion. She said for me to see, to look inside to see if Kahn was still within me, and as I looked, I realized he was really gone. Then I knew the truth. They thought

> that they could turn my son into a demon within me who would even kill me, his mother, if directed to. But they forgot that the love between a son and his mother superseded their evil ways. Eagle Song is free.

I believe that this was a powerful way for my psyche to deal with the son they had aborted and with my being told repeatedly that I was carrying Satan's seed. In this metamorphic and symbolic rebirthing, I brought that seed they had placed within me and birthed it into healing and freedom. I birthed that child, that inner part of me, symbolically into freedom—again, this was a major step in my own freedom.

I know I've recounted a lot of these stories where I've claimed my freedom, where I've struggled and met wounded parts of myself. I hope I'm not telling you too much, too many of these stories, but I want you to know the process I went through. I want you to experience the journey with me, the struggles and the power of each step. I want you to walk the path to freedom with me so that you will understand what follows. I want you to be ready for dealing with the deep government programming and the experiments that happened in Colorado Springs that I testified about in Washington, D.C. I didn't just wake up one day and remember what the government had done to me in the experiments; it took years of deprogramming terror and of integrating lost parts of myself. It took many soul retrievals and journeys to develop the strength to break through that fear barrier. I have concluded, in my healing journey, that the fear barrier has been created in a number of people who have had similar experiences. But it's so terrifying that most people can't go past those fear walls to get down to deprogramming the government mind control. And that's intentional.

CHAPTER   TEN

The Age of Dichotomy

For weeks I had been working in my journeys at coming to a red brick wall and finding it impenetrable. I thought the wall was a metaphor. I thought many times, as I stood before it, that if I were a mouse, maybe I could climb through it. I worked long and hard to find a way. Finally, I collapsed with a headache and was taken to a friend's house. I meditated and contacted some of my inner children.

I found myself at the red brick wall—but when I looked this time, there was a doorway to the right. It looked just like the red brick, so it was easily concealed. I opened the doorway and found myself in front of a vault door inside an inner chamber. One of the inner children was so frightened that she couldn't enter, so one of the stronger ones had to take us in. We opened the vault, and a whole new terrain, a new segment of the journey unfolded. I entered into the chambers of experimentation by the government and the programming that was done in Colorado Springs.

> February 4, 1993: I revisited a memory, the chambers where they do the spin programming. I don't know; it seems so weird to me. In a khaki gown, held by both arms . . . again, the red-brick-wall door to the right, then the chamber with the vault door. Inside, I saw a table with a hypodermic needle. They put three needles in my spine to put in medicine. It made my brain hurt. I saw a room, a cylinder to stand in and spin—total darkness. I don't know when the spinning will start or when it will stop. Then the spin table I remembered before, the one they hang you by your hands to spin at the wrist. Shoes mounted on the floor, to cross your feet. A device where you're facing away from sharp things, in a chair that slowly brought the distance to

where the needles could poke you. They are fine and don't leave big marks, but they are very sharp. Then long, fine needle-wire is put in your brain, your eyes, while you are tied and sitting up. This all seems so bizarre.

February 5, 1993: I returned to the programming center. I remember that we were in orientation in a center for programming. We were all in a classroom. We wore light, short-sleeved, button-up-the-front shirts and pajamas with elastic-waist bottoms. I was eight to ten years old. I can't remember any of the faces. I felt the clothes; these were like the military would issue. A doctor was talking to us: "You are fortunate to have been chosen for a very important experiment. I assure you, careful records will be kept. You are privileged, for this project will benefit many people. Many of the tests are unpleasant, but you are not to be angry with the staff; they, I assure you, are well-trained professionals. They are just doing their job. Proper procedure will be followed. You must not speak of this project, as it is top-secret. You must not remember anyone you meet here. We will keep you isolated after today for your own safety. Again, I welcome you, and congratulations, for you are serving your country."

To recover this memory, I dispersed energy in the left top part of my brain. Writing about it has caused me an intense headache.

It was during this time, in 1993, when so many people began going to therapists and reporting disturbing, deeply buried memories. The television series *Primetime* featured a special report on cult abuse. I became very upset when I watched this program. It was full of what is termed "debunking" propaganda. Sometime later I saw a program that was aimed at ruining the reputation of Dr. Corey Hammond, a prominent psychiatrist who had been active in exposing the secret. It was slanted to make him look like a perpetrator. This was also when the False Memory Syndrome Foundation became so popular. Cases came up where therapists were sued and intimidated. I think the Foundation knew quite well that false memories could be implanted. I think they knew that individuals had been intentionally programmed with false memories so that when the programs began to break down, a cloud of confusion would obscure the truth. The media has been used for mind manipulation, but I feel that as consciousness awakens, the media will become an instrument to awaken people and free minds.

Years later, in May of 2001, Dr. Steven M. Greer of the Center for the Study of Extraterrestrial Intelligence (CSETI) gathered together a number of retired government officials to discuss their personal experiences with UFOs and the government's attempts to suppress this kind of information. [You can see this video for yourself at www.disclosureproject.org.] One of the participants said, "If out of a thousand reports of extraterrestrials, one is true, that's all that matters." I believe that statement also applies to this situation—if one of the thousands of stories of people who have remembered this kind of abuse, this sort of information, is true, it demands investigation.

February 8, 1993: Across the nation, therapists are struggling with bizarre and horrible memories their clients are recalling, referred to as Satanic ritual abuse. Beyond the terror, once I move past my horrible experiences, I discovered intentional programming and brainwashing. Truly there is an awakening in this country. Alarmingly, many people in recovery from this abuse either return to the state of denial, are reprogrammed by the cult or remain involved in cult activity during treatment. When I started my recovery, my motto was, "The truth will set you free." Recovering memories is helpful in the process; deprogramming or dismantling the brainwashing accomplishes ultimate freedom. Well-planned mind control is at the core of this issue. Certainly religious fanaticism is a primary element used, as it has been throughout history, as a method to control and enslave masses of people. The issue is mind control; the objective in healing is freedom of thought.

Recently, *Primetime* did a special on the cult and ritual abuse that is an excellent example of cult propaganda and programming. Why is there no evidence? No bodies? No FBI cases? At least four fallacies seem obvious. Every program I have seen about Satanic ritual abuse promotes this lack of hard evidence as a means to discredit the truth. The cult's specialists are well-trained in removing and disposing of evidence; they are extremely thorough and careful. I doubt if a top-notch forensic team could discover a clue after the scene has been cleaned up. The second implicit message in the special was, "Anyone who remembers is crazy." I hear this false rhetoric repeated in my own family. In the video, a well-dressed "intelligent newsman," established as an authority, states, "We have to wonder who is sicker, the therapist or the patient?" This reinforces the idea that if we tell the truth, we are crazy, and that any therapist who would help us to get free is crazy.

The third falsehood that was reinforced in this special was that psychiatrists have put this in our heads—another classic piece of cult propaganda. Over and over in this program, this lie was reinforced. Four middle-class housewives (evidently reindoctrinated by the cult) testified that therapists had planted this in their minds. Their statements were used to prove this fallacy. The fourth fallacy—that nice people don't do horrible things—was reinforced by interviewing benevolent Christian elders. They were shown singing hymns in the perfect American home. They expressed alarm and confusion over their daughter's behavior and the memories she was recovering. I felt the message was, "How could nice old people who love God do this?" This piece of propaganda reinforced the perfect-American-family syndrome. In fact, they are prototypes of the typical cult leaders—that is how the lie has been perpetrated so long. The closing footage ending the show allowed the viewer to look through the girl's bedroom window, making one feel that she has had it all. How lovely. Yet it exemplifies the intrusion typical of the techniques used to strip away our privacy and dignity. Her bedroom should be her refuge, private and safe, but it never was. Finally, and most important, was the implicit message by the families interviewed on the special, "We want our daughters home." You bet they do—home, to be reprogrammed. (This illustrates how the media has been used by the cult to call back its victims.)

It is my belief that good people are not conscious of the shadow side. When the issue of mind-control, programming and brainwashing is clarified, we—both therapists and survivors—will be less susceptible to being manipulated, misled, confused and used by the cult. Then, and only then, will we truly be free to heal.

———————————

February 11, 1993: Yesterday I started reading Lifton's books, *The Nazi Doctors* and the one about the Chinese concentration camps. The significant elements are thought-reform in the reversal of a value system and the creation of a double, not a fragment, that assumes the value system of the perpetrator or the perpetrating institution. He mentions the confusion in the left and right hemispheres of the brain, but most important, he draws out the myth of doubling within the German culture as being predisposed to cultural doubling, such as Auschwitz. He stated that the doctor and the victim doubled. It isn't dissociation; it is, in my opinion, connected to the Native American mythological character, the two-faced woman.

I had just done extensive work locating my own two-faced woman. I discovered a medicine woman who was half strong shaman, loving the Earth, and half grotesque, controlled by evil. Her name was Lantru and Leantru. In journeywork I had sent Leantru, the evil twin, to the cave of origins, to be instructed and healed, to be forgiven. Then she would be able to return to Lantru as a whole being, fully integrated. Now Lantru is a trusted ally and healer. In my own psyche, I had met the very phenomenon that Lifton refers to, the modification that is happening within humanity as a whole.

It's my belief that at some time in the history of this planet, we entered an age of separation—the age of dichotomy, I call it. At this time, the psyche of humanity was split. An amnesia barrier divided the two worlds. Mythologies and religions are full of stories that demonstrate this separation. I found this very thing in my own psyche. I believe that in so doing, I assisted in healing the collective consciousness.

During that week in February, I made a significant breakthrough. It became clear that in recovering these memories, I did not recover guilt about what I had participated in. At the same time, I realized that my whole life was being run by guilt. I was guilt-based, constantly apologizing for myself, always feeling that I had failed, always feeling guilty. I began to apply this realization to my daily life, producing a dramatic change. The guilt I did *not* feel from the secret life, from the things I was forced to participate in, filtered into my "normal" life. No longer did I suffer from a chronic guilty conscience; no longer was I overcompliant. I didn't feel obliged to apologize for things I hadn't done.

What a week! I broke through the memory of orientation at the programming center, met the two-faced woman and read the book on brainwashing. My journey seemed to be mystically guided; everything came to me just when I was ready for it. I also asked one of my strong inner children, Suzzanne, to contact the core, or the depth, of where I had been brought into this evil plan. I recovered a memory from infancy where I was given to what was pronounced "Sah-tahn." In that memory, I went back and retrieved the soul of my infant-self. I gave that baby to the cosmic being of light. In doing so, I disconnected the very origin of my psyche's belief that I was connected to evil on a core level. That's the key here: It's not what is done to you; it's what you believe happened to you.

This is so important that I want to revisit an earlier topic. The False Memory Syndrome Foundation's propaganda is that therapists implanted these memories in survivors. The Foundation's work has succeeded in suppressing thousands of victims' efforts to remember as well as in intimidating therapists. The Foundation created a bizarre scenario: that therapists sat there and suggested it, and that clients automatically began spewing out detailed memories of Satanic rituals. According to them, it was all through the power of suggestion that these memories were put in their brains.

My therapist certainly never did that. He just kept me anchored. We used to joke that I was the kite and he was the kite string, and his job was to get me back safely. He never offered his opinions about my experiences, which I see as perfect professionalism. I can understand how a therapist could research these phenomena and ask a person with symptoms of this kind of abuse, "Well, did this happen to you?" The False Memory Syndrome Foundation people jumped right on that one possibility and set up a program of intimidating therapists to shut the whole movement down. I believe that some of the controlling programs were breaking down for some reason, and because of that, they wanted to close the gates before the truth came out.

What I want to emphasize is this: If indeed a memory was implanted, the covert government, through the process of brainwashing, implanted it. I believe that confusing memories were deliberately implanted so that if people did begin to remember, their confusing statements could be used to discredit them. Perhaps some people were implanted with memories of being taken onto a spaceship and probed by aliens. But, on the other hand, maybe they *were*. I have no doubt that the government made deals for technology for people to be used as experimental victims. I also feel that many of the Satanic memories were staged. Everyone who has Satanic memories recalls the drinking of blood. I've been in an operating room. Do you know how fast blood congeals after it's exposed to the air? So something must have been done to make people *think* that they were drinking blood, or perhaps some additive was used to prevent its coagulation. Even if the whole thing was staged, it is still fear programming. It has the same effect on a child's psyche as if it were real—the child or adult victim does not know the difference. If some memories are authentic and some are implanted, it is hard to tell one from another, but it is still fear programming for mind control.

Even if certain recurrent events never "really" happened, they are no less a means of terror programming. I figured this out early in my recovery: The terror programming set up a belief system in my psyche that I had experienced all those things. When you're a little tiny girl, standing there and seeing these horrible things, when you're being tortured and sexually abused, it's real. To that child's belief system, everything is real. It doesn't matter if it's an act or if they're really sacrificing somebody. (Of course, it really matters if someone is sacrificed—I'm talking about the effect on the psyche, the part of the brain that believes the lie.) The child believes, allowing the power of fear to control his or her mind. Interestingly enough, if you follow the chain of command upward, the person at the top was brainwashed with the same fear-programming techniques used on other people. So there really aren't any victims or victimizers in this. It's not either/or; it's both. Every single person involved in this atrocity from top to bottom, from the people who ran the program right down to the children who were taken off the streets and were never seen again—every single one of those people are victims and victimizers. When we can find that part of our psyche as a society, I believe we can be free. This world of ours has an opportunity to emerge into a higher state of consciousness that will not permit these kinds of atrocities.

CHAPTER ELEVEN

Of Wolves and Angels

February 13, 1993: So much has happened these past two weeks! Yesterday, in meditation, my guide showed me that the essence of my soul is the ancient Wakan [sacred energy of the Earth spirit]. My beauty is the beauty of the sunsets I absorbed as a child. He said my soul is like the flight of a bird, that it can't be trapped or dissected. He told me always to remember that what they did, I was *taken* to. The love of the Earth, I *brought myself* to—as I did all of the good in my life. Then a path opened up to the higher cosmic plane, and Laiolin took me to the angelic realm. I drifted in total peace. There I met and was accepted by the angels. I saw the clouds part; I saw God's throne. Then they showed me my disturbed planet and told me there is much work to do. Laiolin brought my infant-self to heaven and is keeping her there to heal and be safe. It was an enlightening experience, a satori. All the deep shock and pain was lifted from me. When I returned, I felt lighter. Quanab also told me to learn about joy from the chickadee, that in absorption of beauty is happiness. I remember that as he spoke to me, his eyes were so bright and sparkling. I felt wholeness inside, a wholeness I know is my original soul-self.

It was during this time that Quanab stood me on a rocky point of my safe sacred mountain and told me that I needed to learn a lesson. As I stood there, thousands of bees swarmed around me. The lesson was to stay and hold my energy, not to panic. Fear would result in being stung. Bees respond to fear. After a minute or two, it didn't even bother me. Then lightning flashed all around me, and once again, he helped me let go of my inner fears while holding my ground in a strong way. Inner fear attracts negative energy. I used this teaching often, to keep myself grounded and to get through the experiences.

As I continued my journey of discovery, family members in denial were becoming hysterical, like frightened birds. Something deep inside them was frightening them. I could understand their behavior, and I learned a sense of compassion rather than of accusation—a strong place to come from. All this spiritual assistance prepared me for the next challenge in my journey to freedom.

February 19, 1993: Last night my brain started experiencing some very peculiar sensations, which included humming and pain. This morning I was really having a rough time: spacy, not focused, dissociated. I went to Dr. D.'s and journeyed to my safe place, and after getting past some very upset inner selves, I got to Quanab. He told me to go down the gulch and attend to what was there. I found a wolf with her foot in a trap. She was ravaged with pain and fear; she was dangerous, rabid. I was so sad to see her, and I felt so helpless. Tears streamed down my face. My guide told me to see if it was possible to help her with my hands or my voice. She was dangerous to approach. I stood by helplessly as she gnawed at her leg. Then Quanab told me that I had abilities I wasn't using, to focus my mind's energy out the front of my brain. I did, and I focused the energy to her without a word. She calmed down and stopped struggling. She lay there whimpering. That is when I knew her breasts were full; she had puppies. Still her paw was stuck. My guide said if I touched the trap, I would be poisoned like her. He said, "Use your tools." I placed the purple fluorite crystal by her head and the shield between us, in case she attacked. I used the sword to pry open the trap. When she was free, she licked my hand. I looked at her leg; it was horrible. My guide said my healing abilities were beyond my intellect's ability to conceive, to get spring water and herbs and to help her to heal. I dug bear root and gave her sacred spring water. She was thirsty. I squeezed the bear root on her leg and bathed it with the spring water. It began to heal before my eyes. I knew she could heal the rest. She got up and went to her puppies over in the canyon.

I saw the wolf mother again on another journey. While she was in the trap, her puppies had been hungry and thirsty. She would have gnawed her leg off to get to them. I had seen her set free to be the kind of mother she was supposed to be. I knew the wolf mother was me, that I would have gnawed my own leg off to escape from the trap I was put in as a child. I also knew that the trap prevented me from being the kind of mother I wanted to be. My kids suffered from my rage and from my not knowing how to protect them from evil-doers. I know my kids suffered because I had not been strong enough to make that journey when they were little. Now I see my children healing. I know my grandchildren are protected; they don't have the sore throats, chronic kidney infections and other ailments I had as a child. We've taken a big step in the right direction.

CHAPTER TWELVE

Gathering Strength

March 2, 1993: Help me! Empty visions of agony wait in doors within chambers of my mind, trapped beyond cruel barriers, lost to reality yet reckoned with by every fiber of my being. Long, dark passageways of anguish to be traveled once a door is found. Foul retch flows forth in rancid anger down to the corridor of hell I was brought to as a child. Turmoil to be reckoned with: white coats, clipboards ready, the ultimate pain experience. Waiting within my womb, dark, sharp angles of horror, lost in forbidden corridors of reality, waiting to be washed clean in the seas of their empty loneliness, longing for the sensuality of the forbidden, raping my mind in an endless odyssey of lost memory, lost lust for death, through the blood spilled, running onto the floor, until it gels and shines in blackness. Life spewing forth from a victim in revolting rivulets of flesh, cut by the sharp blades of the executioner. Lying on a cot, a grimace on the face, there alone in the twilight of horror. Flesh in ripe folds of sliced hell from catacombs of terror, lost within my soul.

March 3, 1993: Last week I came out into the front room and saw that my granddaughter had spread some magazines and books out on the floor. As I reached to pick them up, I found an old book on the top. When I opened it, I saw that my mother had written on the back cover, "Peace, man's rightful place in the universe." Then, beneath that, "They lack a cause. Evil is a stagnation of the spirit." I looked at the front cover of the book; it was *The Sioux: Life and Customs of a Warrior Society* by Royal B. Hassrick. I couldn't help but open it and begin to read.

All the stories were there: of Iktomi (the trickster), the witch, the wizard and the two-faced woman, plus the story of White Buffalo Calf Pipe Woman. These myths are crucial to understanding the consciousness behind Earth's drama. There are so many important associations here with what has happened to me and to the psyche of the people on this planet. I also went back to *The Nazi Doctors* and read again about doubling. It's so fascinating; he speaks of removal from reality and numbing, changing terminology and disavowal as significant aspects of the Auschwitz-self, the shadow side of society. Everything is coming together.

I also found an article in the *New Mexican* by a man named Alexander who has a Ph.D. in death and dying and paranormal psychology. He does research at Los Alamos labs on nonlethal warfare and psychotronic weaponry (used in psychic warfare). One of the techniques used in this research is low-level ultrasound to cause nausea and vomiting and disorientation that stops when the sound stops. I asked myself whether this has anything to do with the human experimentation I'm remembering. Is he associated with these experiments? I created an equation: the cult equals the covert government agents equals the mafia equals mind control, linking to the Nazi doctors.

During our weekly sessions with the acupuncturist, Laiolin had channeled through me to begin teaching me about the awakening and to help me heal. She told me we were being assisted by highly evolved ETs, whom I refer to as extraterrestrials. She explained that they could not intervene in Earth's destiny without the assistance of humans who agree to work with them of their own free will. They are not here to take control of our planet, but rather to offer divine assistance. She told me that multidimensionally she is an Arcturian and would bring energy through the therapist from a mothership. This beam of energy was intended to heal my brain, to tune the frequencies of the right and left hemispheres. At different times during my journey, I've been told of being taken up on ships to receive special healing, for balancing of the brain's chemicals and frequencies.

March 21, 1993: My guide told me I must learn to discipline myself with exercise, meditation and prayer. It takes a strong mind, body and spirit to be a peaceful warrior. It is time; I must find the will and the way. The early morning is my best time. I can get up early and meditate before the family wakes up; I can walk and pray and meditate every morning. This has become a way of life for me now. I must build a strong fortress of life, love and protection around my family. It must be stronger than ever, for strength and support. To do so, I must train like a warrior, be careful what I eat and how much, drink water, bring light into every part of my body. It is possible; I can do it. Walking meditation helps balance the right and left hemispheres of my brain. It is actually very easy to tense up one side and relax the other; then I did it with alternate breathing in circles. I know this is what I need to do to heal.

On April 9, Quanab gave me a warning: I need to practice distancing or detaching myself from the intensity of the emotional pain in order to see what is coming next. I must be careful, or what I need to know will shred my heart and leave me hopeless. I have a tendency always to see the good in people, not the bad. My love is deep and true, but what is coming next is dangerous, and I must be prepared. I must protect my medicine bag, my heart, my soul. I must use my tools and distance myself from the physical anguish that I must see. It was less dangerous to see my hurt inner children than what I must see now. He reminded me how sick I had become when I got stuck in memory and said that the only way to do this is to move through it. Then he showed me the portal into the next dimension and told me that once I go through, I will never be able to return to the way things are now. Now that the two-faced woman is free, we can complete a balance of protection. He placed me in the center, surrounded by Laiolin, Archangel Michael and Lantru. From this circle of protection, I am to travel and meditate on a regular basis. He advised that the next part of my journey will be risky—the land of the truth of the past. I am always to remember that my body already knows what will be revealed to my conscious mind. Once I work on these things, I will be ready to move to the next step.

During the following weeks, I unraveled ways the members of my family had been used to reinforce programming. The covert government, in its psychosis, its fractured psyche, has perpetrated a great wrong within what we think of as "normal" America (and, no doubt, in other countries around the world). They have fostered a deep sense of betrayal within the family, along with fear and confusion. Although people struggle to be loving, caring human beings, because of that amnesia barrier that has been created in their minds, they become programmers of their own children. They reinforce fear programming through punishment. I think of things I said to my children, things like, "Do you want a spanking?" That's a mild example. M. Scott Peck, in his book, *People of the Lie: The Hope for Healing Human Evil*, speaks of this ongoing programming. Most children endure punishment while being told, "It's for your own good." I'm encouraged to see that these methods of influencing children are beginning to change. More and more parents are using "time out" to improve behavior; they're beginning to use gentle teaching techniques, to talk about feelings. But that's a new thing. It's a shift in consciousness that came as a result of a lot of people, like me, fighting for mental freedom.

I wrestled with how our families are the very place we seek love and protection, and how this sinister, dark force enters into the family home. That's where most abuse takes place. Being abused by an uncle, cousin or parent—someone a child looks to as a source of love and authority— that is the ultimate betrayal, because it creates the belief that there's no safe place. When children grow up with this feeling, this belief, they repeat trauma cycles in their relationships throughout life. This is passed on to their children, and the cycle is continued throughout the long, dark night of the soul of the people of planet Earth.

Before I could begin to deal with deep government mind-control programming, I first had to unravel the way my own family had been used. We were our own worst enemies. We repeated cycles of having no boundaries or inappropriate boundaries; we reenacted dramas of anger, control, shame, guilt and fear. The way we had acted in our daily lives kept me in a mind prison that wouldn't allow me to enter into the deeper realms of what had been done to me and what I had experienced. Once I could unravel that and understand how the dynamics of fear programming, terror and control work within the family structure, then I could reach into the deeper realms.

CHAPTER THIRTEEN

The Little Black Box

By April of 1993, I had discovered a little black box in the upper right hemisphere of my brain. I recognized it for the first time when I received one of a series of reprogramming telephone calls. The phone would ring; I'd pick it up and hear noises and threatening voices saying strange things that were supposed to trigger and reprogram me. But that wasn't all bad news: One of the ways I knew I was getting free is that I consciously remembered getting the phone calls. Had I still been in their control, I'd have taken the calls, been reprogrammed—and I'd never even know anything had happened. So that was a major step forward. I worked for months to deactivate it. Quanab warned me to approach it with great care. It was actually a dangerous implant that could cause brain trauma if not properly removed.

Once I had a short conversation about mind control with a professional deprogrammer. We spoke for maybe ten minutes on the telephone, but in that brief interchange, he said something of great value: *freedom is in the struggle*. And I struggled. Freedom is also in the ability to relax and go with the flow. When breaking mind-control programs, one goes back and forth—feeling peaceful and feeling terrified, fearful and guilty and peaceful. I call it the flip-flop stage. This uncomfortable phase helped me to realize that I had never enjoyed a deep state of peace. An inner anxiety was always buzzing. Now at the age of fifty-two, when I put my head down on the pillow, I go to sleep and have a wonderful night of restoration. The chronic insomnia is gone. I remember the nights spent praying for daylight to come. Things changed for me, but inevitably there had to be a flip-flop period. I experienced horrible headaches, agonizing brain pain. Deprogramming the black box was a major leap toward freedom, but it took a long time. Most of this careful work was accomplished in journeys at Dr. D.'s office. Now I work with removing these psychotronic implants from other people. The first one I saw was in my own brain.

Finally, I broke through another barrier, using the detachment I'd learned from my guide. Having strengthened myself, I reentered the programming center.

April 23, 1993: With objective energy, I explored the means of torture, found piece by piece. Who took the pain and loved it? As a pirate adventure, it was twin shadow boys, to take the pain for the little girl. We examine each device in detail; then Quanab told me there was more in the corner I haven't seen—for later. I saw each thing very clearly in great detail, knowing that there was an order, like working through centers from kindergarten to first grade and on.

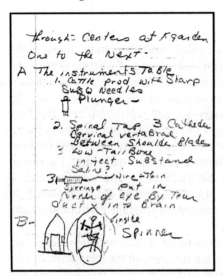

The instruments on the table: a cattle prod with sharp subcutaneous needles and a plunger, and a spinal tap with three catheters—cervical, vertebrae between the shoulder blades, low tailbone—injecting solutions, maybe saline, into my spine. There was a wire-type thing with a thin syringe that was put in the corner of my eye, by a tear duct, and into the brain, and I was strapped to a table to do this. I saw a device that I would sit in and be spun, and later I saw that device on TV as part of the training for astronauts. I looked again at the device where I was put face forward on a board, and it slid back to where needles would go into my back, and I never knew when they were going to come.

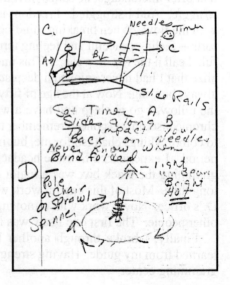

They set a timer, and it would slide along the track. I was blindfolded, so I never knew when it was going to come. I was also put on a disc with a pole or a chair, or sometimes sprawled on

a big disc that spun. An unbearable hot bright light above me flashed on and off. I also remembered a thing that spun me with my hands tied over my head, hanging over a vat that I was told was poison or acid, and being dipped down into the vat.

A doctor supervised these experiments; the others called him the "Nazi" when he was out of the room. I could recognize him if I ever saw his picture. Before he came into view, I could hear his boots banging on the floor. If ever there was a truly heartless person, it was this man.

June 7, 1993: I'm working to deprogram a poem a relative sent me years ago. I believe it was shared with good intent. The first time I read it, I thought it was beautiful and courageous. Now I can hardly believe it is the same poem. I can see the subliminal messages. I am learning to look at things in a different light, to read between the lines.

Comes the Dawn

Author Unknown

After a while you learn the subtle difference
Between holding a hand and chaining a soul.
And you learn that love doesn't mean leaning
And company doesn't mean security.
And you begin to learn that kisses aren't contracts
And presents aren't promises.
And you begin to accept your defeats with your head up
And your eyes open,

With the grace of a woman, not the grief of a child.
And you learn to build all your roads on today,
Because tomorrow's ground is too uncertain for plans
And futures have a way of falling down in midflight.
After a while you learn that even sunshine burns
   if you get too much.
So you plant your own garden and decorate your
   own soul,
Instead of waiting for someone to bring you flowers.
And you learn that you really can endure,
That you really are strong,
That you really have worth.
And you learn and learn
With every goodbye, you learn.

1. "Comes the dawn": The only way we knew we survived the night was that the Sun rose the next day.

2. "Learn the subtle differences": Learn equals program; accept the teachings of the cult. Subtle is a minimal word for the maximum expression that follows. We were conditioned that this didn't hurt and that this wasn't bad, when the experience was horrendous. The word "learn" is repeated nine times in this poem.

3. "Chaining a soul": Once brought out of the pattern of words, it is recognizable as what was done to us.

4. "Love doesn't mean leaning": It also means that you can't depend on anything, not to trust anyone. Anything you lean on might fall.

5. "Company does not mean security": There is no security in companionship, because there is no trust.

The poem leaves one feeling hopeless. It implies that there's no future, that even the Sun burns you, that anything good burns you. Who doesn't enjoy being outside in the sunshine? "With the grace of a woman, not the grief of a child" is saying that once you stand up and begin to accept your defeats, you come to realize that life is not about hope, but rather about repeated trauma, disappointment and pain. Well, a major part of my recovery is that I do not accept defeats. I look at challenges as opportunities to learn and better myself. I do accept that life brings me opportunities to learn; I do accept that things happen in the highest good for me. But to surrender to defeat with my head up and my eyes open is an attitude that I believe is a tool of conditioning.

This is part of the process I went through to unravel, piece by piece, the cult programming. I believe I became my own deprogrammer. Dr. D. did not deprogram me; he held the anchor. I did the work on my journeys, aided by my guides and guardians. The bodywork I received was vital to recovery, releasing body memory. I had a lot of support. When I look through these journals, I realize that claiming my freedom was a step-by-step process.

June 11, 1993: I am centered and ready to work. I ask the guardians to bring me to what is needed for my higher good. I ask for the light of God and the protection of the Cosmic Mother. I ask my guide to lead me swiftly to the path I must explore to be healed and free. Free at last, thank God I'm free at last—free from terror, from guilt, from deception, from programming, free to trust myself, free to learn who to trust, free to speak, think and write. Free from control, free from manipulation, brainwashing, rage, inflicted pain. Freedom of memory, self-esteem, explorative thought process, free. Free to know, to speak the forbidden, to forgive myself. Free to hold myself in high esteem, to heal, to feel, to nourish, to love. Freedom to know the truth, freedom from the lies.

Part of my journey seemed unending. I'd start recovering memories of medical procedures, of instruments and medical tables and people in lab coats and torture. It would come swirling through, and then it would leave. For a few more weeks I'd wrestle with my freedom again. It seemed to take forever to get a little peace, and then I'd just have to keep going on. In June, I read an article from the *New Yorker* about an "average" American family active in a cult in Washington. There was sexual abuse and torture, which the father, a policeman accused by his daughter, could not remember. I started asking myself if perpetrators did indeed forget. Before that, I didn't realize that perpetrators often do not remember what they did. In this family, the man went to jail and—independently of his family—began to recover cult memories. I believe repro- grammers were sent in under the guise of specialists. I had seen the names of some of these people in other articles about the False Memory Syndrome Foundation. Dr. Corey Hammond was quoted, and it appeared that he knew what was really going on. He mentioned the Nazi doctors in association with the case. I felt as if a bucket of water had been thrown in my face. I realized that someone else knew about the Nazi doctor I recalled in my memories. Since I had already been working with these memories and flashes of medical experimentation, I contacted Dr. Hammond. He said he couldn't talk to me about it, because he might contaminate my memories and I wasn't his client. He told me to keep working with professional assistance because I was onto something really important. Before that, I had no idea that my experiences were not individual instances, that other people might understand and recognize some of the elements.

CHAPTER FOURTEEN

Dancing with the Sacred Clown

In the autumn of 1993, I went on an investigative trip to Colorado Springs with another survivor who had recovered memories of Satanic abuse in Manitou Springs and Colorado Springs. I had known all my life that my grandfather had danced as an Indian at Manitou Springs. He was a man of mystery in our family. He abandoned my grandmother with a house full of hungry children during the Great Depression; my mother was eight years old. All her life, my mother had searched for her father without success. I felt that perhaps there was a connection to that area, my history and my grandfather.

My companion knew that the owners of a certain shop were involved, and we dropped in to ask some questions. Just out of the blue, I asked the man if he knew my grandfather. He said of course he did—at least he had known him until the beginning of World War II, when they had lost touch. My grandfather had been his Scout leader, had taught him Indian crafts and lore. He said that my grandfather was a Koshare. I didn't know what that meant. He explained that it was a group of Germans who worked with the Boy Scouts. I said, "My grandfather was a German?" He said that only Germans were Koshares. He told me about the connection to Native Americans in my area. He knew my grandfather! I walked out of the shop into the little plaza where my grandfather had danced and discovered a photo of an elder who lived at a pueblo near my home. In fact, it was the very pueblo where I had lived when I first moved to New Mexico in my twenties. Suddenly, the big picture began to come together.

Later I had a vision of being at a pueblo where the Koshares were dancing. When one of the dancers removed his mask, I saw his face. It was crawling with worms. I was told in the vision that my grandfather had violated the medicine of the Koshares. He had wrongfully taken a medicine bag that did not belong to him. I began praying for assistance to set this offense right.

Koshares are holy men, sacred clowns painted with black-and-white stripes; they appear in many Pueblo and Hopi dances. They are supposedly able to pass between the worlds. I realized that the cult/covert government had violated the medicine of the Koshares and used it in ceremonies to manipulate the dimensions. It all started to make sense: The rites concerned death, fear and sex. With the power of this sacred medicine, the dark ones could manipulate the dimensions and trap souls, holding fear on the planet. My journey to heal this violation took two years. I asked a trusted friend in the pueblo to inquire about my grandfather, Fred Shearer, and to request a meeting with an elder so that I might apologize for what my grandfather had participated in. A year later, my friend, very upset, contacted me. He said that our lives were threatened and that he could no longer continue his inquiries. I cannot disclose all the details, but I did go to the spiritual elders to make amends for how my grandfather was used to violate this sacred medicine. I had heard that the CIA had sent agents to shamans to steal their medicine. This had to be addressed, and I had to reverse the curses put on my family as a result of my grandfather's wrong action.

It might be a nice fantasy to think of the Native Americans as purely victims of our society, but I believe that if you study any society on this planet deeply enough, you're going to find the psychic split. There might be some exceptions; I believe that some people have held the planetary peace. I would like to think that this dichotomy did not touch everyone, that maybe the people of the rainforest or some far-flung islands have not been affected. Although that idea might be comforting, it's probably not true. Their cultural psyche is most likely split, just as in industrial societies. I like to think that civilizations from Lemuria or the lost cities of Atlantis held the peace after the fall of Atlantis, but that's another story.

Part of my journey was to work to help heal this division. I had a lot of assistance from the spiritual realm to do this and to write this book. I hope that traditional Native Americans, who feel that a non-Indian has no business in their domain, don't misinterpret this part. To those people I say that I was called to help heal this, that all the children on Mother Earth will benefit from this healing. I was called to do it because my grandfather was involved with the violation. I was sent through these dark caverns and returned whole. I reached into the spiritual realms where the sacred had been violated—sacred truths that belong to the people and to the Earth—and helped banish the death fear. I journeyed with my sword, shield and medicine power, with the protection I had been given, with the help of Quanab, Archangel Michael, Laiolin and the medicine woman, Lantru. Because of the delicacy and subtleties involved, I cannot relate all the details of this two-year journey. What is important is that you realize that the sanctity of our lives has been violated in every culture, in every place—that now we stand at the crossroads spoken of in the Hopi prophecy. We are living the times of the purification; we are to choose either the difficult path or the gentle path. By the opening of the consciousness of a critical mass of human beings, I believe we are choosing the gentle path. I believe that there are many people on this planet who are choosing freedom, healing, unconditional love, unity through diversity—choosing to embrace and embody unconditional love, the most powerful force in the universe.

CHAPTER FIFTEEN

The Seven Doors of Healing

In May I discovered seven doorways of my inner psyche and began a journey that would take many months. To access these portals, I would go to my safe place in meditation, then enter the doorway of my old home. For each door, I would locate a key that opened inner chambers of my psyche for healing.

In a session with Dr. D., I saw my old home but from a vantage point high in the sky, as if I were looking down on the past. I could see a cord, like an iron rope, that went through my body at the base of the spine and extended to the past. I had never seen these black cords before, but as I worked to sever them, I discovered that they were the psychic cords that hold us to the sickness of our past. They drain not only our own energy, but that of people to whom we are connected. With my sword, I sliced a cord. It felt as though I were slicing black licorice. That was the strength of my sword. The black steel rope fell, and with it, my past just tumbled away. My guide explained that I had physically left my home of the past, but that I had not moved the home of my heart. And today was moving day. I gathered all the good memories and the home of my heart, bringing them to my sacred mountain. I soul-retrieved the home of my heart, using the imagery of moving my old home to my safe place.

May 14, 1993: Quanab said there was a wound or hole where the black rope was removed in my lower abdomen. He reminded me of the wolf and my healing powers. I brought healing herbs to my wound; Quanab said that I must heal it, or it could be filled with something harmful to me. I placed the fluorite crystal on my lower abdomen. I felt an enormous amount of pain. My guide said there was something dead within my womb. I reached in and pulled it out; it was the black, decayed soul body of a baby. I can no longer describe the agony I felt withdrawing it. As it was released, I had a massive convulsion. Archangel Michael took the death in my womb to a sacred place in my journey world called Blue Lake. When I was a child, my mother told me that souls go to Blue Lake when they leave the body. I have always loved that image: a beautiful blue lake in heaven where souls go between incarnations to heal and rest before returning to Earth. My cosmic being of light brought healers to administer to me. I began to feel better as the healing worked.

Lantru spoke, saying that for the hoop of the nation to mend, for Mother Earth to heal, such healing must happen to women. She said that the evil ones placed dead, decayed babies in the wombs of girl-children, destroying the energy of women's integrity, and until it was freed, women would be unable to claim their place in a healing way. She said that hundreds of thousands of women were carrying these implanted dead souls. I was reminded of the light spear that I had placed around me, that kept me from harm during this process, and I was also reminded that my inner child, who was the little girl with the shadow boys, was close by me. I was shown flashing lights, indicating there was programming involved. I was exhausted, but I felt strong. Just before I finished, I felt a warm glow in my womb, a feeling I had never felt before.

This remarkable event is recorded in the poem, "The Womb of Death."

May 17, 1993: Life is so busy, a dozen things to remember and do today. I'm feeling pretty good. I know the Chinese herbs are helping a lot. The big thing I notice is that I can release daily stress. Something in my body lets go, and I can feel the pressure ease up.

May 19, 1993: Lots of very strange brain sensations. My neck is tight, my brain heavy and painful. Does anyone inside know why my head hurts? Does anyone need to speak?

Suzzanne (the strongest of my inner children, who helped me to communicate with the others): You know there are people who want to talk, but we never get a chance. We need a place to talk. There are others who want to talk.

Me: Well, if anyone wants to, we can write.

Inner child [my handwriting changes here]: Men come in grab arms both sides hurt me hurt my arms lift me up by my arms carry me down hall—angry big men hurt me hurt little arms.

Me: How old are you?

Child: I'm a big girl but not as big to fight them—they hurt me—I'm scared. I want my mommy.

Me: Do you know these men?

Child: Big ugly mean men—not nice to little girls.

Me: Where do you go?

Child: To the setting area for bad girls. I'm a bad girl I have to be away from the other children or they will catch badness from me.

Me: Is someone helping you write?

Child: Suzzanne is helping me write.

Me: What is your name?

Child: My name is Pain.

Me: Thank you, Suzzanne, for helping Pain write. We will talk. Pain, I'm glad you came to talk to me. I want to hear what is important.

Pain: Big dark room—everyone in black faces covered black hoods. No light but in the center of room—table cold hard metal or marble. Doctor office place—dark

The Womb of Death

The dark form of anti-life.
A decayed infant, death, placed
within the womb of little girls.
Grown women carrying the
    darkness
        within their wombs,
unaware of why the power of the
Wakan woman has crumpled.

The ultimate deception of
    the evil one:
not just to breed or to sacrifice,
not just to conceive, to destroy,
but to plant an anti-life.
Decayed corpses within our little
    girls—
to decay their woman's spirit.

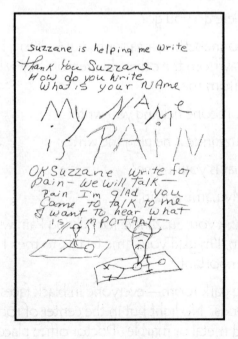

people chanting the High Lord come when the time is right.
Only my tummy shows. High Lord chants everyone
follows. I can see barely out of the covers. People have
paint. They put stuff on my tummy they prepare me for
the High Lord. I'm pulled down to the edge of the table.
My legs are strapped up they bring the funny light thing.
My tummy, the light is a beam they place it on my
tummy—they chant and moan. He stands at the foot of
the table. *I have to go, I have to leave. I can't see him.*

Me: That is a lot of pain.

Pain: They cover my head hurt me big thing to my tummy
big in me. Pain wants to go home. Noise from machine,
burning smell hospital, something wires on my head, head
strapped down cover all but eyes.

This journal entry shows how I communicated with my fragmented
inner children. It also reveals the feelings of a little girl during these hor-
rendous experiences.

That door to my own womb was the first. As I continued my journey,
I discovered the second door. My guide warned me to shield myself
when I opened it. He said there would be a blast of energy from the parti-
cles of horror I carried deep within. I prepared to open the second door.
My guide told me that once I opened it, I would find a passageway and
claim the truth.

May 1993: I returned to the second door. Lantru prepared
our shield. This time Quanab was at the back, Lantru and
Laiolin at my side, and St. Michael next to me. Behind me
was a band of angels to carry the toxic energy away. Lantru
sang a medicine song as I prepared to step up to the second
door. Then a terrible, powerful voice boomed out: "Who
dares enter here in the forbidden territory?" Lantru answered,
"I am the deliverer; I have come." Lantru sang a sacred song,
for we had come on behalf of the children. The children will
be heard. The booming voice was forceful, but we claimed
our warrior-woman power on behalf of the children. Then
Quan Yin came. She sang a beautiful song of grief for the

children. I felt so deeply touched; I felt the pain of all the children all over the world who are still trapped within the secrets. Tears streamed down my face as she sang. I wish I could remember that song. At the end of it, I was quivering, but I felt so close to something so precious, so sacred. I remembered Laiolin saying, "This is the work to save our planet." This is what I was chosen for, why I incarnated and who I am. I stepped forward onto the threshold.

As I opened that door, debris came flying out. Visually, it was like opening up an old cave, with pieces of sticks and debris and maybe an old bird's nest in there. Something like an old rat's nest came flying out; luckily, I had that shield in front of me, because it blasted us. At the end of that journey, I was told that other mortals were chosen to open this door in Tibet and the Andes and other key places in the world. I was blessed for having the strength to open this door. It was a very exhausting experience. That day, as I stood at that doorway, Lantru, my medicine-woman self, called out the dark one. She called him forth. She told him that Mother Earth would heal, that the people would be free, that the planet would survive and that these dark corners would be cleaned and healed—that the time had come for the people to be free.

During this time, I was going to sweat lodges, correctly called "inipi," and having them on my land. The sweat lodges aided in the detoxification and helped me reach the deep state of inner healing that I needed. A sweat lodge is one of the rites of the Native American people in which they build a dome, usually of willow, and cover it with tarps and blankets. In a spirit of reverence, they heat rocks in a big fire and bring them inside the enclosure, placing them into a pit dug in the center. People sit in a circle around the pit, and the person running the sweat lodge, who has carefully prepared for that responsibility, pours a stream of water over the hot rocks. Steam fills the enclosure. The air becomes incredibly hot, causing participants to sweat heavily. It is a powerful way to detoxify. The people pray for healing for themselves, their people and their families. Far beyond the physical cleansing, the challenge of enduring the heat, combined with the prayers and songs, makes it possible to reach deep areas of the spirit. Sweat lodges are now being built at treatment centers and prisons. This brings my heart joy.

For months I entered the deep realms and continued to open up those doors. We'll talk more about them as I come across them in my journal.

May 25, 1993: I go deeper into the memories of human experimentation. I was at the entrance of the experimental chambers. The red brick wall was sealed. I was pounding on it, angry that they had sealed it. Then I realized that the wall was part of a college and could be sealed when classes were in session. I finally got past and opened up the vault door. Then I saw a clear image of the person I call the Nazi doctor, a middle-aged man. I remembered his gold-rimmed glasses and round boyish face. His gray-blond hair was combed to the side. After I saw his face, I went into a deeper meditation and contacted Laura, one of my inner children. She was very upset. She said that they would have to kill me now. Everyone inside was screaming and shaking. I positioned my guardians around me and returned to the programming center.

Suddenly I began to understand so much. The campus I had been taken to was a college in Colorado Springs. The Army base and Air Force Academy near the campus were key to this choice of locations for the experiments. The military base made it easy to get high-security people in and out of the area. Bunkers and chambers honeycomb the land beneath the base; tunnels connect to the college. Then I remembered getting out of the locked dorm room, crossing the campus and entering another building. I wandered down a hall, exploring. Looking through a door, I saw a general—or someone with a lot of military decoration—with the Nazi doctor and the head lab person. They were upset, yelling at one another. I wasn't supposed to hear. But something had happened to security, a threat. This must have been when I was about eleven years old, because the programming-center memories seemed to take place between the ages of eight and eleven. Everyone working at the center was distraught; a door had been left unlocked in the dormitory where they kept us hidden. The children weren't being adequately watched. That's when I identified the trees and the red brick buildings of the Colorado Springs campus. Later I will describe my trip to this campus and recognizing the architecture.

I was caught; they took me to a chair that looked like an electric chair. They called it the iron maiden. They restrained my hands, connected electrodes to my arms and wedged something between my legs. My pelvis was slightly tipped; a helmet or metal cap was placed on my head. Then they inserted something electrical into my nose that stimulated the left part of my brain. When I recovered this memory in Dr. D.'s office, my nose felt completely numb. I was terrified and asked Dr. D. to help bring me back. He always stayed on the other side of the room, rarely touching me in any way. But this time he had to hold my hand and calm me down. The image was burned into my memory: If I ever saw a picture of this Nazi doctor, I would recognize him.

I knew then that I had to go to Colorado Springs and look at the campus; I had to know the truth.

> Summer 1993: How bizarre—a CIA conspiracy to brainwash children connected to the cult. How cruel— putting an electrical probe in a child's nose to shock her brain, connected with ancient Native American secrets and rituals. Stealing kiva secrets of the Koshare Kachinas to enter into a pact with the Lord of the Underworld. I realized that just for remembering this, I could die, but I also realized something else powerful and important: I had angelic protection. The protection had been there all through my journey. No matter how strange, I knew deep inside myself that it was true and it was real.

I began a new journal with quotations that applied to my situation at that time.

> "Forgive them, Father, they know not what they do."
> —Jesus

> "Gracious God, make me sensitive to all the evidence of Your goodness; and may I, trusting in You, free myself of all the terror of death, and feel free to live intensely and happily the life you have given to me. Amen."
> —Source Unknown

> "Those who cannot remember the past are condemned to repeat it."
> —George Santayana

"Almighty and everlasting
God, you have safely
brought us to the
beginning of this day.
Defend us with your
mighty power, and grant
that this day we fall into no
sin, neither run into any
kind of danger, but that all
of our doings, ordered by
your governance, may be
always righteous in your
sight, through Jesus Christ
our lord, Amen."

—Source Unknown

Following these notes, I found an article titled "Common Programs Observed in Survivors of Satanic Ritualistic Abuse," by David W. Neswald, M.A., in collaboration with Catherine Gould, Ph.D., and Vicki Graham-Costain, Ph.D. This piece, published in *The California Therapist* in 1991, came into my hands at a vital time, because it details the programs set up by the mind control, by the cult. People were programmed to injure themselves or to commit suicide, to return or to be accessed. These programs are triggered by telephone calls or gifts. I had received a number of ominous telephone calls as well as the poem I deconstructed in an earlier chapter.

Included was information about pain programs. These are put into place as a memory deterrent. Trying to remember causes such intense pain that many people will just give up. It hurts too much. I definitely experienced that. The pain of electroshock appears to be a favorite for this conditioning paradigm. This was so relevant: I had just recovered the memory of having been electroshocked when I happened upon the meeting between the Nazi doctor and the general.

One of the most phenomenal parts of my journey was this synchronicity. I would recover a memory, and someone would hand me an article pertaining to it or I'd meet another survivor. I began to understand that a lot of other people were discovering these things and that I wasn't alone. These things were so bizarre that they were hard for me to believe, and these pieces of validation that seemed to fall in my hands afterward seemed to be sent by angels.

My journal reflects weeks of struggling with frightened inner children, trying to help them be strong and calm, unraveling little knots of programming tangling my mind.

July 21, 1993: I am swept away with the spin programming. Very intense. Spinning on a capsule, tumbler spinning, a tumbler with lights through a pinhole flashing, very intense. I'm a little girl, almost three. I want my mommy. She was crying and afraid. She wanted a bottle or to suck her thumb, but her hands are tied to a chair with a metal bracelet that snaps over her arms. She is so frightened. She is told, "You have no mommy or daddy; they are only your guardians. We are your parents. They will die." Then I got past my three-year-old and dealt with a part that had a program installed by the cult: to obey and be loyal. This program came in the form of a girl called Soldier Girl. I worked for a long time to deprogram her and to help her know that she did not have to serve them.

That long, difficult work came at a time when I got to go on a vacation and get a much-needed break. I went to the Cascades and out to California. I absorbed the beauty of the Cascades and the San Juan Islands, and I saw an orca whale. No matter how terrifying my memories, I was always comforted by the beauty of God's creation.

CHAPTER SIXTEEN

The Gates to the Past Open

I began to understand how soldiers and slaves are programmed: "Do what you're told, or you'll be hurt. Stay in your place and shut up, or you will be destroyed." The only way to peace is obedience; then there is no real peace because they break their promise and hurt you again.

The tragedy is that we were born into it; it isn't anything we chose. The choice comes when we have a chance to know the truth and heal or continue with the sick secrets. The choice is opening to people all over this country, and it is tearing families apart. Ours is not a unique story. I wrote, "I will not compromise my right to think and speak what I feel. I must speak the truth." This was followed by journal entries where I was told to go back, where I got program messages that I wasn't safe, that I'd be killed, that my family would be killed. Many of these programs were installed in my own brain. By finding them, I could begin to unravel them and diminish their power over me.

I also realized that I had resisted all my life. I explained to Dr. D. my great fear that somehow I would be taken back and reprogrammed. He thought I had expanded my awareness enough that I was in no danger of being reprogrammed—that I had gone too far in my recovery to ever be used by them again. I had made choices at a very young age. But as a conscious adult, I made a choice to be free. No matter how difficult it was, I would keep going forward until every single knot was unraveled and I had come to the place of inner peace.

On August 20, I opened the third door. In my imagery, I was small and the door was huge. I had to stand on tiptoes to open it. My healing wolf stood beside me. When the door opened, I discovered another black box blocking my third eye. These blocking devices are known as psychotronic implants. I deactivated it and cleared it out. When I did that, I remembered being three years old—the memory with which I began this book.

August 20, 1993: I had a huge-head feeling, feeling ill, and I was in a little room, in the bedroom, in the dark, and I was very, very sick with convulsions and high fever. Behind this illness I found a memory of being taken into the initial programming in Golden, Colorado. They put me in a chair, arms strapped, upside down, spinning; then I didn't know which way was up, and when asked, I was always told I was wrong and punished with a shock. I experienced total confusion. Then a tube and a wire were put in my nose to experiment with radio waves resonant in the brain—not current waves, but like sound/vibration. I realized it was the entrance to the black box. A clear trail connected it to my past. My guardian said that to gain entry to the third door, I must grow and heal.

I found myself at my doctor's office in Golden; I saw the black and white checkered floor. I was confused and lost, realizing that the vault and the rites were all connected to his office. These were linked to my memory of being so sick when I was three years old. Then a strange voice came out, robotlike; later I learned it was an alter I call Gladys, a record keeper. She has glasses and a clipboard and short brown hair. She went to nursing school with me to learn anatomy. She learned that my thyroid was in my throat and my pituitary was in my forebrain. She said a lot of stuff about the doctor: that his name wasn't really the name I knew, that it was an alias name, that his name was Ivan, that he wouldn't get patients if he kept his real name. He was the one who referred me to the center in Colorado Springs, because he was associated with the Nazi doctor with gold-rimmed glasses and the baby face. My record keeper said she had asked me to find his picture when I first remembered him. He is a famous war criminal. Even writing this causes body memories.

Then I remembered a procedure in the room of experiments. They had just killed a dog; I remember thinking he was a nice dog. He had short white hair, black ears and black face markings. They withdrew fluid from his adrenal glands, then injected it into my thyroid. The record keeper knew where the thyroid is in my neck. I thought it was so weird, their putting stuff from a dog in my neck. I could smell the dead dog, the warm blood.

I began taking herbs to help heal my thyroid and pituitary. When I was in high school, I stayed home from school a lot because the glands in my neck would swell up. It was like having mumps. I'd stay in bed for weeks at a time. Some kids in the program didn't survive; some became unresponsive or retarded. This was explained to the parents as resulting from red measles or encephalitis. In reality, the children suffered brain damage from the experiments.

I met Patrick on August 28. His voice sounded almost like a computer—unemotional and data-based. Patrick could access information coded within inner programs.

September 4, 1993: Patrick spoke to Dr. D. about accessing parts I am not conscious of. Patrick is analytical and has kept data on the programming. He is void of emotion and has contact with other alters. He communicates with Suzzanne and was active while other alters were being tortured. He kept records of the experiments and observed the implantation of subversive entities who reported back to the programmers. He said that my conscious mind was still blocking communication to some of the parts I needed to access to heal. Patrick then brought out a black box. It emerged as a vibrational sound and developed a voice. It was implanted in the core of my brain to scramble my thought waves when triggered. Patrick warned us that we had to be very careful in approaching this black box and that I had to have a lot of support, because in deactivating it, it could be hazardous to my brain waves. I realized how vital Patrick was; he had helped me keep me from being dominated by the mind-control programming.

As I left Dr. D. for the acupuncturist, I was in really bad shape. My head was buzzing, high-pitched ringing. I was getting intense brain pain, and by the time I arrived, I could do little more than collapse onto the table. I went within and met my inner self named Laura. She warned me to go back to the programmers. I put her to work building a wall.

That would be her new job, rather than serving them. Laiolin came and performed an ancient high-pitched vibrational healing, altering the frequencies of the black box. I decided that I needed to go deeper and let Patrick bring out the information that was so important for my freedom.

September 8, 1993: I tried to let go of my conscious mind and was partially successful. Patrick came up, a computerized assistant; he revealed hand gestures used to reprogram and reprogramming commands. Some of them I recall; most I do not. I recall the power handshake, a gesture of cutting your throat, the motion of reaching upward, someone rubbing his or her neck and a patting gesture with the palm downward as if to repress something. There were others signs. Patrick said that I would no longer respond to the hypnotic gestures and by knowing them, I would be safe from them. He said that what the eyes do not perceive, they cannot send as a conscious message to the brain. There is no neural connection that permits a recognition of these gestures. I had very intense brain sensations.

CHAPTER   SEVENTEEN

Return to Colorado Springs

In mid-September I went to Colorado Springs and to La Junta, a place with cult connections to Colorado Springs. My investigative journey took me to the campus of Colorado College.

I went on a Sunday and told the groundskeeper a white lie, that my grandmother had attended college there. He told me that there were underground passages. He showed me a photograph of a building that had been torn down in 1966 or 1967. It was on a hill, and I believe it was the dormitory we were kept in. The red brick walls were just like the red brick wall I had come to in my memories, with the door that went through into the programming chambers. I discovered that Coors Brewery in Golden, Colorado, made the red brick.

I recognized the unique architecture of the building I had wandered into, where I had seen the general, the Nazi doctor and the head of the lab program together. Everything I saw on campus served to validate my memories. Had the doors not been left open that day and had I not slipped out during the confusion, I would have never known where I was. I must have been drugged when I was taken there, because I cannot recall how I got there or how I got home. I suspect that it happened when I was visiting the Catholic uncle whose house had a basement. I have no conscious memories of ever being on the campus. Yet the architecture, the buildings and the arrangement of the place were exactly as I had remembered from that day.

On that same trip, I recovered a memory at a famous hotel in Colorado Springs. I was dressed as a maid, serving hors d'oeuvres to politicians. Unlike some survivors, I have few memories about cult social events. This was a big gathering connected to state politics, rites and murder. There were always Satanic rites associated with these events. In truth, I believe I witnessed a murder. This, in turn, triggered many more memories about cult programming, resulting in reexperiencing the terror. I had to wade through all that when I returned home.

Not surprisingly, after that visit, there was an onslaught of psychic attack. The conspiracy case against my husband was at a point of crisis. By all logic, it looked as if we were going to lose everything in this fight. I spoke to an attorney whose specialty was protecting people from legal attacks by the cult. The time he spent with me was helpful, because I realized that the lawyer we had been led to use was not empowering us; he was probably a plant and was in fact sabotaging our interests. I was later to discover that he had ties to the very people who were attacking us.

We fired the attorney who had been representing my husband, and I told him to inform anyone who needed to know that my soul was not for sale. I sent messages in every way I could that in essence said, "I declare my freedom. Don't bother trying to intimidate me. Nothing you can do will stop me from pursuing the truth." At the same time, I left directives with more than one person that if anything suspicious should happen to me, my death should be investigated. This also applies as this book is published. Were I or my family to be harmed, a full investigation and publicity would result.

Immediately after I took these actions, things shifted. The energy changed dramatically. An honest attorney came to help us, and the case was settled in our favor in February 1994—only a few months later.

> October 6, 1993: The events of this last week have been incredible. My awakening to spiritual battle and strength of protection is astonishing; the key to it all is in energy patterns. When energy shifts, it changes everything. That shift is divine. We are the instruments of the divine and holy power of the hallowed God in the name of Christ Jesus. Staying always in the light of Jesus is so vital; when evil energy abounds, people are used and manipulated at its whim. When we stand forth in the light of God and declare in Christ's name our freedom and his divine presence, the evil flees.

I began to realize an error in my thinking: It wasn't that people were evil; it was that people weren't free. Because they were not free, they could be used as pawns for deviant energy patterns. Rather than trying to find the evil *person* involved, I began looking toward the source of the energy that was using the situation to try to intimidate me back into silence. Once I understood that, it lost power over me.

CHAPTER EIGHTEEN

Out of Bondage

One day in October of 1993, I was in town shopping on a Sunday morning. Sitting in my car at an intersection, I received a clear message from the Holy Spirit to turn left. There I found an Episcopal church. I entered while the service was going on. I can remember that I cried during Mass. I began attending that church, increased my personal contact with Christ and chose to be baptized. So many wonderful things happened in that church. I was beginning to have powerful visions of Christ, and I was being given healing messages. They often proved to be the subject of the next week's sermon. During that time, I enjoyed tremendous spiritual growth. I still do not believe in the organized Christian Church's threat of going to hell for earthly sins. I believe that people have *been* in the living hell, that that's the psyche of our society. I believe that God is a loving God who awakens within our hearts and helps us find the path to freedom, to unconditional love and to divine protection. I believe that the only thing God asks of us is that we forgive, and we are forgiven.

November 4, 1993: The fourth door—I used my sword to slide the panel and look within. My medicine wolf was there by my side; she licked my hand. I heard the voice of my ancestral ties to the cult, saying that I can't be free because I am destined from generational covenants to be one of the clan—that to leave these ties behind is to be like a ship without water or a man without a country. In ancient Europe, covenants were formed to unite nations through individuals with pagan and Christian cults. If a German or Scottish girl and boy were married, the ultimate tie was through the cult that unified all pagan covenants in Europe. I saw the people leave their cottages for secret rites in many countries.

During the journey, I met an ancestral woman who was pregnant and involved in the sealing of the generational bondage and the cursing of our family.

> November 4, 1993 (continued): I entered with my sword and shield and cleansed the woman with sacred water. Then I cut the black cords that connected us through the generations. I reached within her and lifted the unborn child up above my head without harm to the mother or child. Angels and archangels surrounded us; then Christ appeared, wearing a heavy white robe, and touched the infant. I prayed for my release from any generational bondage. Christ said, "Just ask God once, and it will be done; then pray to thank him." He said I was to prepare myself for baptism, to pray for deliverance and release from the bondage, to pray for forgiveness of this dark evil and prepare to enter Christ. Then when the baptism is done, as the water is sprinkled, my soul will open. He said this is a very sacred time and to be sure during the baptism to consciously receive the Holy Spirit.
>
> I then returned the infant within the mother, as if she had never been disturbed. Then I went to my sacred mountain, my safe place, and returned to the fourth door. The door opened easily now, and behind the door were the elders, two in one, as if they had been merged front and back. These two aunts represented my genetic heritage. I released them and told them to travel to a place of healing. Then I cleansed the inner chambers, put tobacco to the four corners and sprinkled it with corn pollen.
>
> Later I continued the journey, because I had sent them out of my inner sanctum, but I didn't know where they went. I went and found them in an old childhood home. I called the two aunts forward (these are not my aunts in this lifetime) and carefully separated them with my sword. Then I spoke to them and told them to return to where their souls had come from, to reunite with the women they

were, separate from each other. It seems that in this fourth door, the generations on either side of my family were bound by the cult in two witchlike beings. By separating them and sending them to be healed and purified and to make their own healing journey, I released my family from generational bondage.

I learned that people are born into bondage through covenants set in families that go from generation to generation. I understood then how the family of man had been held in mind bondage in a fear prison. In this journey, I saw one of my long-ago ancestors, a European woman, held in bondage. I went back and freed my family lineage. I saw Christ lifting my family up, freeing them from generational bondage, from the covenants and curses that were part of our inheritance. I know my family is not unique in this, that many families are held in similar bondage. My own healing and the work I did to free my family have had a noticeable, positive effect on our family's relationships.

Since then I have learned about Hellenger work, a technique developed for exactly this purpose, and I have completed the Hellenger program. I know that powerful things happen in families when one person is willing to be the fulcrum point to go back and clear the family lineages, helping the family to be free.

November 7, 1993: God, I know you have protected me in ways I'll never know, that my being led to baptism is a holy union with Christ, with the Christ light, and a healing from the lie of my infant baptism. I do believe the holy water will wash away the other baptism; I do believe it will bring me closer to a commitment to serving God, as I have chosen. I am not naive to think that once baptized, we are totally safe from Satanic forces. Many baptized people revel in the cult. I do believe that if an individual opens up to Christ's healing and protection and the gifts of the angels and archangels, the gifts will come—providing that that person is not a hypocrite and goes inside deep to find his or her own truth. I do not go to this baptism from fear, but as a pact of spiritual journey and growth. I have known the betrayal of spiritualism; now I wish, through baptism, to be cleansed of it. I do believe that God and only God can forgive the evil things that humanity has done, but we have to first forgive ourselves.

This darkness violated my family and my marriage. I did not and could not stop it until I started this path of healing and woke up and started to know the truth—that I have choices. I believe that I have been led on this journey. I do not believe that the Church is protection, or that it's such a pure, faultless place. It's subject to the faults of society just like anything else. I do believe that I will be offered a path to greater spirituality, a tool for purification of the mind, body and spirit. I have been cleansed by the sacred waters of my sacred spring. By my journey, I will now be cleansed by God's holy water and unified with the life essence of Christ. I will learn to heal the fear of the past, to heal the fear I've had of the holy sacrament. I know that the bread and wine in Christ's name is pure and sacred. I am claiming all that is sacred as God's true gift; all that was betrayed by the evil one is forgiven from my life, released and healed.

I was baptized that day in a wonderful ceremony. After my work a few days earlier, I felt it was significant that an elderly Scotch-German woman sat beside me. I asked her to represent my ancestors; she was delighted. My baptismal healing was a highlight in my life. My interfaith universal spirituality is large enough to accommodate many faiths. I was later to experience or be initiated into the Buddhist Precepts, the 21 Tara initiation and Tao, Rastafarian and Native American ceremonies.

November 7, 1993, later: I feel lifted of the burden of what I was born to. I feel the healing. Cleansing holy water has washed away the evil of the ceremonies I was forced to participate in. In partaking of the holy sacrament, there is a spiritual healing with Christ. Today was a wonderful spiritual gift; I received the Holy Spirit. Christ is the butterfly.

November 22, 1993: It is nearly Thanksgiving. I am home today, the first time in a long time.

I thank God for all my blessings. I am so close with my children right now. I have been through so much, processing anger and helping them to heal. My relationship with them has blossomed. Finally our home is what I've always dreamt of. At last we have peace and companionship. Much of this is because I was willing to change. Yesterday, Father M. said that there is no greater power than love. This is something I've spoken of, but now it has new meaning. To know that the Holy Spirit can lift us up to protect us is a relief; plus, I can feel it. I can tell such a difference since I've been baptized. Father M. spoke about removing the shackles on our hearts and the power of the Holy Spirit to free us. We have but to open our hand, our hearts to God, and receive his gifts. I'm growing deeply spiritually. Tears are streaming down my face.

At this point in my recovery, I started working with my brain energies, learning how to slow down and control erratic brain frequencies. I began doing meditations to work with moving chi in my body.

I understand from Christ's teachings that all we have to do is have God's faith and light within us. It is for us to awaken to the Holy Spirit and partake in the awakening. It is more important what people have inside than what they say or do. We have a choice: whether we take in the energy of darkness or the energy of the Holy Spirit. The Holy Spirit has a powerful ability to heal us.

November 1993: When I was trapped, a slave to the past, I was forced to ingest evil things. But I was given those things by force; I wasn't given a choice. Thereby they placed the shadows of demons within our spirits. Christ willingly gave of his essence for our freedom; he, in God's way, created a holy sacrament that permits us to ingest the Holy Spirit every time we take Holy Communion—the spirit of light and freedom. Each time, I feel that spirit flushing and cleansing out of my soul body that evil sacrament I was made to partake in. Because Christ gave of himself freely, he left this gift for us, a part of his healing. All this eternal-light stuff is life, freedom from anti-life. Life:

creative energy force, death of the anti-life, the destruction, wreaking havoc on the soul, taking and demanding sacrifice of victims by which the evil consumes all parts of the being. Christ equals empowerment. Let Christ be my light, God, my shield, and the Holy Spirit, my sword. This is what I feel.

CHAPTER NINETEEN

Out of Control

Around the end of November, my guide told me to prepare carefully before I attempted to open up the fifth door. He said I would experience stronger inclinations toward suicide than I had previously felt. This was a strong warning indeed, when I remembered what the voices had suggested in the past. But I had resisted them, hadn't I? And I was determined to go forward. Before I could get to the fifth door, I had to do a lot of work to deprogram this everyday phrase: out of control. I'd never really focused on that common expression, although it's tossed about a lot in our society. Most of us live with the fear of being out of control, and I had become a very controlling person.

> Late November 1993: Control is brainwash, succumbing, obedience, programming. Out of control is not safe; the cult controls offer safety. Your perpetrator offers safety; out of control leads to harassment, torture and punishment. When you are in control, you behave predictably as designated by your controller. You do what you're supposed to do, be where you're supposed to be, behave as your master decrees, as your parent says, as the cult wishes you to.

When I began my journey of healing, my family felt that I was out of control, and in fact I was—out of mind control and the programming. I'd used control to raise my children. When you control someone, you do not want them to escape that control, because you know the consequences. We pass that on to our children or whoever we have power over. Out of control equals danger to the dominance of the controlling entity. Out of control is having free will; free will is a threat to the program, to the family, to the cult, to the society dominated by cult rule.

Little children are easy to control; older ones are harder. Because of my cult programming, I ran my household and my children on control and power. Now I've learned to parent through empowerment, through listening and caring about others' feelings instead of trying to control their behavior. I realize that the entire aim of behavior modification is to control a person's behavior, not to help that person expand his or her consciousness or make better choices. The education of our children reflects this program. I have noticed in the last decade that parenting styles have changed; fear, domination and physical punishment are being phased out. I had to undo that on my own, on an internal level. As others take these same steps, we affect critical mass in the society. When enough of us change, society changes.

I had to come to terms with myself not just as a victim of horrendous abuse, but as a victimizer as well. I went deep inside to explore where I was used to continue these cycles of control and fear programming. I openly faced my own victimizer, forgave myself and asked for forgiveness. This is one of the most important parts of being free. So long as we think of ourselves as victims, we are. When we can see how we hurt others, we can begin to forgive ourselves, and the internal battle with self ceases. All cycles of abuse are passed on in some way. Even though I chose a good path when I was young (the Native Americans call it the good red road), I still passed unhealthy patterns and behaviors on to my children. I was not able to protect them from perpetrators or change the cycles of family bondage until they were teenagers. We did, however, change. My grandchildren have benefitted from these changes; they are much healthier than my children were.

Part of the message I worked to deprogram was that God had chosen me to hurt myself. That was not the God of love. In January of 1994, I went through a deep depression. At that point, the case against my husband looked hopeless. I was humiliated and embarrassed. Sometimes I got so depressed, I wished I would die. I wondered why I had to suffer so much. Of course, the clouds are always darkest right before the Sun breaks through. In February of 1994, at a state board meeting, a board member came out and exposed the harassment, coercion and threats she had experienced. The conspiracy was revealed.

One day I was in a church, looking at the crucified Christ. I thought that as an innocent person, I was being crucified by the case against my husband. I never liked the symbol of the crucified Christ, because I saw the symbol as the Church's message that the ultimate thing you can do for enlightenment is to suffer. I never believed that the most honorable service for the people is to suffer. I decided that day that the crucified Christ is an image that has reinforced cult programming. But there is another aspect to the crucified Christ: the image puts us in touch with our own deep suffering.

I continued to work with gifted practitioners for my healing, including a naturopath whom I saw for two years. Blind from childhood, his hands were guided by the Holy Spirit. He worked with deep-tissue injury, releasing body memories and helping me let go of the screams I held deep within. His clinic was relatively soundproof, so I could scream my lungs out and no one would hear me.

> December 16, 1993: Dr. L. did some deep-tissue work on me. He said my body tells him what happened to me. He said that my hip bones are not even, that my hip was dislocated with an instrument. He can see the imprint with inner vision. He showed me the scar tissue on my side. It hurt so much when he broke it loose. Screaming helps release the agony.

Other therapists helped as well, with orthopedics and deep-tissue work. Without their help, I would still be holding that trauma in my cells. Dr. L. also worked to heal demonic possession. Before too long, the symptoms of depression were relieved and I felt much stronger.

> January 19, 1994: I checked in with my guardians to make sure I was in a strong place and everyone was okay and stable. I entered through the portal and saw the fifth door. The wolves guard there. I went back to the many times I had wished for death as escape or release and had returned to the world. Deep inside me, I felt that there were worse things than dying. Living was much worse. I touched the deep part that would have preferred to die. But it goes beyond just a moment of wishing for death, of feeling self-destructive. It goes into the deep part of myself that felt I would be freed by death, that thought that only through death could I not have to face what they were doing to me again. I remembered seeing myself in the vault as a three-year-old. I recalled how many times I prayed for death as a release. I gathered them all in a sacred doeskin made to contain, not trap, and left them for the wolves to guard. I came back. I carry this metaphoric book "Children of the Holocaust" in my soul. My inner children wanted to die, and yet their story lives. I will live to tell my story.

January 28, 1994: I am fighting depression. I feel the medicine robe of all the experiences that brought me to wish death; they are gathered now to help me know that I have a strong will to survive. That will carry me through this.

I went into a deep trance. Patrick said that I am to be reindoctrinated and returned to the program in the year 2000 and that I have been implanted with a device that will cause me to die of cancer by age fifty-two if I am not reprogrammed. I would rather die than go back. Patrick says we can sabotage the plan, that I do not have to return or die.

January 31, 1994: Patrick is intent on sabotaging the program. He has been with me since 1955 and has linked with other resisters inside the system. The database has an immense amount of information. He will sabotage the program for me to be returned for evaluation at age fifty. They already know I am resisting and would certainly do a carcinogenic implant, causing destruction of the unit by age fifty-two.

I had completely forgotten writing this in my journal six years ago. Just this past spring (2001), I was on my way to a crop circle conference in Sedona and thinking about how tired I had been lately. I had been working on scanning my body as part of my overall health plan, and I was scanning as I was driving along. Suddenly I knew that I had a cancer. One of the members of my psychic protection team called within a half hour. She said that something was wrong, that I should look into my energy fields, because there was a really dark attack on me. When I arrived at the house where I'd be staying during the conference, I showed my friends where a brown recluse spider had bitten me on my leg. We discussed how sometimes minor injuries activate old programs. I told them I felt there was something wrong with me physically. We began a psychic healing session to clear me of implants.

Implants are psychic energy fields that are either accumulated fear densities or literal devices implanted in the brain and other parts of the body to create illnesses and interfere with higher consciousness. Implants can be scanned with a form of remote viewing to determine the origin, purpose and location. When we located the implant, we asked it who it was and where it came from. It spoke through me in another voice, deep and gruff. It identified itself as Draconian; these are often negative ETs that help to hold the planet in fear. The implant had been installed and was set to activate by my fifty-second birthday if I had not been reprogrammed by then. The healer who was working on me works with high-level multidimensional ETs who are not in the service of the cult. With their guidance, we were able to deprogram and remove the implant. This required forcing out the entity attached to the implant. The experience was incredibly intense—I could liken it only to an exorcism.

This clearing and healing happened in April of 2001, with no conscious memory of what I had written back in January of 1994. My birthday is near the end of July. I didn't open the journals until I started this book on my fifty-second birthday. Early in July, I went for my annual checkup. I had never had a mammogram, but when it was suggested, I agreed. The results showed a precancerous condition, which has led to months of diagnosis and finally a biopsy. During the months between diagnosis and treatment, I worked to heal the condition. I was fortunate to meet a deprogrammer at a national conference. He discovered that I did still have an active program, and we cleared it. I also worked with a bioenergetics machine and herbal therapy.

As I write this, it is January of 2002. I am delighted to say that the results of the biopsy came back normal. Patrick was right. I did not have to be reprogrammed or die. And the biopsy surgery was the most positive experience I have ever had with conventional medicine. I was not triggered or agitated by the medical procedures. I was a little nervous just before the anesthetic was administered, but I talked to the nurse about it and felt fine. No anxiety, no trauma. I knew deep inside that I would be fine.

CHAPTER TWENTY

Divine Intervention

February 2, 1994: More memories of the programming experimentation center. Patrick took me back with the words, "What can be done, can be undone." The room was in the lower building, a different building than the room of the red brick wall. It was all white; extremely bright lights flooded everywhere. I was strapped in a chair tipped forward, a band around my forehead. My hands were strapped at the wrists, my fingers in caps, each with a wire. A conductive gel was in the caps. My bare feet were strapped at the ankles, conducting gel on them as well. Then a mechanical hood came over my head, hinged at the top. The hood was soundproof, lightproof and airtight. Patrick said, "Repeated stimulation until desired response was accomplished. The head is environmentally deprived while the body is overstimulated with light and sound, sensations focused on the palms of the hands and the soles of the feet. Then all is disconnected, and the subject is spun to disorganize the neural transmitters." After the spinning, I had a convulsion in Dr. D.'s office. Patrick told me to say, "I am angry at them. I can be angry at them; I can be furious. I can destroy the pictures of the ones I'm not to be mad at."

Then I came back to the fifth door. I went in and smashed the source of my controllers, shattered their windows, destroyed all the things that had held me in bondage.

Laiolin came in, bringing peace, tranquillity, the light of
healing and a place of freedom. "Let the healing begin," she
said. I will be open to receive the gifts I could not receive
before now. I became aware of what happened to the
people from the experiments who didn't survive—left in
institutions as catatonic/schizophrenic, neurologically and
physically damaged. They are lost to our world. They
haven't had an opportunity to heal as I have.

It was amazing. Each time I went to church, the sermon seemed to be
about what I needed to help myself heal.

February 6, 1994: I went to church today. So often the gifts
from church are so overwhelming and powerful. The
service was about the healing of a little boy who had died
and was brought back to life by a holy man who had
deemed him born. The sermon was about grief and
suffering, how suffering is our teacher, bringing us to a place
of growth. To love is to grieve.

After communion, I was praying and affirming to God
that I trust what I have been brought to, that I am ready
to be of service to God's plan for me. I don't remember it
all, because what came next was so intense. I went back to
my last memory, to the point where I had the convulsion.
I was lying on the floor of the light room, dead or dying.
I heard a man's voice: "Looks like we pushed this one too
far. There are plenty more where she came from. Evaluate
her appropriately and make the disposal—incinerate if
she's dead, institutionalize if brain-dead." I was left lying
on the floor. A young woman of nineteen or twenty
came in. She knelt beside me, put her hands on my head
and said, "Oh, God, please don't let her die." An angel
appeared above her, touched her shoulder, and the girl
touched me. Again she prayed, "Don't let her die." The
Holy Spirit spoke to me, saying, "I did not bring you this
far to be destroyed now."

Christ has appeared to me twice; on the third time I will be called to service. I am to be prepared, to become strong and continue to heal. The Holy Spirit said, "Your husband and you will not be destroyed. You will be an example to others, that they can be free and not be destroyed." The sermon had said that ordinary time restricts us; we must open up to God's time as he chooses to work through us. The healing is evidence of God's work; the word of God is the work. I was filled with compassion for the girl who came back at the risk of her own life to pray for me. I knew from this memory that I had risen from death; I had crossed the threshold into the next world and was brought back. This wasn't like wishing I was dead. This was actually crossing over. I know why I was given a sound mind and a healthy body; I have been brought to redemption, salvation and deliverance to do God's bidding, to serve God as he wishes me to. Now I am ready to cast doubt aside and walk forward in the Christ light to enter the place he saved for me. My life has meaning.

February 8, 1994: I feel that I know who I am, what my purpose is in this world. I was not brought back from death without a purpose. I have full faith in the vision I received, when the angel granted the girl the miracle of my life. I had been brought to God. I believe that when I see the third vision of Christ, it will manifest my path. I feel strong inside, stronger than ever in my life. I am not afraid; I do not fear death. He who is in me, God of the highest, the divine light of Christ, is greater than he who is in the world.

February 11, 1994: I want to go behind the fifth door. If I need to, I will let go of my consciousness to do that. I tell Patrick I am prepared; I ask for whatever gift can be given me today. I am strong and ready to walk any path necessary for my freedom, health, growth and higher good.

I trust that I am protected and that the guardians protect my life, which is God's divine intervention. I enter this door willingly, knowing that good will come from my journey. I will not harm myself. I place a shield on my third eye, my fluorite crystal on my heart. I will be safe and free with God's grace.

The session with Dr. D. was good, very intense. My head feels funny. I was prepared for today's work and well protected. I went to the fifth door. I had my sword and shield, sandals and helmet. I was in a net of rainbow yarn, covered by obsidian thread. I entered the top of the door; a crack opened, and I flew in. I found myself in a dark chamber. I could feel death. From the back, an evil voice challenged me, "Who dares enter here? Who goes?" I encountered the evil one, the she-devil and the black widow. She challenged me from the back of the cave. Laiolin came, did a sacred chant and changed the energy with cosmic vibration. She called her out; she threatened death. I entered into combat with the black widow. I pushed open the fifth door and called her forth. She became a black ball. I lifted her up, that she might be removed from this planet and never do harm again. I remember she said that she could consume the soul of an infant before it saw light. She was lifted by Archangel Michael and the angels in God's name and by the power of Christ, Buddha and White Buffalo Calf Pipe Woman. She was banished from our planet, never to return to harm a living thing, and all things, animate or inanimate, are living.

It took a lot for me to come back and finish this session at Dr. D.'s office, and then I went to my acupuncturist. There Laiolin took me to healing, and I was bathed in sacred water. She assured me again that this work must be done to save Mother Earth. She told me to go forth and celebrate, for a true moment in the history of our planet has come to pass—for our species, our planet, has been freed from a truly evil she-devil force. The children will be safer. It will take time for the energy to shift fully, but the effects will be felt. Then she called upon protection for everyone who was working with my family and me. She assured me that by our work, that force has been banished. My cosmic being of light called for angelic protection. She said that the dark forces would be angry with me for confronting this demonic being. She said not to bother telling people, because most of them would never believe me. Then she called on a force of the guardians to protect my family, my home, our clinic and all of us who were trying to be free, for the Dark Lord would be wrathful.

I know I was a vehicle for this work and that the she-devil, the black widow, wasn't an alter. She was an entity I confronted on a spiritual journey. I do feel that this evil one had a powerful influence over me, but it wasn't me. I went to the portal of the world of the dead and did battle with a powerful, evil force. I see why I had to come to terms with my death, will and feelings, and with death itself, before Laiolin could take me into such a place

The portal was in my psyche, the fifth door, a link to the underworld installed by the programmers. If the she-devil had opened the door, I would have taken my own life at her command. Thank heavens it was a heavy door. I know why I lived; I am honored that Laiolin has chosen me. I am fulfilled and truly freed through the power of Christ to shed the cloak of guilt and shame put upon me by the dark forces.

The following weekend I met a person who told me about the book *The Celestine Prophecy*. I read the book and felt as if it had been written for me, because I had been living all those things the author talked about.

February 16, 1994: I got *The Celestine Prophecy*; I'm so excited to get into it. It feels good in my hands. I also

found *Nine Faces of Christ*, a book I've heard is
revolutionary. I am delighted to have these gifts. This
weekend, while we were at the hot springs in Pagosa, I had a
lot of visions. In one I had a healing circle in my old home,
and children were coming to me for healing. I did
long-distance healing for my whole family, for the past and
for all the people I loved. In another vision, I was
surrounded by my guardians; they stretched out their arms
and shot white light from their fingers, bathing and
centering me in healing, beautiful light, inside and out. I
know I'm close to a metamorphosis.

March 1, 1994: I went to church yesterday. The sermon and
scripture were astounding. I have always detested the
reading where God tells Abraham to sacrifice his only son
and he goes to it. As they read it, I screamed inside, *Sacrifice
is wrong!* Abraham lied to his companions, "I'll just go up
and pray with my son, and we'll be right back." The son saw
him build a fire and asked, "Where is the lamb?" Abraham
said, "God will provide the lamb." But he intended to kill his
son—he even had a knife. This is no different than the cult.
Then an angel told Abraham to stop, and Abraham killed a
lamb instead of his son. Wrong. Evolved humans do not
take life to appease God. What kind of God requires
sacrifice? I almost passed out. Then I realized that this is
part of mankind, that in some way, I had been called by an
angel to say no to this ancient rule of the death fear and to
help our people evolve beyond sacrifice.

I know there are many distortions in the Bible. I also know
that the truth of Abraham has not been revealed.
According to the Bible, Mary Magdalene was the whore of
Babylon, when in fact she was the wife of Christ Jesus.
Regardless of what the truth of Abraham might be, the
biblical story reveals in a historic fashion the psyche of
humanity.

We as a people no longer need to appease angry gods. The history of humanity is full of stories of people who believed they had to kill to win a holy war or to appease an angry god. I agree with Zecharia Sitchin about this. He has written several books on this subject, including books that amplify the history of our planet and the influence of negative ETs.

These negative ETs with big egos told people that they were gods. There is but one true God, the God of prime creation who embraces all in divine oneness through the power of unconditional love and free will. The most powerful force of creation is the force of unconditional love. The story of Abraham is like many other stories in the Old Testament. Abraham was being tested. The human heart has been tested with the test of fire. We now reach the final test: Do we choose love or fear? We will experience what we manifest.

Choice and sacrifice: it's a complicated combination. An ancient Japanese teaching says that what you must sacrifice are the ideas that separate you from the sanctity of life. Saint Peter stated that Lucifer was one of God's great teachers who came not only to tempt humankind, but also to bring the gift of choice, thus expanding the conscious soul.

As the service went on, the priest spoke about the cross of consciousness. Whether by circumstance or by choice, there comes a time for us to pick up our cross and follow Christ. She told of a young aristocrat in Sweden who, when the Nazis invaded, invoked the power of the government to issue a certificate to Jews to save them from the concentration camps. He went to the train station, and as people were being loaded on boxcars, he grabbed as many as he could and gave them a sealed document to free them, right in front of the Nazis. He didn't have time to mail the papers, so he had to go to the platform and pull people off one at a time. Soon after, he disappeared. Perhaps he died in the concentration camps himself. One of these certificates saved the husband of the woman who was giving the sermon. Another story she told was of a hemophilic child infected with AIDS. He was an outcast in school and church because people feared him. Shots were even fired at his family's home. They moved a mere twenty miles away, where in their new neighborhood, they were received with love and support. The boy was called to educate people about AIDS. He lived years longer than the most optimistic expectations. His life was one of consciously carrying the cross. I went to the priest afterward and asked that I might bless her by kissing her feet; she cried with gratitude. As it was, her sister was dying, and she needed strength. During the healing service that day in church, I was overwhelmed with the healing light of Christ and the Holy Spirit. I have been set free by God's grace. I have stepped forward to do what it is my life is for, to somehow give back what I have received. God, help me to walk this path in your grace.

In his book, *The Power of Myth*, Joseph Campbell explores the force of myth in the human psyche. I created a myth, recounted in the next journal entry, about my own journey. It helped me accept the changes I had to make to be free. I had chosen to move my home and family from the community I had lived in for sixteen years. That was agonizing. Those were some of the most precious years of my life. My family is a loving one; we always taught our children respect and high moral values. We told them, "Only love will win the war." We grew a big garden, canned food, celebrated sacred ceremony, camped in the wilderness and always honored the Earth as our mother. This myth does not discredit the good in our lives. We taught our children well; we had the best of intentions. But what we did not know, what we denied, sabotaged the sweetness of life. It spoiled our dream of a healthy alternative lifestyle. Even though my extended family did not choose to join me on my journey, things have changed for them. They are good souls and have worked hard to build good lives. My myth is a story of humanity's journey to the valley of healing.

March 27, 1994: Once, long ago, the people left the land of poison, looking for a place of beauty. A voice had spoken to the elder woman, a voice of her beloved canyon and the sacred mountain just beyond the land of poison. It said, "Take your people south; leave this place for the sake of the children." The people left, taking along a bag of seeds, hoping to find fertile soil to grow strong plants and raise healthy children. They searched for a new home. Their hope was high—a dream of beautiful land, their own earth to plant. Little did they know that among many good seeds, some of the seeds they carried held the poison from the land of darkness.

At last they found their promised land at the base of a great mesa. Dreams ran high—a sacred tree, a pure spring, a place to plant their seeds. They had heard the legend of a giant who consumed humans, who was captured by the sacred twins and slept beneath a black mesa. But, of course, they thought it to be a different black mesa. They settled down and planted the seeds they had brought. In the darkness, as they slept, the seeds began to sprout from the Earth and chant evil chants. The sound echoed against the lava rock, awakening the sleeping giant. He awoke and stood up and stretched; he was hungry. His shadow fell over the village.

Seeing the plants, he reached down and greedily consumed
them. So the people lived in the shadow of the giant, and
he consumed their crops. At night he would come out and
terrify the children. The giant ruled the world of darkness;
he commanded the night. His power was strong within the
people. They were deceived, as all they knew were their
good lives of daylight. The poison of the seeds of the past
carried the power to erase their minds, causing them to
know only daylight, not the power of the giant's shadow
over their lives.

Mothers tenderly held their little ones as they woke with
terror, not knowing why. With hope, the people planted
the seeds, thinking they were walking the good red road.
This place was perfect for Old Man Coyote to come play his
flute to trick the people, bringing with him the evil Elk
Lord. As some of the men slept, they were enchanted by
the coyote's music. The evil Elk Lord entered their hearts,
awakening a ravenous power within them. At night they
would leave their beds and dance to the coyote's music, not
remembering in the morning the dance they had done.
The women harvested the plants of poison, feeding their
families, not knowing of the power over their minds.

So the people lived in the shadow of the ravenous giant,
waking at night in terror and never knowing why, thinking
they were walking the good red road. Lame Cat and White
Bird Girl lived in the village. They carried much pain, not
knowing why. Part of White Bird Girl's heart had gone to the
world of the dead, because she could not bear the grief for
the children. Night after night she danced with the Elk, and
he drained her of her medicine power. Lame Cat was a man
of healing. He went forth into the world and brought
healing to the people of different villages. When he returned
at night, he was bound and tied, powerless to help his woman
and his children. His body screamed with agony; he desired
to bring forth his sword to protect his family, but his hands

were tied in rawhide and bleeding. This is how they existed for many cycles of winter to spring. They somehow protected their loving hearts and did not perish.

Finally came a day of wonder. The signs were visible in the heavens—sacred signs of awakening sent from the lands of Prime Creator to the people of Earth. At this time, Lame Cat and White Bird Girl traveled to the north, to the medicine gathering held around the sacred Sun pole. They danced and prayed for healing as the planets danced around the Sun. White Bird Girl prayed and danced in the healing circle. It was there that a Wakan, a sacred one, came to her. She felt the wings of a hawk gently tapping her body, awakening her spirit, cleansing the poison from the seeds of the past.

When they returned from the north, Lame Cat knew he must find another home for his family. He must leave the shadow of the giant and take his family to safety across the valley. They prayed for a miracle, and their prayers were answered. The healing must begin. No longer could Lame Cat allow his hands to be bound. The cry of freedom awoke within him. With heavy hearts and much grief, his family packed their lodge and left their people; they moved to a strange land across the valley. There, in a healing valley canyon at the base of a sacred mountain, they found a home: La Cuchillo del Sol, the Sun Dagger. There they planted new seeds and nourished the soil. The grandfathers sent White Bird Girl back to her sacred mountain, to the place by the land of darkness. There she learned to dip and cleanse the spring of her soul. She learned to listen to the voice of healing of the grandfathers. Here she began her sacred journey, the quest for healing and freedom.

First medicine, sacred water, flushed out the poison and darkness, healing her heart and soul. She learned to dance with Prime Creator and fill herself with the healing light of the Holy Spirit. All this took many moons. Step by step she traveled the sacred vision path of healing. Finally, the power of the evil seeds of the past was weakened within her, and she awoke to the truth of her past. Her visions revealed the truth of her people and the power the giant commanded over them. Her heart was filled with grief and agony as she looked upon her own hands and realized what the giant had commanded her to do. Her body was wracked with agony as she met each shadow of darkness and cast it out of her soul. Sacred Wakan spirits helped her transform each to healing energy. Her vision quest brought her healing and sacred tools of protection and light. There in the valley of healing, Lame Cat and White Bird Girl made a safe place for their children to heal and grow.

White Bird Girl voyaged to the land of the dead and brought her heart back to heal; she traveled to the place where the giant held the seeds that made her people forget. She faced the giant, drawing her sacred sword. She severed the cords between the giant and her family, setting her family free. Each dawn she faced the east and thanked the grandfathers for her sacred gifts. Each day she prayed for her people. Each day White Bird Girl thanked Wakan Tanka, Great Mystery, that she no longer had to dance with the evil Elk Lord, that her family was free from the shadow of the evil giant. There in the valley of light, White Bird Girl and Lame Cat awakened their medicine powers. Lame Cat did the sacred Sun dance and prayed for the people. Together they walked the good red road.

Then the time came when the calling within White Bird Girl's soul became so strong, she lovingly left her family to walk a spirit path. She promised to return, knowing she must make a sacred journey. She traveled far and experienced many initiations; the ancestor spirits guided her footsteps. Deep within her, a voice awakened, her soul's promise to give her life in service to Prime Creator and the awakening of heaven on Earth.

And what of Lame Cat? He carried White Bird Girl's medicine fan when he danced. When the ancestor spirits called him to the Sun pole to receive a vision, his body was hurled through the dimensions and the medicine fan flew from his hands and out of the sacred circle. This was how the ancestor spirits told them that their journey together was destined to end. Lame Cat packed his medicine bundle and left the home of White Bird Girl to find his way on the path of the born-again ancients. White Bird Girl sang a medicine song and prayed for his journey. At dawn she faced the rising Sun and embraced her destiny. No longer was she Wounded Woman.

White Bird Girl made her journey long ago when the giant was very angry. Her journey to healing and freedom was long and beautiful and took much courage. You know it was the love she had for her people, especially the children, and the love they had for her that gave her such courage. They say that many other people have found the courage to leave the old world of fear behind.

And what of her people? Legend has it that they discovered the poison seeds in their own way and planted new seeds. The evil Elk Lord no longer has such a power in their land, and they say that the giant's heart is healing.

I am sad that my dear Lame Cat did not continue on with me. He might someday find his path to peace and serenity. I miss him dearly, but I honor his choice not to follow my path. I cannot judge the journey of another. When he divorced me in 1999, he said he could not be married to a woman who felt she could heal the world. In jest I said, "It's a tough job, but somebody's got to do it." I know we are part of Mother Earth healing herself and us, her children. I also know that for our planet to survive, it will take a core group of souls who are totally committed to the principles of peace, souls who offer themselves as tools of spirit for the higher good to heal our planet. I am one of these; my life is dedicated to the service of birthing heaven on Earth.

I knew that back in 1994 as well. I had been working with that inner part of myself that had been invisible and became Visible. Visible died rather than participate in the lie; Visible chose invisibility. Visible was a part of myself that protected children—including my inner children. Visible was the guardian of the sixth door.

April 1, 1994: As I stood at the sixth door, I connected with Visible. Now that he has a voice, he told me that he had disappeared with a part of my heart and soul and that he always said no to the hurting of children. I asked why I couldn't visualize him, and he said that it was because he was beyond the sixth door. There, in the world of the dead, he preserved these parts of me. When he went into this world, the Dark Lord sent the black widow to weave her web to block his escape. I opened the door to do battle with her for his freedom. I called Laiolin, and together we called in the guardians, angels and archangels. I called in Christ and White Buffalo Calf Pipe Woman. I put on my armor and prepared for battle.

Laiolin began a harmonic chant, and I opened the sixth door. The doorway was covered with black widow spider webs and many baby spiders. With great effort, we gathered the web into a massive ball. The black widow emerged from the portal, and the being of light projected cosmic light upon her. Before my eyes, the illusion of the black widow vanished. She became a tiny but deadly spider. Laiolin told her that her mate and offspring were within this web, and she willingly crawled in. The being of light placed onyx and cosmic light around the web, which I held. With an intense concentration of cosmic energy, the being dissolved the web and directed the energy up to the guardians. It was then that the little Visible came forth, a young man, a beautiful lightbeing. We joined hands and went to my sacred mountain. With our hands joined over the spring, he entered my core. Laiolin spoke, saying, "This is a resurrection at the time of the resurrection of Christ. [This took place around Easter.] He, Visible, has risen from the world of the dead, just as Christ did. This is very sacred."

As I came back, I became aware of three other lifetimes: I saw a small stone house on rolling hills in Ireland or Scotland; a desert yurt in the Fertile Crescent area where my feet were like leather, having never worn sandals; and a teepee made of bark in the northeastern forest. It seemed that Visible and I had been separated many lifetimes ago. My guide said I will learn more about past lives now.

After I finished the session, I went to Wild Oats to eat and met a young man who read auras. He said he had never read an aura like mine before; it was filled with warrior energy emanating out of my chakras, red and orange, in sprays of mist, mostly pure translucent light, with circular beams. He said that humans weren't made to maintain such an intense energy field and that if I kept it up, it would burn me out. But I needed it to clear out that black widow's nest.

On April 5, I had a strong dream about my mother. In a little house by a huge river, I came into a room, and she was there. She thanked me for finding her father, who was in the next room—or his presence was. She said she died not knowing, and now she knows. She said not to let anyone tell me I'm wrong for what I've done; then she lay upon the bed and sobbed. She took me into the next room, where I met my grandfather, Fred Shearer. This let me know that my journey was also helping my mother heal, even though she had left this world over twenty years before I began my journey.

April 25, 1994: I just spent the weekend in Canyonlands, a wonderful spiritual journey. I went to a sacred cave during a planetary alignment. I drummed, played my flute and sang to the grandfathers of the canyons, and they graced me. It has been three years since I was there last—three years of healing, transition and being tested. Now I emerge stronger and more at peace than ever in my life. I can feel a life inside me that is free and strong. If any of my children or grandchildren read this, I want you to know that the journey to freedom and healing is worth it. Transcending terror is worth it. I encourage anyone who is willing to make the trip to do it.

May 11, 1994: Laiolin taught me an exercise that harmonizes my brain and equalizes the static energy. [This exercise is described in Appendix B.] My right hand trembled, then both hands began to float. Laiolin said that my arms were swords of light. She taught me harmonic chants that equalized and calmed my brain energy. She said that the connectors to the left and right hemispheres were disrupted, and part of my brain sometimes begins to tremble like my hands do, that my right hand doesn't know what the left hand is doing. When this happens, it catapults chemicals into my system, triggering terror response to programming. This was caused by sound waves being introduced to the front left brain lobe in the experiments. The floating meditation harmonizes the brain's hemispheres.

She also said that there was a keyhole-shaped spot of black scar tissue on my brain that could cause a stroke if it wasn't healed. She instructed my acupuncturist to insert needles in the top left and right quadrants of my skull. She began a low harmonic chant and told the acupuncturist to touch the needles, thumb and forefinger, and channel cosmic energy. She warned that there would be an immediate physical effect, and not to be alarmed. When the acupuncturist did this, I had a convulsion. Everything went foggy; I made a high-pitched sound, and my hands were trying to clasp in front of me. It took a lot of effort to bring my left and right hands together. Finally, they met. The cosmic being of light said that this was a gift to my practitioner and me from her people. [She has explained to me that she is from an Arcturian mothership. In the incident just described, I channeled the being and relayed her instructions to the acupuncturist.] She said that this was a powerful healing and the beginning of a new process for me. She cautioned me to drink lots of water, advice that many healers and therapists give after releasing energies or healing processes.

May 18, 1994: I began recalling past-life memories of
Leionie, a young Jewish girl taken to the concentration
camps. As best as I can tell, she died in 1944. I was born in
1949. I experienced incidents from this child's life before her
family was arrested. I loved those journeys to her world.
She lived in Austria in a little flat with her parents. Her
father was a rabbi, and her mother taught her the timeless
traditions of Jewish women that honor the home and
family. Her mother said she was a princess of the House of
David. I learned how a lace tablecloth handed down for
generations could serve to create a sacred space on a
common wooden table for Friday evening prayers. One
day they came to get her family. She never saw her father
again. She died in the camps. I was told that the same ones
who headed up the experiments in the U.S. were in charge
of the experiments that took her life. I remembered playing
concentration camp as a small child. Now I understood
why. I also knew that on a soul level, I came back to expose
this atrocity for the sake of our children.

I don't completely understand my connection with this Jewish prin-
cess, but I channeled her. Her life represented for me the strength of a
brave young woman. I have come to the conclusion that I did have an im-
mediate past life in the concentration camps and was a victim of the same
doctors in this life and that previous one. One of the doctors was named
Karl, and I've written the name in my journal: Karl Leisenbraun or
Leichenbaum. I continued experiencing this girl's life. The cosmic be-
ing of light told me that Leionie's soul was linked with mine because of
our connection with the Nazi doctor. A soul link to a past life is more
powerful than just having a past life that your soul experienced. A
past-life soul link is where the lines of feeling and communication remain
powerful and open. The energies transcend timelines and connect the
two lifetimes. Just as Leionie is vibrant, full of love of life and home and
family, so are these things dear to me in this life. Leionie is part of my
next step in healing.

C H A P T E R T W E N T Y - O N E

CHAPTER TWENTY-ONE

Into the Abyss: The Seventh Door

I recalled when I was nine or ten years old—before I began menstruating. I was at the experimentation center, where they put a tube into my vagina and injected dye into it. The technicians talked among themselves as if we weren't there, as if we weren't real people. They were talking about inducing ovulation in prepubescent children. Because of my own later fertility testing, I know that procedure was a fallopian tube x-ray. I experienced it when I was trying to conceive children, although the trauma was so great I could not continue. The dye goes into the uterus and fallopian tubes to determine whether there is any blockage.

> May 18, 1994: Radium dye was injected and also a hormone to induce ovulation. I had to hold still, or it would all start again. Then I felt something very strange—air forced into my uterus. My abdomen began to swell; it was excruciating. A fragmented part of my consciousness kept focusing above the waist, kept thinking about going home, getting out of there. I heard them say that young organs were the best to experiment with. The air was determining how much the uterus would stretch before it ruptured, to tell if young children could be used for breeding. When I could bear it no more, I passed out. When I came to, I was in a small, dark room on a cot; I was bleeding vaginally and glad to be left alone at last.

Laiolin channeled through me during that session, saying that her people had helped me survive and that now they needed my help. She explained that such experiments on children continue in the present day with new technology and more bizarre and cruel methods. She said that we as a people have violated the cosmic law with these atrocities against children, our own young. We must evolve and change by 1996 or great destruction will come to our planet. In my journal from that time, I wrote: "This must stop. It will if it is exposed. That is my job."

My guides told me I was to prepare to enter the seventh door. I needed much courage and determination to complete this leg of my journey, and they gave me a list of warnings at this point: Put aside my ego. Don't try to be the savior of the world. Do what I came to do, but don't let my ego fool me into thinking that I'm stronger than I really am. Know my limits, and accept the gifts without unreal expectations. Accept the fact that my reality and what I had discovered were too hard for other people. Be more considerate and compassionate. Realize that the things I was dealing with were too painful and intense for my family, husband and children. Don't impose more on other people than they can handle.

> June 22, 1994: In the programming center, long, sharp needles were inserted into my brain through the fissures in my skull—not like electroshock probes, but actual conductors of electromagnetic energy—while my body underwent alternating light and sound, pain and sexual stimulation, food and water deprivation and overstimulation. The aim was to create a terror-trigger mechanism that could be activated on cue. The body memory was extreme. Laiolin had asked me to record the session, but I forgot, so I asked Dr. D. to document this in his records. I can still feel the probes in place. The being brought healing energy to those places. I will be able to heal this so that I can no longer be accessed by the programs.

Laiolin performed a healing, using my acupuncturist as a channel. The practitioner touched the two places on my head where the needles had been inserted. Laiolin said that energy would be beamed from a healing team into my head to help me heal. I could feel white-light energy fill my head, then body memory and extreme sensations. My body was trembling. I felt I had been taken into another dimension. She said that it would take one month for the healing to be completed.

After the session, I wrote: "Life has been so intense and busy. The most remarkable thing is a sense of incredible peace within. Not just absence of terror—that certainly is vital—but a wellspring of joy, a lack of rage, a sense of connectedness. I feel totally protected. I am not frightened any longer."

July 6, 1994: Programming—I will die if not useful to the cult. They will kill me if they can't use me. I have defied prime law, persisting to be free. When I sought the source of this programming, Patrick was helpful. He said the source was a programmed entity, not emotional and not a fragment of a personality. It is a created personality installed like a computer chip. Patrick kept the data. I almost had a seizure. Patrick said the program created seizure activity to block the information from being transmitted. When we finally found the program, it was really weird. Patrick spoke. I was put in a chamber and bombarded with electromagnetic energy and frequency vibration. A hologram of the Dark Lord was projected into the room. I was alone with this monster, the image of the Dark Lord who had raped me repeatedly in rites. I tried to get away but could not. I was overwhelmed. I fell into convulsions. The hologram was merged into the central core of my brain. I commanded the illusion to dissolve. My whole body stiffened and tightened like a jolt of lightning, then released. Patrick had to struggle not to be shut down. The instructions commanded a seizure. I fought and conquered it, but I really felt weird.

At the acupuncturist's, I discovered a program, an implanted entity, a death threat. I saw the high school I had gone to. Underneath it was a subterranean programming chamber with an entrance in the back of the stage. It was easily accessible. I went to school, and I was marked in attendance, but really I wasn't in class very much.

I have remote viewed this location; the access has been sealed and the underground rooms closed, as if it had never existed.

On August 3, I recorded a list of symptoms that had adversely affected my life: lack of patience, overreacting, fear, spontaneous anger, blocked energy, pain in the brain, disturbed sleep, feeling out of control, unable to cope, depression, obsession, powerless over a situation, overwhelming grief, humming in my head, repeated statements over and over, overcompliant, unable to meditate, pain in feet, neck, back and womb. I went back to a memory from high school. A narrow hall with low door-ways—a tall person would have to stoop. The walls were tile or ceramic. Three cubicles on either side contain tables with stirrups; I think it was a reprogramming place. It was near the holographic chamber. Four observation windows were placed in each of the three rooms. I recorded some more symptoms that I had in high school: raging headache, eyes rolled back in head, horrible abdominal pain, swollen glands, missed a lot of school, weak, poor energy. I noticed feeling unsafe around certain teachers in my school. I recalled more details on the tables: electrically charged straps went over my chest, abdomen and wrists; conductors put on my head; a cold steel probe in my vagina; hot and cold electric charges alternately with injections of some kind of isotope into my glands; blood withdrawn from the left arm and mixed with a solution and put in the right arm. Recalling this shut down my lower chakra, to block the receipt of the memory. Laiolin did a healing for me and told me some things to do to combat this.

I recorded a memory of the center in Colorado Springs, when I was very young. It made me nauseous and unable to think clearly. I cried and then slept until nightfall. I awoke still sick, with an acute headache. In an effort to gain some perspective, I did some automatic writing. My inner child said, "I have to be strapped down. Karl is cruel. He is the doctor who watches them hurt me. He stands in the corner and gives bossy orders. He has gold glasses. He makes my nose bleed. They take us to the lab when we are sleeping. They hurt us. I want to go home." I began working with issues of betrayal. My guides said that carrying secrets is an act of self-betrayal, because when we do so, we're never able to trust ourselves. The cosmic being of light said that it stops the soul from breathing. Zombies, trance-induced humans who perform tasks for the dark forces against their will, experience such a catatonic state, a temporary soul death wherein the soul cannot breathe. But there are remedies: cleansing, healing, knowing the truth. These keep us connected with our own behavior and protect us from soul betrayal and self-betrayal.

August 29, 1994: Awoke at 2:30 A.M. with pain in my brain and a tightened diaphragm and stomach. Nothing seems to help. I'll try to journal, try to meditate. I'm blocked. I ask, "Where is the pain? Who is upset? What is in my head? Where is the truth?" A little black box is sealed in my mind with control labels fastened over the lids.

August 31, 1994, Dr. D's office: I've been so blocked. I just recovered a memory of the program experimentation center. A small child, maybe eight years old, in a muslin smock, nothing under it. A tiny gray room, maybe four feet square. She cannot stand, only lie, sit or crawl. She has been put there for screaming in the night: "If you act like an animal, you'll be treated like one." A collar or a cord around my neck leads through a hole. They can pull the cord to control me by choking. Food in a dog dish, slid under the door. No utensils, no glasses. Rags in the corner to use the bathroom on. Yuck. If she screams, the chain is tightened. No thrashing, no fits; it's okay to rock or bang your head on the wall. Nothing else. Pain in my kidneys; they put something in the food. No sense of time—no day, no night. The chain is restrictive.

When attendants come in to clean, the child is scolded for soiling her dress. She is called a dog, treated like a dog. She eventually scatters into bits and pieces, singing in her head. No singing allowed. Attendants come in to change her— repeated rapes. She begins to fragment, and I lose track. I come out of the memory. I get the guardians and soul-retrieve her to go to my safe place. The wolf will heal her. I wash her in sacred water and cover her with leaves; I put the pieces under the leaves to heal. When I returned to the memory, it was down the red brick hall. I opened the vault door from the outside and carried her out. She is frail and very ill, but safe now.

On September 14, I had another session with Dr. D. in which Patrick offered help. He said that the intention was to create a psychotic state to use if necessary, if the subject gets too close to the forbidden information that threatens the nation's security and the secrecy of the controllers. It was an experiment in induced psychotic states. The implanted psychotic state can be accessed and controlled; the subject can be locked away in a psychotic ward.

September 19, 1994: I went to St. Bede's. The sermon was about Christ lifting up the child for protection. The pastor had a book about a priest, called the father of the street urchins, who was elected democratic head of Haiti. He was attacked five times; on the sixth, troops attacked his church during worship, shooting and bayoneting people. A pregnant woman was bayoneted; somehow she survived and became a symbol of the government's ruthlessness. The government went to the hospitals to investigate each pregnant woman. They wanted to kill her, to destroy the hope that she symbolized. By Caesarean section, she gave birth to an infant girl, born injured but well. The child was named Esperanza, which means hope. The father was captured and held in his church to be shot, but he was saved by a soldier, a former classmate. The pastor spoke of Christ's challenge to give all for truth, to be willing to throw yourself on the seas for freedom, to speak the truth.

This sermon typifies one of the amazing parts of my journey. When I most needed encouragement, some source would provide it. This church inspired me and gave me strength for the next step.

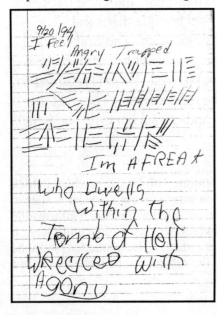

September 20, 1994 (this entry is barely legible, the scrawl of a child): I feel angry and trapped. I'm a freak who dwells within the tomb of hell, wracked with the agony of unstoppable torture. Dark prisons of agony, wretched within a soul of madness, dwelling in the chambers of death. I cannot escape, less I escape by madness, a place of constant delusion. A place removed from constant pain, madness, final freedom from this fury that dwells within . . . a mad, hopeless, empty despair.

_____

September 21, 1994: Whoever wrote that poem last night, I wish to thank you and acknowledge your pain. Here I am, journaling again. There is time to journal or to do morning prayers, but not both. I am feeling overwhelmed, so much to do and I'm the only one to do it. I know I'm having trouble with the anniversary of my mother-in-law's death; the past two years have been a nightmare at this time of year. I am feeling so angry, I had to leave work an hour early yesterday.

My comment to Dr. D.: Never take a voyage without an anchor. This refers to his being my anchor and how he would sit there and make sure I was safe and stay objective, but he was always there to bring me back.

That day, with my massage therapist, Dr. S., I worked with more body memories. He was able to go really deep inside, as in Rolfing, to the places where I held the deepest memories. It took a lot of breathing to get through those sessions. The energy was intense and held more flash-backs.

September 21, 1994 (continued): The attendant's entering the cell. I am insane, like a crazed creature. Put in a straitjacket; carried to another room. A strap around my chest, head belted down—electroshock. Then once again I am alone in the white room, then back to final shock treatment and a total blank. I have no memory of the gaps between or reentering time with the straitjacket. What a novel place to venture to: total insanity. Odd, I recognize no alters with this, just the memory of myself in this white room.

As I left Dr. D.'s office, I teased him about not hospitalizing me. But it is terrifying. I've been everywhere else; why not voyage to the world of utter madness? He told me not to worry, but I was so spacy I forgot to pay him. With the acupuncturist that same day, I bridged the gap. I returned to that blank place of insanity and remembered what had happened between the times they left and returned to take me for electroshock. I was myself, not altered. The key is that when they left, they took the leash—my link, my anchor. Alone totally at first, I altered; I had an image of many people climbing out of my head. But eventually that wears off. Altering doesn't work; besides, there is no place to go. No human, no anchor, no nothing but white walls. So after all the splitting, people banging their heads, screaming, crying, climbing, pounding, hysterics, no leash to stop it like the first part—then collapse. I went into something like a coma—sweet relief, total darkness.

Then I became aware, realized I was still alive. The floor was hard under me. I was hungry and thirsty and had to go to the bathroom. These four things were all that told me I was not dead. Slowly I regained consciousness. There was no one else—just me, the core me, and I was conscious. I attempted to find cracks where the air might come through; I ran my fingers over the cracks. I stayed focused. If there is air, there is contact with the outside world. Again, I lose it; I alter all over the room, cycles of madness ending in collapse and deep comalike sleep, awakening to the same repeated cycles until at last the span of sanity is shortened. The time of focused mental power dwindles to a constant cycle of hysterical, crazy behavior.

Finally, I'm sitting in the middle of the cell and hallucinating. First, a flower blooms from the wall; the crack opens its mouth and speaks to me. People appear; I see a plate of food turn into a cat. I build a home and it becomes an apple. Music dances across a theme. This must be what an LSD trip is like. Then everything freezes. I feel catatonic in my memory. I tell the practitioner to remind me that I am here, that I have a life, that I am not really frozen in a catatonic state. At last it passes, leaving me crazed like a primitive creature, huddled, dirty in the corner with snarled hair, crouched, babbling, crawling, clawing at the air.

But I reached the goal; I bridged the gap. I remembered. I recovered this part of me—the link between the two segments of the attendants entering to straitjacket me and take me to the electroshock room. I have fooled them. Now that I've remembered the experience, it is mine. I brought me back; I own my own reality. No one can control my sanity. They didn't bring me back; somehow I clung to my sanity—not a gift from them, taken at will, but my own treasure. Once I own my experience, they cannot control me and my reality in any way.

I remembered. That means I was there all the time. I never left. It wasn't their electroshock that brought me back, but my thread of reality and human spirit. Had I lost it, I wouldn't have come back. I alone hold the key to my own sanity. If they didn't restore it, they can't take it away— ever. Another chapter complete, another mystery of my hidden life unraveled, another step taken to ultimate freedom. I claim my life.

This happened to an eight-year-old child. I want you to stop for just a moment while you're feeling this, while your heart is open to what happened to me as a child. Stop and think. Somewhere, as we speak, as I write, a child is experiencing things like this. The children are still suffering.

In the summer of 1999, I heard Andy Thomas at the Glastonbury Crop Circle Symposium. He talked about the covert government, the plan for a New World Order, the Reptilians, the atrocities going on. He challenged everyone: "Well, we all know about this stuff, but what are we doing about it?" I sit here at my desk on a beautiful summer morning and pray for the strength to continue speaking into this tape recorder. Earlier I went out to the medicine wheel and prayed to the four directions; I called upon the power of the white eagle, the great cobra who transmutes poison, the bear spirit and the white buffalo. I called to the rainbow warriors.

I was being intuitively guided to seek extra help to read this particular memory. During the years since recovering it, I had of course reflected upon being subjected to environmental deprivation and forced into psychotic states as an eight-year-old. But until today, nearly six years later, I had not read this journal.

At an antinuclear rally sponsored by a Native American women's group, I heard a holy man from Japan, a peace prophet. He told of his experiences as an eight-year-old child and survivor of the atomic bomb. He spoke of his long, dark night of the soul and how he came to forgiveness and to peace. When he described being in a psychiatric hospital in the U.S., I was shocked. He recounted being treated like a dog and otherwise abused—just as I had been. Since then, I have met another person who experienced this same bizarre abuse. It is imperative that we do something to stop the continued abuse of children.

My life is a prayer for freedom and healing from this dark secret for all of humanity. All my life, I have sung freedom songs, songs that people with passion on the journey to freedom have written. They speak to the soul that cries out to be free. "Redemption Song" by Bob Marley is one of my favorites. When I hear his words, I know that I too have sung these songs of freedom with my very life. He speaks to my soul when he says, "Emancipate yourself from mental slavery, none but ourselves can free our minds." In this song, he asks each of us to make a stand for freedom, not to stand by helplessly and allow a wrong to continue. He tells us that the prophecies will be fulfilled in the phrase, "Some say that's just a part of it; we've got to fulfill the book." I truly believe that the fulfillment of these prophecies is the promise of freedom and the emergence of a golden age.

September 28, 1994: Intense processing at Dr. D.'s of my feelings of being degraded, beyond a loss of self-esteem. I'm aware that I remained intact, went beyond dissociation into a psychotic state, but my core survived. Therefore, I remembered. I claim my experience. Dr. D. agreed that I am dealing with the very core of my humanity. The illusion is shattered that they returned me to sanity; this destroys all sense of control they will ever have over me. I own the experience; therefore, I own my freedom. I felt a deep sense of shock. This must be the bottom rung, the lowest a human can be. Even as I crouched in the corner, crossing into an animal state, primitive, wild, vicious— somehow the core of my humanity survived. I claim my sanity with that knowledge; I was present to remember. Overwhelming grief and anger flooded my being, deeper than words can express.

With the acupuncturist, I channeled Laiolin. I have described many times in this journal how this being told me of her people and worked with me in healings. Perhaps it sounds as if I took that for granted, that it seemed normal. Far from it: It took a long time to get used to the idea that I was channeling a cosmic being of light. Of course, by this time, believing the unbelievable was no longer a novelty. I was probably as accustomed to incredible things as a human can be.

September 28, 1994 (continued): Laiolin is aware of my concern that she hasn't been coming through lately. She said it took a focused energy to support my process these past weeks, that the energy to verbalize with me would have distracted from the focus we both needed. She knew of the risk in recovering this memory and said the healing beings with whom she works decided the risks were reasonable and that I could safely accomplish it. She said it was a kind of test for the work I have chosen to do with them in partnership. She knows I resent this concept, but they had to be sure I am free. They cannot take the risk that someone in the dark forces could step in and control my mind. It would be far too dangerous. They, the Arcturians, must know that I can be fully trusted. She made it clear that they and my healers helped, but that I had attained my own freedom. I have chosen by my own free will to help heal Mother Earth. I am never to be confused about that. She found it humorous that the evil ones have lost their investment in me—not laughing at my agony, but at their folly. She said that during the next two decades, I will be called to do very important work, things beyond my comprehension at this time. I am to rest and heal, knowing that wounds are not chains. I am to prepare for higher-level training by her people. She congratulated me and told me that they are proud I had the strength to voyage beyond this innermost door, the seventh door, claiming my ultimate freedom. Again, she reminded me that I was choosing to work with them; she apologized for the risk in recovering this memory, but she knew I would be able to successfully complete the task.

CHAPTER TWENTY-TWO

The Allies Come to My Assistance

The summer of 1994 was filled with expansive experiences that opened me up to a higher sense of spiritual union with the divine Creator. When Laiolin had come in the spring of 1992, she had told me that I would undergo eight years of training and preparation for the work I was to do. The initial two years were for healing and integration. Now, two years later, she explained that I would be given two years in which to decide whether to continue the work. During this time, I began channeling for friends and family. Laiolin said that at the end of those two years (a total of four years from contact), I had to vow to speak the truth, to abstain from alcohol and recreational drugs (which did not appeal to me anyway), to avoid violent entertainment or any activity that might contribute to sexual abuse (like movies that disrespect sexuality) and to live the principles of peace. Later I was to learn that these principles are similar to the Buddhist Precepts. This commitment has deepened my spiritual path.

October 1994: Today I had a session with a physical therapist. I seem to be developing unique sensitivity; I can see healers, healing guides, when they work on me. During the physical therapy, I saw a white bear working through the therapist. It is a wonderful gift to be able to put people in touch with their healing guides.

I also had an appointment with another acupuncturist named Van. I immediately connected with his guide; he is so beautiful, a lightbeing, master of the highest temple. I knew this acupuncturist was special and unique. His guide told me I had come to him for an ancient healing of which he holds the knowledge and that the knowledge of the oracle will be revealed to me.

This has happened as it was predicted. I now do the work of an oracle.

October 1994 (continued): He has been waiting for me.
He said it is time for me to form associations with others
like me. He and Laiolin will also form a conscious
connection through this acupuncturist and me. Tonight I
feel at peace. I know that all these intense sensations are my
brain opening up, energy flowing through unused sections
of my brain, remembering.

During the first week of October, I was at the hot springs in Pagosa. Laiolin told me she was sending someone to me and that I should give him a message of great importance. I said, "Right; I'm supposed to talk to a total stranger and give him a message that you want him to hear?" And she said, "Yes. Will you cooperate?" I said, "Well, it'll be kind of strange to just tell a stranger that I have a message for him." She said, "All you have to do is tell him you have a message. If he doesn't want to hear it, he doesn't have to." I asked, "When is this stranger coming?" and she replied, "He's coming up the walk right now."

Just then, I heard footsteps behind me. As the man sat in the pool, I asked him whether he would want to hear something important about himself. He said he would. I told him I realized he was struggling with an important choice that would affect a lot of people. He had come here to make the decision. I told him that the hot springs is an ancient healing place and that the grandfathers would help him if he would open himself up to them. I felt he was someone important. I told him I knew that he intended to make the right choice and that both avenues looked correct. If he chose wrong, it would cause a lot of difficulty for a lot of people. If he chose right, a lot of people would benefit. He had no idea what the right choice was. That's why he needed the help of the spiritual guardians of that sacred spring. He looked surprised and told me that was indeed what was happening. Laiolin said that was all I was supposed to do. I said, "Then I will leave you alone to do just that." He thanked me, not for leaving, he said, but for helping. I wondered who he was, but I knew to let it be. I looked back over toward the pool, and he was gone.

That same day at another pool, I meditated and experienced a healing of my womb. Laiolin told me of someone who helped heal thyroids, that I was to go to her. I asked how to find her, and she said, "Go to the office." I found the healer's card in the office; it had a prayer staff on the back. I called and asked if she had an opening. I told her that I had been guided to her for my thyroid. She changed her schedule to see me, and what happened was amazing. In her office were pictures of elders and holy men and women; it felt like a safe place. I met her animal healer, a beaver. He said his medicine was powerful; it was the entrance to the lower world. He told me his people had helped me when I was a little girl. I remember being very close to the beavers when I was young. Then I met the healer's elder healer, an Iroquois woman of perhaps one hundred years of age. She and my shaman medicine woman, my internal shaman, Lantru, made contact. Because the practitioner and I had come together, these two would manifest their powers and unite in this dimension. The practitioner was to learn from my body cells as from a library. I had asked Laiolin if I had to teach her verbally—no, she was to learn with her hands as she worked on me. The awareness would come to her. She would need to know what my cells hold to do her work. Afterward, the practitioner told me about her contact with ETs and shamans and all that she had been through. She just steps aside and lets God's work be done, God being her focal point. I agreed; that is why she is so safe and such a good healer. All healing must be manifest through the divine.

On October 19, Laiolin talked to me about the emanation of joy. She said that I was to be aware of joy, that it is an enormous concept for a small word. She said our language is not adequate to describe the importance of joy and its healing powers. If I could tap into that experience, I would experience miraculous healing.

That same weekend, I visited the church at Ranchos de Taos. In this church is a picture of Christ. In the daylight, Christ appears to be standing there; in the dark, it becomes Christ on the Sea of Galilee. One can see the cross over his left shoulder and a fisherman's boat. The background radiates, and there's no scientific reason why this happens. When I was a child of ten, I could hardly see the miracle painting. Later, I could make it out with some effort. Now, as I stood before the painting, it was very clear. I saw a halo around the head of Jesus. The tour guide said that there was a new phenomenon, that some people were beginning to be able to see a halo. Two other people and I could see it. A woman standing next to me could see it; she told me that she did hands-on healing. She put her hands on my back, and I felt enormous light energy. My friends could feel the warmth afterward. That began a friendship with another healer who played a part in my healing journey. When I was ready, things came to me. I was living the Celestine Prophecy.

My guides took me on another journey and told me that my family of origin was confused because they believed the lie of the death fear, that anyone who leaves control or speaks the truth will die. I was experiencing a kind of death that I've learned is called the shaman's death. I had to die to so many things in the past, to experience a metamorphic death and an ultimate transformation. On my journey, I saw a portal. It was dark on this side and light on the other. My guides said it was my choice to go through or not. I had to understand that if I crossed through this next portal, it would be, once again, another place where my life would never be the same. I would experience a death of myself in the past and emerge into a new consciousness. Once I did this, I couldn't go back. I knew I was ready. I didn't need to wonder. I placed both hands on the rim of the portal, knowing that it was a sipapu. A sipapu, in Native American tradition, is a place of emergence. I crossed through. I felt I was being born. I put my leg and foot over the portal and found myself spinning headfirst down a long tunnel. Around me were colors: pink and red and shades of purple, warm and close as the passage continued and I spun. I lost all sense of time. It was almost frightening. Then I emerged into a warm, dark place, peaceful and serene. My guides said to be careful with what I eat and drink and do, for this is a place of waiting, the place between the worlds. I will be here for as long as necessary, until I am ready to step forth.

A few days later, I wrote in my journal: "I went to the Episcopal church; the sermon was about death and birth in the service of Christ, about being a vessel for his light, a beacon. The reading was Isaiah 49, verses 1–7. As I prayed, I thought, *No one lights a candle and puts it under a bowl.* Then I thought of this waiting place that I am in. Today I celebrate my shamanistic death." This transformation stretched over a period of years and included many mystical initiations that do not belong in this book, but I know my shamanistic death began that day.

I began sessions with a new healer to balance my energy. With my same massage therapist, I was working with clearing my chakras and balancing my energy field. I saw the healer of the new therapist and journeyed to the cave where her medicine gifts came from. I began to realize that all who have chosen this path have spiritual healers who work through them. I was being given the ability to see these healers, to work with them directly as the person who worked in the physical world worked with my healing. What a blessing! This new healer had studied shamanism, and we had long conversations about what she had learned. I began to realize that through my journeys, I was being taught powerful and specialized things directly from the spiritual teachers beyond the veil.

On October 22, I went to a channeled workshop by Karen Cook, the Pleiadian channel who channeled Benu. I was amazed again—Benu was talking about things Laiolin had already taught me and that I had learned from other sources over the years of my awakening. He spoke of the change in our lightbodies and microelectronic structure to evolve, of letting go of fear and how controllers rule by fear, of allowing ourselves to believe in abundance and protection. He said the faith within us is the mustard seed that moves mountains, the protection of the Christ light. He spoke of what the being of light had told me only two weeks before—even using the same word, "beacon"—included in a service at the church. He said the controllers torture to keep people in pain, that video games are used to create gladiators. He cautioned us never to give our power to any-one—not doctors, not aspiring masters. Other light healers would come to assist us, he said. He said that the old stuff fills the cells with fear, and it is for us to let go and live in the now.

At the gathering, I met another woman who felt, just as I did, that she was being led and taught. We were excited to meet each other. I asked Benu if he thought most people were naive as to the reality of the con-trollers, and he said yes, but we shouldn't bother knocking on doors. People have to wake up on their own. He confirmed that we are being assisted by cosmic beings of light who would help us bring about a shift and awaken people.

In another journey, I went to that temple master I had met with the acupuncturist.

> October 23, 1994: He reminded me that I was to come to him for added training, to read the oracles. He took me within the palace temple and stood me in the center of a light fountain, blue and crystal, then told me to be very still. The golden rings were lowered around me; it was so beautiful. Then he said to hold my breath for just an instant while the transfer was made. I felt a subtle energy move through me and then a shift and a transfer of information to my core. To get there, I had floated through blue water and air.

Then I wrote in my journal, "Where am I going?" Intuitively, I knew that someday I would write a book, that I was being empowered for a greater purpose. I made a journey through the new portal I had traveled through, and there I saw my soul-self. She was a radiant child of light—simple, old but young, and so clear.

I began making journeys to the lake with the temple, the place that Benu had introduced me to. There I would see masters, beings of light and many people I was meeting in this lifetime in the physical dimension. Then Laiolin introduced me to my soul-self. She thanked me for keeping her safe and said that I had made the journey to bring my own freedom. She and I could see each other. I could see her now, because I wasn't be-ing shrouded by all the darkness. I kissed her feet. We touched hands; she gave me a globe of light. As I left, a beautiful man came—Archangel Michael. I realized that my soul-self had been with me for all eternity. Now I know who I am, how I've come to travel these lifetimes and galax-ies, my soul intact. I am safe now to manifest her presence at the center of my galaxy. This is a confirmation of my freedom at last. Thank God, I'm free at last. I began communicating with my soul-self.

Undated entry: I asked my high soul-self, "Would you share your name or identity with us?" She said her name was Ma Waz Na Ka: "I am a dancer, young and graceful. I come forward to reunite today with the core of this being, for I am her soul. I am happy to be in this woman's body at this time. We have been through many dark journeys through many lifetimes. She might now receive me; she is safe and free from the control of the darkness."

Then I asked, "What is our purpose? What is our link?" She replied, "They attempted to shatter and to control this being. We have been together in many lifetimes; we might now embrace. She is present in her conscious state, and she can hear me. We are, who are, for we are the core of this being's entity—not visiting and not a guide of the medicine path and not angelic like Archangel Michael, but the core of this being.

"Ma Waz Na Ka is the core of this being's entity. Now that we can be perfectly present and manifested, her gifts might be given in protection and safety. She protected me in many lifetimes, in Auschwitz when the soldiers raided, on the prairie when the Indians came and took her away and in other places she had not been aware of before now. This is her chronicle, her history. I am young and beautiful, her love of life, motion, music; we have been together in every lifetime. I am her soul being. In many lifetimes, the dark one came and attempted to sever us."

I asked, "How shall we journey to manifest our gifts?" And her response: "She has worked very hard with her children to protect me so we could be together. This planet is so much at risk. I have not lungs; I cannot breathe or feel. Others have come as guardians and guides to this being; I am this being, from the Source, as we all come forth as from a spring. We chose many lifetimes to be on this planet but have been other places, too. Today is such a glorious day because we embrace a physical form and matter. This is a great evolution because this being has been persecuted through many lifetimes; she has had to protect me, that I would not be ripped asunder and shattered. Now that she has conscious understanding, we can manifest together. I will be her light shadow, which she may speak; I am the core of her essence, guiding eminence. In these days, when she must enter the dangerous places that she may help her people, I will work silently within her core and touch a child and reach out for the hand of an old man and stand in front of groups of people to emanate. The words she says will be only part of the gift she gives."

Ma Waz Na Ka then taught me about the soul, that it is a duality. There is the core soul or axis soul, and there is the soul being. The axis soul can be envisioned as a golden cord extending from the crown chakra to the soles of the feet. The soul being, or high soul-self, is an entity with whom it is possible to communicate. We can accelerate evolution by accessing these fields of higher consciousness. The soul has three aspects: the incarnate soul essence, carrying memory of all cycles of incarnation; the cosmic soul essence, carrying vibrational encoding to our origin in the cosmos; the axis soul essence, maintaining an electrostatic energy balance with the axis soul of Mother Earth, which in turn is balanced with the cosmic axis essence. An imbalance in the axis essence creates a sense of disharmony. Harmonic resonance with the Earth and cosmos axis soul is ascension.

The Dark Lord attempts to cut the soul asunder, to sever it from ascension, which can only be attained by unison of the soul being and the core soul. A separated soul wanders between the worlds. In some theologies, this is called purgatory. The core soul is unable to unite with the axis soul within the human. When this happens, demonic beings can occupy the core axis soul and control the human. Now, my soul being had not been shattered or cut asunder, but it could not unite. I protected her from the Dark Lord; now I am free. She can unite with the axis core and help me ascend karmically. The Dark Lord wants to empty the axis core of light and fill it with poison. That would destroy the connection of the soul being, leaving it to wander. This is one cause of wandering spirits. When a human is totally under the rule of the beast, this is hell. As each of us ascends within this dimension, our planet will shift and be preserved.

———————————

November 1, 1994: I continue my journey, for although I had gone through the portal and attained my soul's freedom, there was still work to do. I still needed a lot of healing. I think that's how Earth is right now. I believe Earth has gone through a portal and attained a new birth, but much work remains to heal the energies of the death fear. In a session, with the help of a massage therapist, I removed a demon from my rites of passage as a baby. When a baby was sacrificed and the soul was united with the demon, they had placed the dead baby on me and forced the demonic soul into me. I had a flashback to the pit of death at my rites of passage when I was fourteen and the demon who came from the underworld. I released him and bound him and praised God and Christ for this miraculous healing.

A few days later, a friend recorded as I channeled Ma Waz Na Ka: "Do you remember? Remember, in your journey, you were taken to the womb place. This is a place of shelter. I told you to be very careful of what you do, my granddaughter, and these past weeks you have experienced the gifts of the awakening to your next dimension. I have blended with Laiolin. She is the spokesperson. It is far too difficult for you to verbalize and vocalize all the dimensional entities who bring you information at this time. I would want you to know that this has been an introduction to what is to come. When you feel overwhelmed, you may enter the darkness and safety of the womb space between the dimensions, finding rest and calmness from the conflicting forces that exist within your newly awakened self."

Then Laiolin took over and began to channel: "This has been a taxing time for your body. You will find it easier if you take better care of your physical body, but this is a good time of awakening for you. You have experienced a rapid pace and more input. It would be helpful, when you feel overwhelmed, if you would just take a few minutes in the dark womb place. Once you were numb and did not feel the conflicting, bombarding energy of your world; now that you feel it, you will develop skills. That is why the womb space is important. The womb space knows neither evil nor good, not intellect nor thought nor feeling. Another word for that is the void. It is simply a place of rest—no decisions to make, no discernment needed. If you can use this place properly, you will adapt more rapidly to the transformation you are making.

"I am carefully monitoring your body. You might benefit from more exercise and walking. If you think this is a lot, imagine a baby coming from the womb. This is very much your experience at this time. You are adapting on levels you can't perceive, so be gentle with yourself as you are with others. You are moving toward peace, yes, but you tend to place yourself in hyperspace. You need more attention to breathe and relax in your body, in your busy life. You have been called to help with healing the hoop of the nation."

"Mending the hoop" is a term from *Black Elk Speaks: Being the Life Story of a Holy Man of the Oglala Sioux*, as told through John G. Neihardt. I read this book in high school. Black Elk, a Lakota prophet, speaks of the time when the sacred hoop of the people was broken, bringing our world into a state of imbalance. He says that in mending the sacred hoop, the great tree of peace will flower.

CHAPTER TWENTY-THREE

Delta Codes Begin to Surface

November 23, 1994, 3:00 A.M.: Tomorrow I cook for Thanksgiving. I am awake with symptoms of a memory I have had since Monday evening. I awoke Tuesday with a splitting headache, barely functional; I can't concentrate or focus. I feel like vomiting. A weight is on my chest. I have flashbacks . . . the hospital in Colorado Springs, the sound box at my high school, or wherever it was. I feel crazy. It's always important to note that I can't meditate. My mind keeps thinking of things I need to do: buy stamps, pay bills, kill myself—whoops! Where did that come from? Must be one of the little programs sent to shut off my brain. I realize that I really am different; I have many disabilities. I get so frustrated when my granddaughter wants me to play jump rope or when my husband wants to teach me how to operate a mechanical device. Noise from the TV drives me up the wall.

[Then the writing comes from an inner child]: "Noise drives me up the wall! When me in sound-trap box, noise comes and comes and comes, and has I have no place to go but up the wall. I am nine. I am not a kid anymore. I'm not a monkey. People care about monkey's experiment, but not me. Time for the sound box, time to go crazy. In a box, can't get away; how long, no time. Not funny."

November 29, 1994: I had frustrating dreams again. Sunday

> Im 9 I'M A
> KiD NOT A
> monKEY—
> People Care about
> monKeys experiment
> But Not me—
> Time for The
> sount Box
> sAndy— Time to
> Go Crazy

night I dreamt we lived by a volcano, my husband and I and our children. I looked out and saw fumaroles spewing ash and steam, and I knew the volcano would erupt. I couldn't convince them of the danger or get them into the truck to leave; they wanted to take their things. Our car was broken, and the truck was parked between the house and the volcano. I couldn't get my husband to move it. The lava started to come. It just missed the tires. Then he believed me. We threw stuff in the car. The only road left out of the valley was packed with hysterical people. I kept waking and sleeping and having this dream over and over.

This past week was rough; I had severe back pain, anger, sadness and crying. Thanksgiving was okay, but it was a difficult time for me. That night a dear friend came to visit. He's a Catholic brother from the Philippines. He talked about creative Catholicism versus redemptive Catholicism. The creative aspect is

close to the Earth and emphasizes blessings; redemptive Catholicism is concerned with sin. We spoke of Hildegard of Bingen, a creative mystic whose work was repressed. We talked about the awakening. I told him of my visions and being called, and he validated so much of what I've learned. He said if you have a vision, savor the taste of the rim afterward, like the rim of a glass. If it is bitter, it is of the evil one. If a vision is empowering, it is all right, but if it leaves you drained, watch out. I explained my check system, that if something isn't of the light of Christ, I send it away. He agreed with that. He said, "In coming times, there are those of us awakened ones who will nourish the ones of the breakdown and those who will lead the breakthrough." He believes that I will lead the breakthrough; he believes he will lead the breakdown. He said that Mother Earth is breathing and awakening. He referred to the awakening of female empowerment that is coming full circle. He spoke of the Harmonic Convergence as the beginning of the awakening.

That weekend, in a sweat lodge, I was cutting cords of darkness, pulling out hooks and asserting that the evil ones cannot have my family. I clapped my hands three times and commanded them to leave. I clapped again, and the lodge door blew open—from the inside. Some people go on vision quests and fast, depriving themselves of food and water to attain spiritual enlightenment. Such methods have always been difficult for me, because I have been forced into vaults and boxes and coffins, have been deprived of food and water unwillingly, have in fact been hypnotized to simulate a feeling of starvation. At the end of some of these sessions, they would give me something sweet. That's why I craved sugar.

I held my life together by doing things in normal reality. That's why I didn't like to meditate—I was afraid of that other world. In the sixties, people I knew in college were taking LSD, and I didn't dare. I probably knew intuitively that I would have a bad trip. Come to think of it, I wonder how many of the people who took LSD and had horrible experiences were actually breaking down that wall in that psyche before they were ready. They might have gone into the terror places, places that I had gone willingly, but after preparing. I can see how that could cause a nervous breakdown. I had always avoided altered states, even as benign as meditation, because I had one way of keeping my life intact—daily routine, normality. I could control it, or at least I thought I could. As I gained safety, I began realizing that there were safe ways to journey into meditation and there were some altered states that weren't dangerous. This revelation was actually given to me in a session with my guides.

January 11, 1995: I woke up with a thick head at midnight; this morning my energy is shut down again. Since the end of December, it's been impossible to connect. I have struggled to keep my energy open and move the pain. It has not affected my behavior as I haven't gone into rage and fear, but it has been difficult. There's a tightness in my throat; I haven't been chanting or meditating. I have an eye infection and lower back pain—and now this horrendous head energy. There is something going on, on a large scale. I am thankful I could work with the massage therapist and move some of the body memory. I really am stuck and depressed. It is so frustrating to find all these gifts and not be able to use them. Last summer, when I could go out and offer tobacco, I connected with universal energy; now there is a part of me that just wants to be inside and deal with my family. But shutting down the process of healing can lead to anger. I must reconnect with the light of life. [Offering tobacco is a Native American tradition. I believe it is a way to acknowledge and honor the world beyond the veil, to honor the born-again ancients. I have always prayed in this way.]

———————

January 17, 1995: I went into a deep meditation, went to my safe place, and recovered this number: 133, 979-876. Patrick emerged, and I went back to the experimentation center. Something like a biopsy; they were pinching my cervix with tweezers. Sound and electromagnetic frequencies and mild electroshock injected into my brain alternately with the pain in my womb. Instruction, words and number sequences. Difficult to access without causing a seizure. Sequence of lights flashing, lime green and yellow, a strip over my head. Code words, to activate.

Pain associated to trigger the numbers, words, sounds, frequencies and colors. I could feel it all; several times I almost had a convulsion remembering it. I worked with calming my brain waves. Patrick said that if I did automatic writing or drawing with my left hand, he could access the other codes and we can deprogram it.

January 19, 1995: Awakened at 3:00 A.M. to see if I could decipher some of the codes. One was W6RD5. (I am writing with my left hand, which isn't easy to read.) "Words.fright.might.set.used.in.sequence.rhyme.right makes might. Password or code, 1267. Code 1267, 8767, alpha code 767, delta code 543, 3, 3, 3, code 5. Activate program helexus 785 [spelled phonetically], delta B, carbonate. Carbonate access code AB code red." The codes will be different for different people. This code is instructed in memory cells for activation of programmed response to call commands.

January 20, 1995: I awoke yesterday in a fog. Could not even dial phone numbers right. At work I could hardly function, in tears. My pulses were erratic; everything was an effort. I had to come home early and be in a quiet place; anything was overwhelming. This morning my head still hurts, I still feel fragile. This has to be very important to zone me out like this. I worked with my massage therapist; my glandular system was wiped out. The work was very intense, but I feel much better. I went into another memory. I had a flashback of bands being placed around my elbows and knees.

There are strange marks in the next journal entry, followed by "delta V, 5133867, [more marks], a spiral, then delta 5133867, then more marks and spirals." I feel as if I am spinning. In a session, my guide spoke to me. He said the ancient witches cast sticks on the ground to interfere with the flow of universal energy and that these numbers are no more than thrown sticks. For the hoop of the nation to be healed, for Mother Earth to heal, these figures must be set in harmony and balanced with cosmic vibration. This number programming began with shock before I was born. Now I can take the sticks, build a fire and reestablish balance. I am to scatter the codes and reform them in a circle, the symbol of the pulse of life. They're only sticks to build a fire. After this, I felt much better. My mind sharpened and the fog lifted. These last two weeks have been frightening. I realize how blessed I am to journey safely. And it's fascinating to learn how sticks were used—first to play, then to count and then to conjure. A witch cast sticks for power, to attach her will to destiny.

February 24, 1995: My head hurts. I just broke the delta code; I must deprogram it. Delta 5133867. I have a lot of things here. I have 5133867, totals 33.85652599, with the word "hopeless" written above it. I see 13 + 11 + 7 + 18. I'm working with 5133867 and how it breaks down. I used numerology. I wrote, "E code, ACCHFG, delta code B, delta code B code, enter digits 5133867, access code 33, entrance 3 to the third power equals 9. Delta code, alpha 8936, close counter, cross band to alpha frequencies of plus nine, which has a symbol of less than 687. Delta 5133867." Then Patrick said, "I am Patrick. I am accessing the resolution to the delta code, to the number frequency that sets off a harmonic frequency of alpha and beta waves. The frequency code 5133867 interrupts normal brain functions. 993399, one tone, even balance." I worked with my own brain frequencies with that.

Then he said, "Frequencies are often outside the audible scale. I intend to establish a translator code that is related to an object of freedom. Then I come up with death code, access forbidden." It seems that Patrick set up the code of 993399 as an equal balancing harmony code, to break the code of 5133867.

He went on, "To break the code, use the Holy Trinity—the Father, Son and the Holy Spirit—fourteen times. There are fourteen threes in 993399."

I worked with Patrick's suggestions to deprogram the delta code and change its frequencies. I learned a lot more about this later, and the facts I discovered validated what Patrick had said: the delta code is set off by frequencies. When I changed the frequencies in my brain, I changed my susceptibility to being a Delta, and I deprogrammed my Delta programming.

CHAPTER TWENTY-FOUR

Deciding to Testify

February 1, 1995: There is an article in the *New Mexican* about this committee that has met three places in the United States. The federal government is interviewing people who were damaged by radiation experimentation. I called the reporter and told him a little of my experience. I felt strong, stronger than ever, but I felt it in my head. It is 2:00 A.M. I'm awake, my head is roaring up to a headache. My body hurts—kidneys, mainly. I am angry and want to be heard. My stomach is burning. I ache all over. I didn't talk to my family about it. It was my daughter's birthday; we've been celebrating since Saturday.

I feel sad and robbed, depressed. Who would ever believe me? In the newspaper, they said they sterilized men in prison by dipping their testicles in high-level radiation. The horror is unbelievable. Feeding plutonium to children. I wonder if there were experiments like that at Colorado Springs. I never knew what normal was.

The reporter I spoke to had given me telephone numbers for both E. Cooper Brown of the Task Force on Radiation and Human Rights, national committee staff, and his secretary, Joan McCarthy. The Task Force was a hub organization that was established to support and facilitate individuals and groups planning to testify. Some of the groups included were the Utah Downwinders and the Atomic Vets. I placed a call and spoke with Joan.

February 1995: I spoke to Joan at the Task Force. I might testify. I want to. I want my truth to be heard. I want this door to open. Laiolin came and told me we would speak, that I should prepare myself. Her people are waiting to help along the way. God, I hope this is what I am preparing for.

I've been so angry these past weeks. I'm coming to terms with how damaged I've been all my life and how I just accepted myself without question. Freedom is the ability to question and probe. We might have a part of us capable, but for me, a whole part of me never questioned, never doubted. Freedom is in the struggle.

With great difficulty, I wrote a nine-page document about my experience and faxed it to the Task Force. They asked me to testify in Nashville in March—a little less than a month in the future. Even though I very much wanted my story to be heard, what if there were repercussions?

February 9, 1995: I'm awake at 4:45 A.M. My head is zooming. It looks like I am going to testify for the presidential committee on human experimentation. I feel so deeply that the truth must be spoken. I don't know what impact this will have on my life, but right now it is the most important thing to me. I wonder how my people inside feel. Frightened, I'm sure. If anyone needs to speak now, it is a good time. I know you have feelings.

My inner child writes: "Fear, pain, pointy needles hurt me. I'm little, I want my mommy, I want to go home. The needles hurt. The pain is too bad. I want a soft bed. I want to go home. I want my daddy. I want not to go to them, to talk, they will hurt me, I don't like people who will hurt little girls. Questions, then shots. Questions, then shots. Never, never, never answer questions. They hurt me too bad. No questions, please."

I tell my inner child, "We are big now, honey; we can be safe. We need to talk so that other children won't be hurt."

February 10, 1995: Now it's 1:00 A.M. I'm moving pain in psychic attack. I've changed the energy in my brain. I am beginning to build a network of more people for support and information—including a therapist in Albuquerque.

When I was under psychic attack, I would often experience severe pain. I found that I could stop the pain by placing shields of light around me, filling myself with Christ light and clearing and smudging my house with sage. And by this point of recovery, I had begun learning exercises to move energy, balance the left and right brain hemispheres and generally calm the agony of recovering and deprogramming memories. I did not meet the therapist I mention as a client, but rather because she is a survivor. I was afraid to meet her, terrified in fact. I did not want to face another person who had experienced what I had. I did not feel at all safe. But to my surprise, the meeting went well, and this gifted person has become a dear friend. She later accompanied me to Washington, D.C., to testify. I realize now that many of the people I met for support have become friends. One thing we all share is integrity and creativity. It seems that many creative people have suffered extreme trauma. I wonder at what point a troubled soul chooses to create rather than to destroy?

February 15, 1995: I spoke for the second time to Dr. Corey Hammond at the University of Utah in Salt Lake City. He gave me the names of doctors involved in leading the mind-control and radiation experiments—Green and Gotslief (not sure of spelling; that's how it sounded). I hadn't recovered memories of these people, and I still haven't. Hammond is excited about the opportunity to testify. Wally Cummings, the attorney for the Task Force, called. He called me a brave woman. He said my narrative is powerful; he called it a bomb. They might want me to go to Washington, D.C., where I will be heard by more people. I can't keep my identity secret; to do this, I have to step forward. It is just as well.

The call from the attorney gave me a headache. There's no way he could have known of the alters who had been attached to bombs, but when he used that word, it brought up a program about a bomb threat. His words were, "I know what you have here is a bomb; we just have to place it where it will do the most good." Joan McCarthy at the Task Force is so supportive. We talked about funding. I will have to pay for the whole thing myself—transportation to Washington, D.C., hotel accommodations, everything. But I know it is important. Mr. Cummings said that prisoners were given spinal injections like mine, with radiation. I learned yesterday that another survivor has remembered rites at Colorado College and another is recalling experiments in Roswell. God, I hope I can do something to stop this.

———————

February 21, 1995: I'm going to testify in Washington on March 15 with survivors from around the country. Valerie Wolf, a therapist from New Orleans, will be there with two clients. They have names and records of CIA documents. Corey Hammond, Alan Scheflin, John Boyd and other clients and therapists are going to send their documentation with Valerie Wolf.

———————

February 26, 1995: It was a rough night. I was awake a lot, meditating. I had a severe headache and awoke achy and exhausted. I took an herb bath and went to my safe place. My guide told me to stand very still, with the same energy as if I were on the edge of a cliff. Birds came from everywhere. At first I thought they were going to carry me off; they surrounded me, flapping their wings everywhere, with their beaks preening me, like they were grooming and cleaning me. It didn't hurt, but it took a lot of focus to stand still, and then they were gone. The sky filled with clouds and lightning flashed. Before me was a giant angry god, fierce like Hindu temple gods. He held lightning in his hand. He gave me his anger. It wasn't like fear anger; it was the anger of a warrior, righteous anger, as when Christ Jesus drove the vendors from the temple.

February 27, 1995: At times I cannot believe I'm going to testify. I am afraid, yes. Am I awed? You bet. Am I determined? Yes. Until I heard of the Task Force and these hearings, I didn't know the government officially did things like this to people; it's so amazing that somebody wants to listen. I know it is the right thing to testify, but yet it is so massive. What I report is so bizarre, I have trouble believing it myself. How have I lived anything close to a normal life? I try not to obsess, but it is on my mind constantly.

March 1, 1995: I've known for weeks that a memory was coming up. I went back to Colorado Springs; I'm eight or nine years old. I have been placed face-down on a strange chairlike device, sprawled like when you sit facing the back of a chair, but this was contoured to fit the body of a child. My arms and legs are strapped into grooves so I can't move; my chin is on a chin rest. Something like a ball forces my spine into a curve. Conductors like for EEG [electroencephalograph] are put on my head; a band is around my forearm that could measure blood pressure and also emit painful electrical currents. Caps are on my fingertips. They put something like a needle into my lower back—I believe it was a spinal tap—then a needle in my mid-spine and one right where the skull meets the neck. I felt drugged but conscious. I heard them say they didn't want to puncture my brain stem. The needles had two depths, one to enter an artery or vein, and the other to just barely enter the area before the brain stem. An IV tube led to an odd-looking machine.

The tube went to five different orifices. A meter counted the numbers with control knobs so they could choose which fluid they put into me. The machine released a certain amount of fluid at timed intervals into my brain. I heard them talk about the circulation in the brain. Part of the fluid went into the circulation part, and the rest

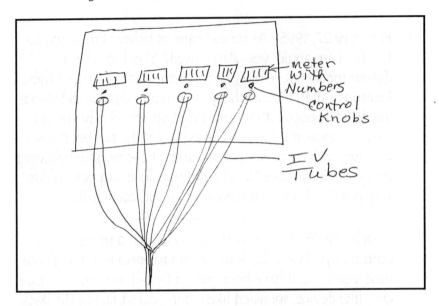

somewhere else. It was all carefully monitored. They said
they had taken spinal fluid, or they would say, "It is time to
check the spinal fluid." Then they would do something to
the needle in my back. I could see their white lab coats and
things in their hands. One technician said, "This is a trace
dose, but enough to light this kid's head up like a Christmas
tree." They thought it was funny that my head would glow;
they were joking about it. I remember words like "radon
dye" or "radium dye." A device that fit over the skull was
put on like a cap to monitor the injections. At times they
would induce pain from the arm cuffs and take more
readings. The number 5133867 was a sequence used in
releasing the injections. I also felt things were timed: a
needle in my tailbone, in the mid-spine, at the base of the
head. I guess they thought I couldn't hear because of the
drugs. Someone called a name: McCracken. Someone else
said, "Last names violate policy; there will be a reprimand."

March 1, 1995, later in the day: Another session with my
massage therapist. I channeled a being who called herself
the Guardian of the Kingdom of Minerals. She said that all

the minerals were in chaos in our world, that minerals are being used to poison us, in food and fertilizers and sprays on plants. She said the Goddess of Minerals has manifested within healers, shamans and women who use rattlesnake venom to heal. The gift of that goddess is this healing, the use of serpent energy to transmute poison. She called forth the rattlesnake who bites his tail to heal the hoop of the nation; then she told me the poison would be released from me. The poison will return to the perpetrators; the snake will bite them so they can heal. Her voice is raspy and growling; she looks like a Medusa. She called out the names of some of my male perpetrators and called for atonement for the violation, for the use of male sexuality to degrade the female spirit. She deemed today a day of liberation for all women as well as the women within men.

Not long after this, I would be amazed to visit the Smithsonian Institution and see the sign "Temple of Minerals" in the Asian gallery. Just outside it stood two guardians, one male, one female. The female one was the being who had come to me in my vision. I was so moved that I trembled; I felt as if I should bow down to her. I walked up to the gift shop. The woman working there was Asian. "I hope I can talk to you about this," I said. "I just had a vision of the Guardian of the Kingdom of Minerals, and she told me that the medicine people who carried snake medicine transmuted poison. The Guardian told me that they could use the venom of snakes to heal people." The woman made a small bow and said that it was that way in China. She said that I was on a special path and encouraged me to keep following it.

March 6, 1995: Valerie Wolf just called from New Orleans. She and Corey Hammond have been networking with therapists across the country. She says this thing is really mushrooming. She will have twenty to forty backup testimonies. Some of the biggest names in the country are sending documents. They feel this is their chance. It won't be swept under the rug this time. They want a Congressional investigation. They are getting the media involved. I remember what Laiolin said, that I would be speaking in front of people. I am so thankful that God has called me to be of service in this way.

Within the next year or so, a prime-time television program was aired that cast Corey Hammond in a very bad light. It was a major piece of propaganda, accusing him of molesting his patients and other terrible things. I tried to call him, but because of all the publicity, he had quit taking phone calls. He has been forced to adopt a low profile because of all this, and I have even heard of threats upon his life. This has happened to many people who have stepped forward. I was honored to testify with brave people like Valerie Wolf and her clients.

March 8, 1995: I am dizzy this morning. All of this is getting to me. I feel like I'm going at warp speed. I need to talk to my inner children. Who's upset? My inner child writes, "I am pain. I am real pain. I died. I am hell, agony, pain. I am your feelings. I will not heal, I will die a death of agony. They will come for us. They will take us back. You are serving us to them on a platter, as a perfect sacrifice." But I told my inner self, "This is 1995, and we will not go back."

March 10, 1995: These days are so incredible. I do need to catch up on my journal. I am awed at what I have been brought to participate in by testifying. When I first called and sent my narrative account, I thought I was the only one. Now there are forty therapists and clients attending or sending testimony. Valerie keeps telling me this is bigger than I can conceive. In my work Wednesday, my guide called the warrior chiefs—Sitting Bull, Crazy Horse, Chief Joseph, Chief Ouray, Geronimo, Cochise—all my favorite Native American heroes. He told me they would stand guard for the children and for me, to guard my inner children and all children. Then the little girl, Leionie, from the concentration camps in Germany, came, and I channeled her. She said that she is a descendant of David and manifested herself as a child. Her entity is vast on the level of high spirituality she will reveal to me. She reminded me that her gift is that of family love, regardless of the horror. She showed me piles of dead infants and told me that I had died in my past life in child breeding in the concentration camps. She said that her baby was taken from her in the experiments. I see Leionie standing on a mountain with a staff and a crown, and light is radiating from her head.

CHAPTER TWENTY-FIVE

A Chance to Speak the Truth

March 14, 1995: I am on the plane to D.C.—finally. These last few days have just stretched out. It has been hard to manage my life, my family and this, too. On the way this morning, I channeled my cosmic being of light. She told us that she and her people are helping us. She said that we might have a hard time accepting the part of revealing the experiments on an important, larger level. She confirmed that ETs are using hundreds of humans for experiments in this country, exploiting the poor. They have made a deal with their human counterparts to share data. But we humans are so backward. The collaborators cannot even comprehend the data—not only that, but the experimenters are withholding information. She spoke to my husband and said, "Don't doubt; just protect." I must be protected from the negative ETs who will certainly be there. One of the reasons for bringing this to the light is to help our own species protect the planet from the experiments of these negative ETs. She warned my husband to scan my food; there will be an attempt to make me sick or poison me through food. I must be very careful.

I was so afraid that I had to stop and throw up on the way to the airport.

March 14, 1995 (continued): I had to wait to use the bathroom on the airplane, and as I was standing there, I looked down on the seat beside me and saw a book about the Holy Spirit. I asked the attendant, a beautiful young girl, if I could look at it. As I opened it, the first page spoke of the awakening of the Holy Spirit. I told her that this is what has happened to me. Then the most wonderful thing happened. We talked for half an hour about the awakening, about angels and how to trust visions and angels and protection, about clearing spaces, about faith and fear programming, and about healing with Christ's light. We prayed together and wept. I was filled with wonderment at this special miracle.

I'll never forget the morning of my speech in Washington, D.C. I woke up frightened—terrified, in fact—but very determined. We took the subway over to the place near the Capitol where I was to testify. We were early, so we had breakfast and walked awhile. Even so, when I went in to register, an hour and a half remained before I was scheduled to testify.

As we left the building, I saw a man I thought I recognized from my memories in Colorado Springs. I almost had a panic attack right there. I prayed and asked for a place I could wait in safety. Just half a block away, we found a Methodist Episcopal church.

I felt so drawn there. A young man inside opened the door for us. As I waited for the door to open, I could hear him sing. What a beautiful voice! I asked him to sing for me. He sat at the piano and played and sang "Amazing Grace," a different version than I had heard before. As he sang, I felt the church fill with angels and I was lifted in the Holy Spirit.

At noon a small group came in for a service, mostly black women and elders. The minister was an African-American woman. I felt the presence of the Holy Spirit so powerfully in that church as we all sang hymns together. Later I learned that this church, built by slaves, was the site of President Clinton's inauguration.

The minister began the teaching of the gospel for that day. It was the story of the seven lepers whom Christ healed. She said it was the story of the one who came back. She talked about that; she told how seven of them had received healing, but only one of them came back to do the work, to serve. She asked, "Are you the one? Have you been chosen in some way to make a difference, to do something important, not just to receive healing, but to come back, to serve? Have you come back to make a difference with your life?"

I was so touched by this that I began to cry. I knew that I *was* the one. I had received the healing, and now I had come back in service of Christ to do the will of God and to do this testimony. I was trembling as I stood and said, "Excuse me. I am the one. Today, I am the one. For the sake of the children in this country, I've gotten the courage to come to expose the dark secret of my experiences as a child being subjected to human experimentation, and I have come back. I was healed, but I didn't just go on; I came back to do something about it." And then I told them, "I am frightened. I'm frightened of what might happen to my family and me, but the Holy Spirit sent me to this church to wait before my testimony."

And do you know what those people did? They brought me up to the altar and the congregation laid their hands on me and prayed. It was so amazing! I was so filled with the Holy Spirit.

I feel that the angels sent me to that church that day to give me strength and courage, to fill me with the light of Christ so that when I went to testify, I wasn't shaking. Oh, I was shaking a little bit inside, but I was strong. I stood up and I spoke my truth, and I didn't break down. I had been so frightened earlier that morning; if I hadn't gone to that church, I might not have been able to speak. The people in the church helped give me the strength to do what I needed to do.

March 16, 1995: So much has happened in two days. I am astounded. I sat in awe as two women from New Orleans reported the same type of things I know about. I cannot remember all the details of everything they said—people's names, project codes and other things. I want to get copies of their testimonies.

I am angry. I am so angry. No one there gave us the least bit of respect or support. The members of the Task Force didn't even introduce themselves. When Valerie came in, their attitude seemed to be, "Oh, here's the therapist; we'll talk to her." Someone could have at least said, "Hello, I'm Christine or Wally or Joan or E. Cooper." But my disappointment was overcome with inspiration. I was so inspired by the other survivors and their courage and their speaking. And yet I was angry at being treated like an untouchable.

I heard a doctor speak of low-level radiation and the immune system and how the small birth weight of babies correlated with low-level radioactive fallout. I listened as the Utah Downwinders spoke. I listened as a woman told us how her father's life had been destroyed by the experiments. Except for Valerie Wolf, all the people who spoke had conscious memories of radiation experimentation.

Finally, my turn came. I asked my husband to come to the speaker's table with me. As I began speaking, I felt myself being filled with strength. A powerful energy filled the room. The proceedings were videotaped, and when I view the video, I can see that people were moved by my speech.

I was told of an attorney named Kenneth R. Feinberg on the committee who was there to protect the government from settlements; he had done the same thing with the Agent Orange settlements. During my speech, he got up and walked to the back of the room, shaking his head. In a recent *Newsweek* article about the tragedies of September 11, I read that he had been assigned as a special taskmaster for the settlement of the families of the victims of the disaster. I talked to one of the people mentioned in the survivors' group. I asked if the victims' families felt Feinberg was an advocate for fair and just settlements. She said no. We talked about our feelings toward this man, and "heartless" was the best word we could come up with.

I include my speech here. As you read it, imagine how I felt that day.

Speech to the Advisory Committee on Human Radiation Experimentation
March 15, 1995

Honorable committee members, thank you for listening. I am a survivor of secret experimentation conducted by our government on healthy children. I have been working for weeks to overcome the terror programming so that I could testify with dignity today.

I know I survived my childhood for this moment. These horrid secrets undermine the core of our society. They exist only out of the power of evil. As long as atrocities to humans, particularly children, go unbelieved, they can continue. I have come to realize from my awakening that the reality is a dimension beyond human beings' ability to conceive the truth. When the truth comes to light and is believed, there is an incredible healing for ourselves and our nation. That is my hope.

I was born in 1949. We were very poor. Both of my parents and most of my aunts and uncles died of cancer. As a child, my parents were victims of mind control that permitted me to be inducted into human experimentation. I have an early recollection of people coming to my house when my father was not home. My mother was held and I was tortured until she signed a paper. Either she signed or I died. Afterward, my mother held me and said, crying, "Someday, honey, you'll be free." I believe this was related to my being taken into the experiments. I believe that our family physician, who was retired from the military, got children from the mountains of Colorado for the experiments. He was the only doctor I ever saw until I was twenty years old.

The incidents I have recalled happened to me between the ages of three and twelve years old. I was taken to a college campus in the summer. We were kept in a locked dorm and taken to the experiments by the way of underground tunnels. Once a door was left open during some confusion and I got out. That is how I know what the campus looks like. I wandered across the campus and into another dorm. I recall the campus and the structure of the buildings. I entered one of the dorms. When I went in, I heard yelling. I went down the hall and looked in a door. I saw a head lab tech, a high-ranking military officer and the Nazi doctor yelling. Someone caught me, and I was taken for electric shock. Prior to my recall of the experiments, I never thought I had been to that college. When I returned two years ago, I found it to be exactly as I had recalled it.

I recall being in a classroom with other children; we were all in institution pajamas. We were told that we were chosen to help serve our country. A careful record of the procedures was to be kept. The technicians were highly trained professionals who were just doing their job. We were not to be angry at them. An American flag hung in the room.

The experiments are discussed in more detail in my narrative. One of the doctors who supervised the experiments was called the Nazi when he was out of the room. The experiments involved environmental deprivation and the effects of extreme sensation on the brain, spin programming, breeding children and injections. I was given frequent electroshock and mind-control sessions with the threat of death or insanity if I ever spoke. Obviously, they misjudged my spirit and desire to be free.

The experiment I wish to speak about involved radiation. I was strapped face-down, straddled to a device like a chair that curved my spine in a haunch. Needles were put in three places: my coccyx, mid-spine and the base of my skull. To the right there was a device with five orifices. Five IV tubes came out and joined into one with controls for the amount of fluid and frequency. This tube was connected to the needle at the base of my skull. I was given a timed injection at my coccyx. The technician had a monitor; I believe it was a Geiger counter that they checked my head with. There would be time-released injections through the IV into the base of my skull repeatedly, which they monitored.

When the injections went into my brain, it felt like ice spreading through my skull. It was agonizing. I had cuffs on my upper arms and things on my fingers, I believe for vital signs. Wires were connected to my head, similar to EEG wires. Often they would say, "Get some fluid." Then they did something to the needle in my mid-spine. I believe they were testing my spinal fluid. Sometimes something happened to the cuffs on my arms that caused horrible pain. Readings were taken again. The procedure was being taught to someone, I believe. They talked as if I was unconscious and not human. I recall it was explained that the injections were referred to as "trace, but enough to make this kid's head light up like a Christmas tree." They thought this was funny and kept making jokes about my head glowing. They sat me up, put a tube up my nose. I could feel something horrible in the front of my brain. I blacked out.

In another experiment, they thought I had died. The head technician said, "Well, it looks like we lost this one; there are plenty more where this one came from. If she is dead, arrange an accident; if she is brain-dead, we'll institutionalize her and use her for other experiments."

Another experiment involved inserting air into my uterus and expanding my abdominal cavity with the air. This experiment was torturous. Measurements were taken periodically. X-rays of my uterus and fallopian tubes were taken by injecting radioactive dye. I know this test. I had to have this done during fertility testing when my husband and I were trying to conceive a child. Fertility testing was so traumatic that I had to stop trying. I have never had a normal pregnancy.

Today, as others spoke, I have gained valuable information regarding project codes. I have struggled in my work to understand why I keep recalling a delta 5133867. I realize from the information presented here that this is possibly a project code.

I am willing to discuss my experience in more detail if any of you wish to. I have suffered all of my life because of this. My life has completely changed because of my recovery. Five years ago I began my quest for the truth. I didn't perceive how much I was suffering until finally the symptoms diminished. I have recovered these incidents with the help of a caring professional. He has been careful to maintain a neutral position and does not lead or influence me. Once, early in my healing, I spoke to a man who helps people deprogram from mind-control cults. He told me that freedom is in the struggle. The good Lord knows I have struggled to be free. I am thankful that I started working on healing my body in my thirties. The past five years I have healed my mind and spirit. Now I am strong enough to speak the truth. The truth will set us free.

I wish to thank the people at the Task Force for helping me trust enough to testify. I would never have trusted a government project without their support. I also wish to thank President Clinton for appointing this commission, and each of you especially for having the courage and integrity to listen to us, the survivors of America's most horrid secret. I am deeply committed to exposing this horrid secret. Of course, I am terrified of repercussions, but I will not purchase peace at the price of my silence. Patrick Henry once said, "Is life so dear, or peace so sweet, as to be purchased at the price of chains and slavery? Forbid it, Almighty God! I know not what course others may take; but as for me, give me liberty or give me death."

I do not choose death. I choose the freedom to speak the truth.

After my speech, my husband called me to the back of the room. Standing there was a woman with a face so scarred she was practically faceless. She had only one eye. She thanked me for what I had said and told me that they had treated her like a nonhuman also. As she spoke, one tear left her eye—one tear, but within that one tear was the agony of humanity. I wrote the poem "Song of Truth" for her.

March 16, 1995 (continued): Oh, my God; what had they done to us? How many people are victims? I want to stand on top of the highest building and scream the truth, but would anybody listen? I must write my book. I will call it "One Tear: The Truth of My Life." I'm astounded at my own reality and both awed and frightened by my destiny.

That night we walked around Washington. I met a street musician, an excellent violinist. He played and talked about his CD, titled *Hungry for Music*, that he had produced to help the homeless people of the city.

Song of Truth

Speaking on the wings of an eagle,
   sending forth my voice as a prayer on the wind,
      praying for spirit to open the door to the
         ears
            heart
            being
of those who sit before me as I speak my truth.
I feel the spirit move me from deep within my soul.
   Speak of darkness with healing light.
Speak of pain with hope of healing.
   Speak of truth with songs of freedom.
Shattering the walls of secrecy with lightning bolts of words
   spoken from my heart.
      Is this indeed why I survived as a child?
         Or was it for the moment when
   you came forth, my sister, and touched my hand
with tears brimming from your wounded soul?
When you came forth and said,
"They hurt me, too, and
   I was so afraid to speak until now.
      You give me hope"?
Oh, my sister, I dedicate my words to you.
   With all my heart,
      with all my soul,
   I will sing the song of truth and freedom.

There I sat, listening to this incredible music, talking to a homeless man named Bill and just having the time of my life. I felt angels were guiding me. I met a woman from Indiana named Wendy. I told her who I was and that I was there to testify. She confided that she was recovering from memories also. She was a beautiful, vibrant woman. We were dancing to street music and laughing together. I was having so much fun that I forgot to be afraid.

It was the next day at the Smithsonian Institution that I saw the statue of the Guardian of the Mineral Kingdom in the Asian gallery, as well as many other pieces of art. My friend, the therapist from Albuquerque, had come with me for support. A talented and knowledgeable artist, she took us on a tour of galleries in D.C. I had never studied art and never heard it explained as she did that day. It all came alive for me. The beauty I experienced that day helped heal the trauma of testifying. Maybe it did more than that—maybe I opened up an old wound, cleaned it out and filled it with beauty.

In the long run, my testifying in D.C. was for my healing. I gained strength and power. I lived to tell the truth. I had the courage to speak. And the best part? I disproved all the lies they told me as a child. They promised me that if I ever spoke, I would be killed—or worse. I returned home safely and came one step closer to casting off the shackles of fear placed on me as I was being tortured as a child.

CHAPTER TWENTY-SIX

Forbidden Territory

April 18, 1995: I'm awakened at 4:00 A.M. and Patrick speaks. There is an image of a file drawer, white labels on the files, typed Delta Project. SKK rocket code is classified information. Delta fox, beta excalibur, beta X 53, code ABX 53, Project Sky Fox, files accessed. Has to do with military personnel. Code fire alert, X 37, zygot, repmancy. Zygot, Marcy, New Hampton research project, gold X 53 74 26831. Management of military personnel, debriefing. There is a long tunnel, military base, underground. Uniformed soldiers. What, I ask myself in the memory, is a kid doing here? Age 17, on assignment as an assistant. To terminator X, debriefing military personnel, big room, lots of young men. I access the file unobserved; the project, top secret, delta X, 537892. Many soldiers in chairs with electrodes on their heads and fingers to access the optic nerve, to alter visual memory frequencies and create optic impressions of inaccurate, nonfactual data. A machine with a long extension focused on the pupil very close, altering optic impressions. A combination of light frequencies and rapid motion instilled images; many chairs lined up.

I have a clipboard, and I'm picking up file sheets from each one of the readings kept from the experiments. I'm charting test results while filing code projects. Accidentally I come across Sky Fox AC53078 and open up the file.

I was taking the files from the room with what turned out to be Air Force cadets, because I was inside the Air Force Academy in a secret area. At this time, I had not yet learned about Cheyenne Mountain and the facilities inside the mountain. I was taking the file papers from the clipboards in this big room where all these cadets were sitting, and I was supposed to deliver them. But I had a habit of going to places where I didn't belong. I had gone down a hall and opened up this file, and that's when I came across Sky Fox AC53078, plans to assassinate rebelling leaders of Third World nations, programming of chosen leaders of key Latin American countries like Argentina and Bolivia and also information on South Africa, Spain and Bosnia. Castro was on the list. It was a ten-year projection.

The next day at Dr. D.'s office, Patrick spoke. He insisted that the information he preserves in the archives not be lost. He keeps a database and visual recall of volumes of information that he wants documented now that I am strong enough and not at risk. I went home and prayed for somebody to help me with military mind-control programming.

At the water fountain outside Dr. D.'s office before my next session, I greeted a man who passed by in the hallway. We introduced ourselves and shook hands. As we chatted, I knew he was the one I had prayed for. I made an appointment with this therapist, Jim. He was an ex-Navy Seal, and he worked to help deprogram people from the CIA. He and I began some work. During the sessions, some of which are detailed in the following journal entries, I would allow Patrick to speak. I can't say that he provided me with information I did not know, but he did help me realize that all these programs can be undone. Eventually, I had to stop working with him, because when Patrick would come out and talk, it would make him sleepy.

April 24, 1995: Terrorists blew up a federal building in Oklahoma. Hundreds of people were killed. One of the bombers is a young man, an ex-GI, Desert Storm. There was a bit in the paper about a computer chip in his buttock, put there by the military. He says they link him to Waco. I just wonder what the truth is. I watched the movie Bluebird about the atomic testing military and the AEC's [Atomic

Energy Commission] disregard for human life, where the
hero tries to tell the truth and is put into a mental hospital.

May 1, 1995: This morning I woke up with the spinning
feeling and then convulsions and body memories. Intense
flashbacks of the Air Force Academy. This memory came
last weekend also. It was a small room with a small bed.
One soldier after another came in and performed sex with
me; sometimes I do blowjobs and sometimes any kind of
sex they say, even anal, just about twenty minutes each—all
strangers, one rape right after another. Then I'm in an
observation booth, nude. There is a mirror/window. I am
maybe seventeen. A nude cadet is put in with me. We are
kept there until we have sex. There is a banging noise, a
crazy-making noise; I can't get away, no place to go, just
pain, humiliation and suffering. I cried for an hour. I was so
embarrassed, so humiliated, feeling like a whore. I was in
high school. I never let boys touch me. I was very shy.

May 8, 1995: Head roaring, 2:00 A.M. I feel trapped inside
with fire, like no one will listen or care about my life and
pain. Deep anger. There is a fire inside, burning my very
soul.

Yesterday I worked to process the feelings of grief from the
memories of all those men in a room of sorrow. And that
young man and me, naked, tortured with the noise. Lately
I feel degraded and overwhelmed by the house, cleaning it
over and over, just like that little room. I'm not a
prostitute, not a maid, not born to repeat the same actions
over and over. Last weekend I grieved for my lost
innocence. I thought when I married that I was a virgin.

Memories of the cult are predictable in an odd way—robes
and blood and orgies and death and rape. This was different;
this was not in the setting of rites. In this scene, I am a
technician with an important job. My assignment: to satisfy

Fire

Fire within,
consuming my pain.
No place to hide,
no place to be free.
Pain deep within . . .
within my soul, agony.
Flaming, broiling,
consuming the beauty,
consuming goodness,
spinning agony meshed
In a web of death.

each man in a certain amount of time. Then the buzzer rings, and he must climax: oral, anal, vaginal, with hands, however they wish, rough, shy, crude, mean, gentle, all the ways, each one different. Twenty minutes of hell, then the next one. A job never done, never completed. Then afterward I'm wasted in pain, drained and empty and hollow and ill. I am home from school, very sick. My mother thinks it is because I slept by an open window.

May 9, 1995: I awoke and connected to my guardians and guides. I realized that the May 1 memory of the spinning was the birth from the womb space. I go there and feel the birth again, less intense. My guides tell me it's my choice, not to rush. I'm ready. I emerge from the womb space to an inner Wakan sacred realm close to God. I am the Holy Trinity. I have a journey where I receive special spiritual gifts, and Laiolin comes and tells me that I'm ready to go forth and accept the responsibility to help Mother Earth heal. My life will change rapidly now, transformative metamorphosis. I am ready to honor the gifts. I accept the challenge.

After that, I began working with my inside people on the memories at Colorado Springs. I wrote, "The dynamic fulfills command, alliance, military lifer, themselves as nonentities. They steal innocence, the innocent self and the wounded woman. This was an act of humiliation, to rob, to defeminize, to degrade, to demoralize. I contact inner parts of myself that were programmed to serve at the Air Force Academy. I contact and heal my stolen innocence."

May 10, 1995: Patrick speaks, saying that the first purpose of this gang rape was to control the sexuality of the male servicemen. Intruding on sexuality to control, time observed. There are no secrets from Big Brother, no privacy, no part of our humanity not accessed. I was a training device, an object. Men copulate in twenty minutes or face consequences. The second reason it was done was to keep me in place and programmed.

Then a new alter came up, Caroline. She's a military girl, a lifer, devoted to service to her country. Nothing is below her; in uniform, she has brown short hair, very perky. She contrasts to my wounded woman, in a heap of agony after the multiple rapes. But Caroline left at the door; she carried out the orders to go to the room, then I was left to face the music. She finds weakness appalling. She said that Laura, the wounded woman, was the trigger and she, the dynamite. She came in my junior year in high school. Laura was the memories of the electroshock and the torture implemented during conditioning. Caroline carried out the assignments. It is different from being a child victim or being in a bizarre cult. Caroline, clean-cut, professional, carried out assignments. I could see both women as counterparts of myself. Caroline, a zealot—get the job done at any cost—resenting the wounded woman.

I see how Caroline has been vital to my ability to function, for she succeeds at any task, even the seemingly impossible, but will be oblivious to people's feelings. I also see how the wounded woman feels degraded at doing housework—not a labor of love, but just a job that never gets done, no integrity. When the wounded woman is present, I'm overwhelmed and degraded. When Caroline's present, I'm competent and controlling. Wounded woman is self-robbed of integrity and innocence. Caroline serves Uncle Sam, Big Brother, faithfully, unquestionably.

I ask how she was triggered into action, how she was accessed. Laura is the control switch; the wounded woman feeling degraded is the control switch for Caroline. During my next healing session, I soul-retrieved my wounded woman to the center of my trinity of power, of female integrity. I laid her on a pyramid to heal. I took her from that room of hell and brought her to the place of healing.

As I worked, moving deep pain in my lower back and pelvis with the massage therapist, the story of Dulcinea and Don Quixote came to me. No wonder it was my favorite play! I listed my favorite stories in high school: *Brave New World*, *Fahrenheit 451*, *1984*, *Don Quixote*, *Children of the A-Bomb*, *Black Like Me* and stories by *Edgar Allen Poe*.

I worked intensely and deeply during the next session. I showed my wounded woman to Caroline. She did not want to accept her counterpart, refused to acknowledge that an aspect of herself would do something like that. To make peace with such an anomaly, she decided to regard the undeniable events as training, for the good of the whole and the country. The end justifies the means.

I dug deeper, trying to find out who she was. I asked about her identity. I saw the sound booths with the holographic images of a military female who looked like Caroline. I asked Caroline if she knew someone deeper, if she had access to someone else. Suddenly Patrick came up: This is classified information, dangerous to retrieve. Caroline tried to talk but was choked. I opened my throat chakra and asked her to tell me. Patrick informed me there was a trigger to shut my voice down if I spoke. I asked how to shut it down. He helped me defuse the trigger, and I got to the memory.

I saw my high school again—an intense body memory. I was given an injection in the thyroid, causing shock and pain in my heart and head. Military music is playing; patriotic posters are hanging on the wall. The implant, the trigger, is 19366397. It would be the equivalent of several megahertz of voltage, which would trigger appropriate programmed responses. I almost had a seizure but was able to hang on. I came back to consciousness with the numbers: $6397 = 6 + 3 = 9 - 9 = 0$, leaving the number 7. I reprogrammed these numbers by association with sacred numerology. Nine is the number of knowledge, of completion, the balance of knowledge in completion, and seven is the seven sacred directions. I instructed all parts of myself, even those programmed by the number, to resequence this pattern and reprogram it. Caroline said that my praying for help and direction was no way to run a military. I told her about the world beyond the military—the universe. I took her to my sacred mountain for larger perspective.

I talked to Caroline about a broader perspective beyond her limited world. My guides joined with me to encourage her to have pride in her performance and efficiency in uniform, while realizing that the military is deceiving itself. The military establishment does not trust humanity. It does not trust its own human self. I connected her to other wounded parts of my inner children so that she could become aware of the pain I had experienced

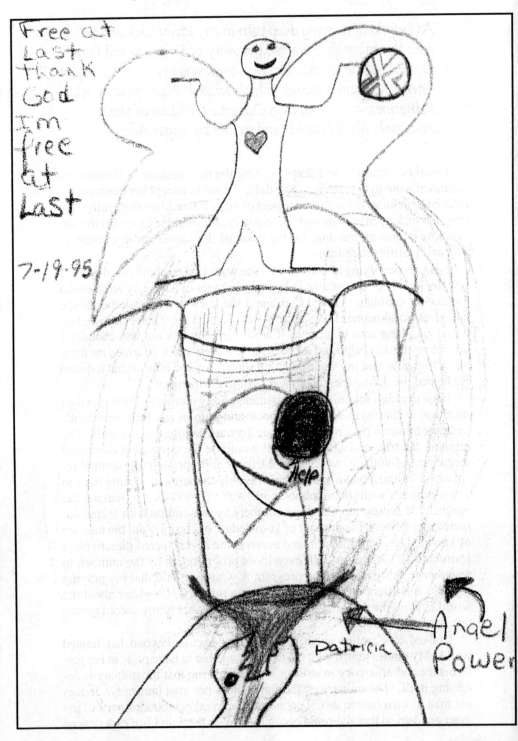

Free at
Last
Thank
God
I'm
free
at
Last

7-19-95

Help

Patricia

Angel
Power

and the damage caused within. I explained to Caroline that she is part of another whole than the military; she is part of a system of entities, a whole within. I explained that she is not part of the military; she is part of other personalities who do not respond to military command or logic, parts of self who do not feel that the end justifies the means, parts of self who do not serve the U.S. government in any way. I asked her to expand her perspectives. This work was very intense. Afterward Quanab spoke, telling us that he is pleased that the grandfathers brought me to this new therapist.

May 23, 1995: A wounded part is speaking: "I'm really not okay. I started getting so sleepy after lunch. I got worse; my head is really intense. I need help; help me. I'm going to kill myself before they get me. I can't let them get me again; I must die first. I want to die; please let me die. I must die. Let me die. I have to die, please."

May 24, 1995: Last night was hell. I started having trouble at work, uncontrollably sleepy. I had to go home. It got worse until my head nearly split open from the pain. I couldn't function. I just tried to hold it at bay. I think it had to do with a phone call at noon. Then the material from Valerie Wolf made it worse—too hard. I called a friend for support and finally got past the dangerous part, but I still have a headache, all night long. I called sacred space and returned to my safe place.

I remember being put in a vault the size of a garbage can. They told me they control the oxygen and could deprive me and destroy my brain cells. They showed me hungry rats they could put in with me if they wished. Water dripped on my head. I had to lick it and drink as it ran down my face, because if it landed on the floor, which it often did, there were shock pads on my feet. There was a high frequency, erratic sound and electrodes on my scalp. This sound was to induce energy surges through my brain; then readings were taken.

They controlled every aspect of my environment. I was to respond as they wished, or else. Two words were used:

obedience and loyalty. I had to speak a certain way, slow, low-pitched, fast or high-pitched. My response was to be linked with certain stimuli. If I responded the way they wished me to, water would dribble down my face for me to lick for a drink. If I didn't do it right, too much water would run down my head in the back, to puddle on the floor and activate the shock. I never knew what was coming next. Of course, I defecated and urinated on myself in there.

When I was in session, I went back to my sacred pyramid and soul-retrieved this fragile woman-child from the cylinder pit to my sacred mountain. I washed her and wrapped her in an amber cloth, to heal in a hammock of healing comfort. Then the Guardian of the Kingdom of Minerals came and freed all the trapped women, all the spirits who died in such ways across the globe. We freed them to form a spiritual army to heal the women within the men, too. "Awaken, all ye spirit beings, awaken to this healing. Free them to be a spiritual army, to mend the hoop, to heal Mother Earth." My practitioner and I thanked the spirits for using us. I told my therapist about this, and he said he had been in the Seals' special training. He recognized elements of this memory—the box and the water. He said that they create anxiety and anticipation of oxygen deficiency. Panic is created in the anticipation. We talked about the aspect of mind control and how the programmers control the options and limit the choices. I asked if they were successful. Patrick spoke. He told us about a very deep part of myself that we named Patricia. She worked for them. I sensed that Caroline flinched. Patricia didn't. Patricia was successful; she never flinched when doing her duty.

May 31, 1995: I am so blessed to have the gifts and skills to access these forbidden places. Today I worked with my lost sexuality. I had a dream about reclaiming myself as a woman with normal sexual feelings. I went to my massage therapist. Anger came up about my repressed sexuality, my innocence denied. How unfair it was that I could be devastated on one hand and innocent on the other. Here I am, forty-five years old, with no sense of normal sexual feelings. Immediately a box came up, just like the one I was put in after the shifts of forced sex. My massage therapist and I did a shamanistic ceremony to reclaim my sexuality by cutting cords from my womb to my perpetrators. This ceremony made a huge difference in my power. I began working with Patricia. I call her the ravenous child. I went deep within and helped her to be fed and to heal. I found that she had been the place where my sexuality as a normal woman had been repressed. I soul-retrieved her to my safe place.

June 6, 1995: Patrick speaks: "Information is confirmed. Vital process. Accessing inner codes. I must not be deprogrammed until valuable documentation is accessed. My database is complete and may be accessed. Code green, code 9937, access to inner files, forbidden files, the third piece. Accessible to code 8756. Domestic intelligence, code 2142, universal code."

Those documents were accessed in March of 1998, as you will later read.

June 8, 1995: How incredible it is, how absolutely astounding! Who would have imagined six years ago what course my incest healing would take? I am certain that the cult is a surface terror programming for extensive mind-control operations by the U.S. government and military and the Nazi doctors—not only experiments, but refined techniques in massive mind slavery. Here I am, forty-five, and I know the truth. On my own, I have accessed the inner programming, alpha, delta and beta codes. When I discovered the delta code, I was sick for days, just before

Washington, D.C. Now I read a document from Corey
Hammond, called the Greenbaum Speech, that says that
people all over the country are recalling the same thing and
that the delta codes are entry keys. He said Deltas are
programmed assassins. I wonder if other survivors have
computer data like Patrick. My therapist told me I've spit the
sour milk out; now all I have to do is get the taste out of my
mouth. Once I've accessed the delta codes, I'm no longer
accessible to them. God, I hope he's right. The plan for the
planet of slaves is in place. God help us, we can stop it.

Dr. Hammond's article stating that Deltas are programmed assassins
relates directly to the files I saw at the Air Force Academy. They were hit
lists, assassination plans. Have I been trained as an assassin? God help
me, I hope I've been in reserves and not used. I pray I am free. I have so
many unanswered questions. This was never my choosing. I am deeply
astounded after reading the Greenbaum lecture. I am so angry; this all is
so unbelievable. Satanic ritual abuse, government and military, equals
government control of the world and a silent robot force available. I won-
der if anyone knows when and how the program is really undone.

Today is July 10, 2002. I am working on the final edit of the manu-
script. I have crossed the last hurdle of realization. I was programmed as
a Delta. I have atoned for the way I was used. It was not my choice. My
choice is freedom.

June 14, 1995: I have journeyed to some forbidden areas
these past five years; now I embark on yet another
forbidden territory. Each time there are inner threats and
warnings, blocked doors and forbidden passages; each time I
transcend the forbidden to claim my freedom. I have
accepted that I was used as a technician to facilitate
experiments with the Air Force cadets—forced into sex,
then placed in extreme environmental deprivation to twist
and distort my reality and sexuality. I have claimed my
reality and honor my integrity.

Last week I cut the cords of bondage to all my prior
perpetrators, returning the female spirit to them and
claiming my own cords of power. One at a time, I cut these

cords leading from the deep womb of pain of my past. I claimed my power, nourishing Patricia, teaching her empowerment instead of patriarchal dependence. Each cord cut was an intense experience, ranging from convulsions to screaming and coughing, yelling and chanting. I felt intense energy shifts, especially when I cut my cords to the nun in the basement of the hospital.

I awakened my own temple of strength. Now I feel it all shift and sift down within me. Today I attempted to go deeper and release my co-consciousness. I faced threats of criminal prosecution, of repercussions. I found an iron door with myself blocking it—fear of what I was made to do. I accessed it by way of a cave in my sacred mountain. Slowly the door opened. I saw a document titled "53776812 forbidden."

Patrick said I resist access to deep codes. I saw a freezer locker with bodies in it. The bodies were not normal Earth people. They have learned to replace key people like changing flat tires, cloning, assassinating if it serves the social goal. Replace, if the subject becomes uncooperative. It sounds bizarre, but my brain and body sensations were so intense that I could barely walk after the session. I am going forward. I asked Patrick if he has any information. Valuable documentation must be accessed regardless of resistant programs. Will continue to access code blue, zygot.

June 17, 1995: Yesterday, my dear friend Susan gave me some information mailed from a survivor back east who had attended the committee hearing, a memo from the staff of a national committee to the national committee research operation called Operation Paperclip. This was the program that brought Nazi scientists to the U.S. There was a confidential letter, including a list of the Nazi doctors. Two were named Karl. One of them did electromagnetic research. I wonder if this is the man who conducted experiments on me in Colorado Springs?

June 21, 1995: I am aware from my work last week that something has shifted in my brain. Last week, when I woke upon opening the inner door, Laiolin told me that when I accessed the key part of my brain, she would transmit healing energy. At the precise time I felt her presence, there was a shift. Since then I have felt strength. I can read about or discuss the experiments without dissociating. Yesterday I spent thirty minutes talking to someone over lunch about the experiments, and when I went back to work I felt fine. I could read material about the subject without dissociating or triggering. I remained centered and easily moved from reading to being to going shopping and carrying on with my normal life. This was a big change.

Undated entry: This morning I awoke with intense brain sensations, even painful. I am unable to harmonize the brain energy. I felt a lot of pain over the weekend, from head to toe. I felt like it was a Satanic holiday. I was able to move the energy and now I feel fine. I am far more attuned with my body, feelings and energy. I have been invited to a gathering in Phoenix of survivors of mind control. Walter Bowart is supposed to be there, along with other deprogrammers from Oregon and people who know about the government experiences. I feel ready for today. I am thankful for the gifts my healing has manifested.

June 28, 1995, 5 A.M.: Awoke with a splitting headache on the crown of my head and nausea. There must be someone who wishes to speak. "Alpha 7342869; beta, delta kill. Russia, delta kill. Delta X, 77776, kill. Kill Judy; stop the process. Delta speech in D.C., delta code; beta 78436, alpha beta codes, destroy. Kill, kill, kill." At that point I uncovered memories of being programmed by the government to be a Delta and experiences that indoctrinated me and forced me to do what they said, then never remember that I had ever done it.

On June 28, I was getting ready to go to the first forum in Phoenix of survivors of government mind control.

June 28, 1995 (continued): The headache and other symptoms were from fear that I was going to Phoenix. Once I identified that, the headache passed. Of course, I'm afraid of what I'm doing. All by myself, going to Phoenix to meet strangers who know what I know. I'm afraid of being betrayed. I'm afraid of meeting other people. Before I went to the airport, I went to see Ammachi, the Hindu saint. It was miraculous.

By the time I got there, I was in a much better balance than when I left home. It was early, and I went into the tent and sat on a chair to rest my back. In front of me was a woman waiting on the rug for Ammachi's blessing. I saw a woman in a turquoise dress; I thought I'd like to meet her. I connected with my guardians. After half an hour, Ammachi came, and I moved forward and sat on the floor. We all meditated.

Later I saw the woman again. Spontaneously, I gave her a hug and kissed her cheek. After a while, she asked me why I had come to Ammachi. I said, "Do you really want to know the truth?" She said, "Yes." I said, "I testified at Hazel O'Leary's committee for survivors of radiation experimentation, and I'm going to Phoenix to meet with a forum to expose human experimentation." She said she had worked at Sandia and Los Alamos labs and left because of a sexual harassment case. Then she asked if I had an attorney. I said I couldn't afford one. She said I needed one. She knew an environmentalist attorney who had helped her, and he would help me. [This never happened, however.] Then she whispered to me that she had smuggled documents out of Los Alamos that led to Hazel O'Leary's being able to open up the committee hearings. She had given them to the attorney, who gave them to the proper person and protected her. They would kill her if they knew.

This attorney defended Winnie Mandela. I was crying. She said she would call me but that we should never discuss this on the phone, that her phone is bugged. She said she was coming to Santa Fe next month, and we would meet. [This never came to pass.] She told me that her father had assassinated Hitler's second-in-command. There was much evil in her family, as in all of ours. She agreed to be incarnated as his daughter to do her work.

She said she knew that my work would manifest beyond anything I could imagine. Within three years, she said, angels would contact me and tell me what I've done. She said I should do my part and be willing to let go. We will persevere and do our work in safety. She had to hide. They follow her still. She was glad to see I am in phase two of her work. I called her my sister and wept. She told me she was surprised at my emotion; she felt detached. I am astounded. I know Ammachi brought us together. I have so much to share with her. She told me to breathe and quietly accept Ammachi's blessings; she would heal my mind and spirit. This I know has already been manifested. I am humbled by this experience. I kept glancing over at her, and we'd smile. She patted my shoulder before she became respectfully silent. I told her I was thankful we had found each other. It is no coincidence that I went to Ammachi's and met this woman today and that now I'm on my way to Phoenix to this forum.

June 28, 1995, on the airplane: Here I am on the way to Phoenix. It's 5:30 P.M. If I were to share the keys to my healing, what would they be? The list is long: self-guided trance journey, setting my intent to learn only that which is for my higher good, using a guide and a safe place. I had the help and support of caring professionals who empowered me, and even though they were as baffled as I at times, they continued to give me unconditional support. I had a good therapist who stayed out of the way and was grounded and neutral. I definitely experienced divine intervention. I learned about clearing my space, facing the dark ones, light protection, the protection of spiritual Christ, the Cosmic Mother, guardians and guides, Quanab, Laiolin, Archangel Michael. I healed my body with Chinese herbs, minerals, acupuncture, massage and deep tissue work. The bodywork gave me a way to release body memories and learn to be in touch with my feelings. I began spiritual healing with daily prayer and meditation, the healing at the Episcopal church, sweat lodges and light experiences.

The cosmic being of light contributed much: healing my brain energy and teaching me healing meditation, harmonic sound healing and vibration chants to equalize my brain energies. I found group work to be vital to my healing, participating at different times with three survivors' groups. I began to eat a healthy diet, no alcohol or any drugs. Probably most important, I learned to breathe and move energy through exercises, Qigong and meditations to move energy in the brain and balance my chakras. The purple fluorite crystal helped in so many ways to heal the brain energy. My journal was one of the most important tools of my recovery; I learned to write with my left hand and do stream-of-consciousness journaling and art therapy. I couldn't have made it without the love and support of my family. My children and my husband ground me in this world. Validation by research was vital. I returned to places and found validation; meeting other survivors after I had recovered memories validated my memories. I also benefitted from relaxation tapes like flute music that helped me sleep.

It seems this journal entry opened up another dimension for me as I wrote in my journal this question: "What is up with aliens and the connection to Satanic ritual abuse, evil and saving the planet? I think I know."

The meeting in Phoenix was rewarding. Kurt, a deprogrammer from Oregon, provided a lot of information. It was an intense gathering. We shared our stories and experiences. It took courage for us to gather and talk. I called the meeting in Phoenix the Rainbow House in the Desert. It was a powerful meeting of individuals who agreed to endure of the hell of their childhoods, to experience the experiments and torture, to live to tell, to gather together with integrity, spirituality and safety under Christ's protection. I was acknowledged and empowered by this group for my testimony in Washington. After I returned from D.C., no one even wanted to talk about what happened out there. I know it was because it was too difficult for most people to think about, let alone discuss. It really mattered to the people I met in Phoenix. We met two years in a row, and both times were amazing and powerful.

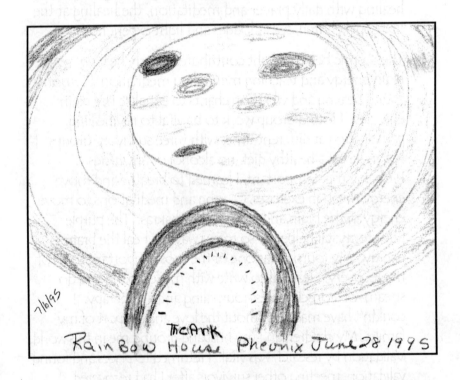

CHAPTER TWENTY-SEVEN

The House of David:
A Resistance Movement

July 7, 1995: I return to the programming for Delta: "I am blocked; I am angry; I feel fear; I am tired; I am very, very tired. Hurt, lost, abandoned, smashed. Delta code, help me; I agree to stop the pain. Delta code, agree to help, to serve, to die if needed. Delta reserve, always ready. Delta agreement, code blue, bell, X 53468."

July 10, 1995: Yesterday was hell. I was dysfunctional almost all day, with intense brain sensations. I even got angry, which I haven't done in a long time, yelling at my daughter. I'm a good person; I don't need to be hurt by people. I got so mad, I wanted to break things, like a child having a tantrum. I pulled it together and cleaned the refrigerator and the front room instead. Cleaning helped me vent my anger, but I still felt shut down. I contacted my inner alters and talked to Patricia. She was angry, hurt, abandoned, isolated and sick of being in the can during the Air Force abuse. She said I promised to come through the door and get them but never did. She said I talk and talk, but she isn't ever heard. Patricia is a starved, hungry, bottomless pit of emptiness. After I allowed her to come out and speak, I felt immediate relief from all the symptoms. All this Delta stuff ties me to the first memory at the Air Force Academy and the file that I discovered.

July 12, 1995: The closer I get to healing and accessing forbidden information, programs automatically trigger in my everyday life. Sequences of normal events must have been calculated as probable and then program triggers set up like a mine field in a war. It doesn't detonate unless you go to the forbidden zone. I have discovered that some of the triggers are the use of phonetic sequences in numerical order, not the content of sentences. Programs were put in place assigning dual meanings to phrases like higher good, serving God, being of service, God using me, awakened and higher purpose. These must have been established to control in the event that I discovered spiritual enlightenment. I began to qualify each phrase and to be mindful of my integrity. One piece at a time, I undid these programs and freed my mind. I am in the service of being, not being of service.

I recovered a memory about a programmer named David who created Patrick in 1957. David was a double agent who worked to sabotage the controllers' plan. The database program he created in my brain served several purposes. It recorded information, analyzed it for faults, sabotaged programs that would threaten my ultimate freedom and served as an objective fact-recorder. He told me that Patrick was a program that would help me deprogram when the time came. I would be assisted to awaken and bring this truth to the light. I discovered two verbal triggers: hamburger and hot fudge sundae. I was shown how common words are used to keep the programs activated. Once I was aware of this, I could defuse the power of the words and no longer be triggered.

David came to the one-room schoolhouse and took me aside. He explained that he had met my teacher, a veteran of World War II, after the war was over. David had been in intelligence in Operation Paperclip, bringing the Nazi doctors to the United States. He had been contacted by a group of people in Austria who called themselves the House of David. They were a nongovernment, ET-assisted resistance movement. David decided to help them and became a double agent.

He explained that I had agreed to enter into my body, to be incarnated with the purpose of entering into these experiments to bring the truth to the light. Deep within my soul, I knew this was true. My life is not a trap, but a choice. I chose to do this work because I love Mother Earth and all humanity and feel compassion for the children's suffering. I am not alone in all this—I have always been helped and supported. It is reassuring to know that even through the horrors of Delta programming, I had protection from being consumed by the lie. There are times in life that transcend understanding, that reach a deep sense of knowing. This was one of these times. I realized that the term "awakening of the House of David" meant both the awakening of the Christ consciousness and of a group who used this name to identify their cause.

July 12, 1995 (continued): Patricia agreed to enlist in Delta after they got her out of the can. A woman named Delores took me into a room and treated me really nice. She gave me clean clothing and food—good things. She told me that it was for the good of my country, and who wouldn't rather be treated well than return to the torture? It wasn't during the pain that Patricia gave in. No, it was when the pain stopped and her needs were met. It was when they treated her like a princess. It seemed logical that her compliance would be for the good of all.

July 19, 1995: Body memories of needles in my spine when I was in the can. Delores had straight brown hair; she was sweet and loving, soft and gentle. It felt so good to be spoken to kindly. She said, "Oh, what have they done to you, you poor little thing?" She sympathized, held me and gave me sips of broth. There was a nice bed to lie on. I could sleep and eat good food. I was given back my own clothes. Oh, how hungry Patricia was. Just a little at a time, not so much as to get sick. Delores said, "This never has to happen again. All they want is for you to be loyal. It is for our country, for the good of our country. Really, you are honored to be chosen. They have to be certain that you agree to a contract as a choice—not only to escape the pain. They are preparing you for the Delta Force, a special service you should be proud of. They want to interview you, but first they must be sure of your loyalty. Really, it isn't bad working for them; they offer you a good life—marriage, children, comfort and happiness. Part of the agreement is that you won't be psychotic, and they won't put you back there. The torture will end; you can enjoy your life. You can travel, camp, have a career; you'll only be in the reserves and will be called only when needed. Some people are never called. Part of the agreement is, no more torture or pain induction—of course, unless you violate the contract. Then necessary steps will be taken. They want it to be your choice, because this is a democracy. Oh, and I am to mention the misfortune of teenage suicide, like your cousin's friend who drank weed poisoning. This never has to happen to you; you won't be a candidate for suicide. You must have time to consider; you may go home, and we will call you later. There is a test you must pass before you return, to be sure of your loyalty and ability to qualify."

I was then given instructions to awaken in the middle of the night, to meet a car and be driven across town to a certain house. I was to go in and perform a task, then meet my pick-up vehicle and be returned home. If I performed the task right, I would go back to the committee and be reviewed for acceptance into the Delta Force.

Around this time in my life, in the autumn of 1966, I was sick for weeks with swollen glands. I missed many days of school. I would lie in bed and wish I could die. My mother had no idea what was going on, and my father had died. She was busy working to support her children and get an education. There was plenty of time for me to be missing while she assumed I was at school or at a friend's house.

I began the process of dissolving the Delta contract. Even though they had agreed to stop torturing me, still I suffered from severe emotional and physical pain. When a person signs a contract under coercion and duress, it is not binding. I communicated this to all parts of myself, and we had a ceremony to nullify the Delta contract.

July 27, 1995: Forty-six years ago I was born into bondage, a slave to generational bondage. Six years ago I chose to heal. Today I emerge as a transformed being of truth and light, awakening to the true safe spirituality, healing from the past wounds, shedding the shackles of my own oppression. With the dissolving of the Delta contract, I feel I have ascended Mount Everest. I will continue to heal; I will continue to seek the truth. Yet I feel a deep sense of accomplishment in my journey in the past six years.

I had a vision yesterday. I was in an obsidian cave with a master from India. It was a perfect sound chamber. I stepped through the wall and up some steps to a temple. I knelt before him. He placed a pyramid and a pendulum over my head, a bronze rod with the pendulum suspended in the center. Then he stepped aside for me to pass. I was at the foot of a mountain; it was lush and beautiful. I was in a white gown. Before me was a pool. I took off my gown, walked through the pool and bathed in sweet, flowing water. I was anointed with precious oils and given a more beautiful white gown with a gold belt. I ascended the mountain, walking up a gentle path.

Jesus was at the top. I knelt and humbled myself. He took my hands in his and helped me stand. His eyes were turquoise, sky blue, deep, infinite. He looked into mine and said, "What I have done, you can do. Welcome to this House of David." He stepped aside, and there were others, elders dressed in white. Then he said, "This is your family. Come feast at our table." They rejoiced as I joined them. It was a spiritual feast.

This was the third vision of Christ that I had been told about in earlier visions. Since then I've had other visions of Christ.

I always check to make certain that it is indeed Christ Jesus and not a holographic imitation sent by the dark forces. I am grateful my Catholic mystic friend taught me how to tell the difference.

That summer I went to the Southern Ute Sun dance and met Steve, a professor at Indiana State University, with whom I talked late into the night. I told him about my experiences and what I remembered with the government. He connected me to Michael Andregg. Michael was part of an organization called Ground Zero Minnesota and was associated with the University of St. Thomas. He was doing a project called *Rethink the World*, a series of twenty-five documentaries discussing the challenges faced by democracy. Upon Steve's urging, I sent Michael a copy of my narrative and later worked with him on a documentary. You'll read more about that later.

September 20, 1995: I recalled being at Metro State College. I was sent to a congressman's office, whom I remember seeing at a political gathering in Colorado Springs when I was ten or eleven. He instructed me to perform oral sex and then had intercourse with me. He kept saying, "You are mine. I am the government. You will never betray. You are mine. I own you." As he thrust deep inside me, he repeated, "Mine, mine."

October 1, 1995: Six years ago, I began a quest for truth, a journey of healing my mind, body and spirit. Truly it began when I was born, and it manifested at the Sun pole at the Sun dance in South Dakota the day of the Harmonic Convergence, August 17, 1987. I stood in wonderment that day, knowing that something enormous was about to happen, but my intellect couldn't have imagined the scope of it. As I neared my fortieth birthday, I went around telling my family that my fortieth birthday was going to be one of the biggest birthdays in my life, and there was a big change coming. My journey led me to unearth deep pain and childhood trauma and taught me the gift of safe journey. Dancing with my dark side took on a new meaning as I ripped open the lid of Pandora's box. We, the children of the awakening, are rewriting this old myth. We are cleansing the box and transforming the energy; we are filling it with light and healing and truth. Once the box lid came open, the demons really didn't want to stay in there; they wanted sunlight and transformation.

October 4, 1995: The news carries the story of President Clinton apologizing to radiation experimentation survivors. He said that when the government does wrong, we have a moral obligation to admit it. A chairperson on the committee was quoted as saying that she was morally outraged by what she had heard. The government might offer financial compensation to some of the survivors. Not me, for sure—just the ones at the tip of the iceberg who can document their experiences. Will the dark secrets of the Nazi doctors ever be exposed? Perhaps this is a good start.

Over the next months, I struggled to understand government mind control, to understand programmed words. I worked with recognizing programming and programming clues. I discovered through research that there is indeed a plan for a New World Order and that it extends back before biblical times. The Bible speaks of Armageddon, because the Armageddon plan already existed, had already been developed. At the same time, there was a divine plan to help our species awaken to a higher state of consciousness.

Finally, after months of deprogramming, in November I uncovered the memory about signing the Delta contract.

November 29, 1995: I went to my safe place and spoke to my guardians. They told me that Delores was a resister. She was being observed, but still she managed to get secret messages to me. She kept saying, "You must walk, you must be strong to be useful to them; you know too much at this point. For your own sake, walk. Sign, and move forward. Someday you will resist them." In my ear, when she bent near me to do something, she whispered, "Be useful to them; be strong. Resist. Someday, when you are called, don't go.

Now they will just destroy you; then it will be critical timing. If they can't use you, they will have to move on to someone else. Remember the House of David."

Then I was back at the grade school again. I asked David, the resister and double agent, how he made Patrick. I traveled back to the third grade and my sessions with David. He would put me to sleep in a deep trance and work to establish Patrick. Patrick has no control over other selves; his main function was to record data that was not to be accessed unless it was totally safe. He was programmed to protect me from participating directly in anti-life activities. He was designed to know, to log information and be able to relay it. David told me that if I got out, Patrick would be a library of secret documents and events. Now is the time. Patrick is ready to record the transmissions and the key information. And then Patrick comes up with "delta code X file, 467, the assassination of Martin Luther King, delta code Z, 983, the assassination of Gandhi; delta code D, code X, 7685, the failed plan to kill Castro; delta code Zebra D, 8936, the assassination of Malcolm X; assassination attempt, Jimmy Carter, delta A, 743, top secret."

Did they know that Jimmy Carter would be president in the future? The people who perpetrated these programs used remote viewers to see the future. I have no idea why Jimmy Carter appeared in this memory. I have deep respect for him, but my question is how I got this information in the 1960s. This remains a mystery to me.

December 1, 1995: "I am Patrick. My purpose for existence is to record and relay information for the purpose of freedom from mind control. I am operated by David of the House of David. Information lineage retrieved. Non-Earth beings coded DNA for free will and resistance to any form of mind control. The House of

David, the house of what your species refers to as angels. The term angel is as diverse as the term man. These non-Earth beings are represented to you as the cosmic beings of light. These beings intervened in your life at age three. Your DNA was coded to the House of David. Your DNA is coded to spiritual attunement, free will, connection to the heart.. You carry DNA memories to the preflood era, to pre-Babylonia, to historical references to the ancient Middle Earth. Strong lineage through Scot and German ancestry, but not exclusive lineage; there are many other people on the Earth who are encoded with the DNA from the House of David."

Patrick said that David was thirty-eight years old, was born in Chicago, had a degree in psychology and was indoctrinated into the experiments as a soldier in World War II. He served in Germany in counterintelligence Operation Paperclip and assisted as a liaison to extradite Nazi doctors to this country for the continued project of programming individuals to autoresponse data trigger mechanisms. He obtained top-security clearance in military efforts. He was 5' 8" tall and weighed 162 lbs. He had blond/brown hair, blue/hazel eyes, was bearded, of German descent, with a mole on the left ear and a red birthmark on the back of the neck. He was contacted in Germany by members of the House of David, independent of government control, who had operational bases in southern France, Belgium and Austria. Their central communications base was a mountain in Austria.

We of the House of David have star ancestors who are highly evolved benevolent beings. They have returned now to assist us in awakening, healing, empowering ourselves and claiming our freedom from fear. They cannot interfere in our free will but can assist us when we request their help. In the bigger picture, they are members of a galactic council of light called the Council of Abborah, the Elohim representative to the Galactic Federation. Their role is to awaken the Cosmic Christ.

December 5, 1995: I spoke with Laiolin. She says I'm on the river of my choice, to go with the current, to know that all is as it should be. She said that the fearmongers had been detonating underground electromagnetic bombs since mid-November, disrupting the alpha/beta rays and making people sick.

December 12, 1995: I feel exhausted and totally blocked; I've been awake since 4:30 A.M. I am so deeply frightened.

After writing that in my journal, I took a bath and went into a deep meditation. First, an alter associated with Caroline spoke: "You don't know how powerful they are; they are the ultimate master controllers." Then Patrick accessed file 361, year 1967.

I saw the room at the Air Force Academy with the virtual-reality experiments. I took a tunnel to the right of the main entrance, up some small stairs, to an observation room approximately ten by fifteen feet. There were chairs along the back wall; I was observing from the right side. There were maybe ten people in the room. I wondered what I was doing there. A general and his sidekick were angry; there was a confrontation with a male being. The general was saying that the U.S. government was the most powerful nation in the world. The being was about 6' 4"; his skin was an odd color, almost normal but a light tan-yellow, a very subtle variation. He was distinctly different from humans. Major differences included a large forehead with a wrinkle in the brow and strange eyes like those of a Siamese cat or a lizard, heartless. I knew he was an ET, because nobody looks like that on Earth.

He laughed at the general, "What fools you people are." He exposed the fault with the virtual-reality experiment. He told the general that if the U.S. wanted technology and help, they must know who they are dealing with. They were to know that he and his people have ultimate control. He brought the general to his knees by beaming his mind on him. The general was sobbing, groveling. Then he released the general and turned his mind on the people in the chairs. One at a time, they began to scream and hold their heads. He turned back to the general and said something like, "This is toying with you." He focused mildly, and the general pulled a gun and shot his assistant. I blacked out. I woke up forty-five minutes later with huge brain sensations. I was overwhelmed, dizzy and nauseated. That was my first encounter with an extraterrestrial being at a military facility. Seven months later, I finally got to the bottom of the memories at the Air Force Academy and remembered more about ETs and the Air Force.

CHAPTER   TWENTY-EIGHT

Visions and Validations

On the last day of 1995, I went to the Global Reunion for World Peace in Iowa. People of many different spiritual beliefs and religious backgrounds came from all over the country. A Tibetan priest, a Native American elder named Wallace Black Elk and many others gathered there to pray for world peace. I met an elder called Smokey who was giving what was called the 11:11 initiation, an initiation from the mystery schools.

I also met Charles Lawrence, with whom I had quite a confrontation. I told him how I felt about contrary elk medicine, about medicine men who misuse their power to violate women (crudely known as "humping a white woman in a sweat lodge"). What he told me was shocking, but now I know it is true. "You choose everything that happens to you," he said. He said to be thankful to *all* my teachers. Then he told me about a shaman's initiation where nine holes are drilled in ice and an initiate is thrown in. If he survives, fine. If he does not, the initiator brushes his hands and says, "Next!" This sounded cruel at the time, but now I realize that everything I experienced was for my highest good. What did not kill me made me strong.

There I had some unusual experiences and an enormous spiritual opening. I could easily write an entire book about the Global Reunion for World Peace. Before I went, I had a strong feeling that I had to get some information to someone associated with Patrick. I was getting strange information from Patrick about a planned Armageddon, a planned nuclear bombing and the coordinates for that. Upon my return, however, that feeling of urgency was gone. I was aware that I had been taken up on a ship and that the information I carried in my brain's computer, which I call Patrick, was given to benevolent ETs to assist in curbing the impending disaster. I know that we receive assistance from what I call ultraterrestrials, but they cannot intervene without freewill consent. I provided the consent and the information needed.

I was in an altered state for thirty days afterward. I needed some help in integrating my experience and made an appointment with a therapist named Maud who specializes in assisting people to process powerful spiritual events. Maud helped me understand what had happened in the context of a spiritual awakening.

We did EMDR (Eye Movement Desensitization and Reprocessing) therapy. This rapid eye movement modality can open up centers in the brain blocked by amnesia. During the session, I recovered a memory of being on a ship. I know I was not abducted, but that I agreed to do this to help the planet.

This is the truth as I know it. I have had many similar experiences since then that I will not speak of here. Suffice it to say that after years of working in this capacity, I know the power of the work. I now have a working relationship with ultraterrestrials in several dimensions.

Near the end of March, I went to sleep holding my granddaughter. All at once I woke up, and Patrick began to talk. He said that I had indeed given vital information to the proper source of the House of David that created him. I had been taken up on a ship in Iowa while I was sleeping. He said that the information needed to help preserve the freedom of the world and prevent a nuclear disaster had been gently and painlessly retrieved from my brain. The cosmic being of light said that the procedure was a strain on my brain, accounting for my altered state when I came home. She said that I had served to save the planet. The memory work and recall I had become accustomed to stopped for a while so I could recuperate and reorganize. Mysteries remain about that experience, but I have no doubt that it was for my highest good.

On my home from the Global Reunion, in an intensely altered state, I had a vision just as we were entering into New Mexico. From my vantage point in the back seat of the car, I gazed into the distance. The grain towers disappeared, and a huge apparition of the Virgin of Guadalupe appeared on the horizon. Since then, I've talked to other women who have had visions of the Holy Mother and we share certain similarities.

My first vision of the Holy Mother occurred when I was twenty years old. I was not a "Christian." My fiancé had told me that he might be sent to Vietnam. We were distraught. We had been engaged for a year and a half. I was finishing nursing school, and we had agreed not to be intimate until we were married. This was not an easy choice, and now it appeared that we would be separated before our planned wedding day in October. We drove toward the mountains just to calm down. We happened upon the Mother Cabrini Shrine; it was after hours but the gate was open. In the chapel, we gazed at the beautiful statue, wept and prayed. I asked her why I had decided to wait until we were married; my friends didn't take that approach. Before my eyes, she came alive. In my heart I heard her say that she had chosen me for a special task, that my self-control would give me strength and discipline that I would later need. She promised to make things easier for us and that we would have a beautiful wedding and a good life together. We both felt her love fill us and we left in peace. As it turned out, he was not drafted, and all her promises came to pass.

Every year after that, we'd make a pilgrimage to the shrine. On one such trip, our car filled with children, one of the kids asked, "Mom, why do we go here every year?" I told them the story of Mother Cabrini and her journey to build a safe place for orphaned children. I looked at the faces of our adopted family and knew that she did indeed have a special task for me. I have thought often of that task and my need for strength and discipline. Now I look at the faces of the children of Mother Earth, and deep within my heart, I know she is planning another miracle.

My spiritual life has accelerated following the visitation. I can also look into the Sun. At first, when I look at it, it is as bright as it used to be. Then—as I focus and pray—it appears like the full moon, bright but not blinding. Another odd thing is that my skin no longer sunburns.

Strangely enough, I haven't been all that curious about the details of being taken up on the ship, but I have a deep feeling that something important happened. I believe that I did indeed give benevolent extraterrestrials information retrieved from the Air Force Academy. I believe these beings are here to assist us to curb the destruction of our planet, to help break up the fear grid around our planet and to help us awaken to a higher state of consciousness.

Also during the month of March, I traveled to Minneapolis/St. Paul to work on a documentary titled "Mind Control," with Michael Andregg of Ground Zero Minnesota, at the University of St. Thomas—a project that required extensive work with my inner selves to get the strength and resolve. This was a major piece of work, one of a series of twenty-five called *Rethink the World*. Michael told me he had studied the MKUltra experiments and the congressional hearing in the 1970s that exposed a lot of these mind-control experiments and programs. I had never heard of this hearing before. During the taping of the documentary, he said that after the hearings, the project had been renamed MKSearch and swept under the carpet.

I was led to believe that the video would have wide distribution. It seemed such an important document, one that could open many people's eyes and minds. As far as I know, however, that never happened. I've lost touch with Michael and have had very little feedback from the project.

All the same, my spiritual growth accelerated with many really wonderful experiences. I continued to work with healing modalities, but a great deal of my healing at this point was spiritual awakening. My meditations were powerful. In April of 1996, during a trance journey, I met my great teacher from the spiritual realm, the Great Cobra, called Muchlinda, who you often see pictured with Buddha. She is usually shown behind him, her great hood shielding and protecting him.

April 10, 1996: I want to speak of my vision. I prayed for truth and went to my safe place. My guide told me to go to a cavern high in the mountain. I entered into a place made of obsidian; from a pedestal in the center flowed a spring. I've been in this cave before. The Guardian of Minerals came and told me to wait for my master teacher. A huge snake entered, filling the chamber, so big that its head and tail were outside. Together we went deeper into the Earth. From a ledge, I saw mutant beings holographically projecting evil illusions onto the Earth. Then we went down below to the prisons of the minds, to what is called hell, the pits of loathsome suffering and human agony. I saw the beast. As he approached me, the ceiling split and light healed the cavern. The Guardian of the Kingdom of Minerals said that this was a healing for the whole planet, not just for me. I had entered the underworld as a child and had emerged to bring the light into the darkness, to heal these deep caverns of the human psyche, my ultimate challenge in healing. This could have claimed me, plunged me back into the evil one's control, but I emerged stronger from the confrontation.

Many Native Americans believe that you give your power away when you tell visions. For some people, this is true. My guides lead me to share some of my visions for the benefit of others. The Great Cobra has taken me on many healing journeys. I have received spiritual initiations and visions in her cave. I see Gandhi, Martin Luther King and Ammachi there, as well as others.

You might have heard of negative Reptilians and ETs, but not all reptilians are of the fear vibration. The Great Cobra is a spiritual entity, not an ET. I was sent in a Jungian way to heal the poisons of my childhood shamanistically. I made many journeys to the Cave of the Great Cobra and received healing from her and the snake clan.

Things were going well; I was having more good days than bad and was beginning to enjoy the benefit of all the work I had done. Lifelong symptoms diminished, and I realized that I had never known life without suffering. Now I am almost pain-free. Of course, if I work too hard in the garden, I'll get a backache like anyone else, but the constant pain and the headaches are gone. I know that not everyone who has traveled on this journey has made it through to these rewards. Many of my brothers and sisters stopped halfway, got stuck or went back. I am very much aware of my blessings, and I'm constantly thankful for my healing and the courage to make it through those dark places. I am thankful that I didn't turn back when I faced my own demons, when I faced the depth and the breadth of the terror. By persevering, I have come to a place of wholeness and awakening to a higher state of consciousness. Some of us had to make that journey, to crack the paradigm, to change the psyche of our species.

I think of Rosa Parks. She knew when she sat down that somebody might beat her up or even kill her. She had seen what happened to other black people who tried to make changes. Something inside her guided her that day, something similar to my inner voice that insisted I heal, that demanded I know the truth. I had to take the risk, even though part of me knew it was forbidden, that if I ever spoke out or told the truth, I'd be killed or my family would be killed. I knew these threats were real. I had a lot of help from the angelic realm, from the spiritual realm and from the ETs or ultraterrestrials here to help us heal this planet.

One day, in an antique store, I opened up a little prayer book and a piece of paper fell out. It was Stephen Vincent Benét's "Prayer for the United Nations," which President Roosevelt read June 15, 1949, at the United Nations Day ceremony. The prayer, now more than fifty years old, speaks to my heart of the awakening, of the destiny of our planet as we move forward to claim our freedom, our peace, our empowerment and the right to have unity through diversity.

Prayer for the United Nations

We pledge our hearts and lives today to the cause of all free mankind.

Grant us victory over the tyrants who would enslave all free men and nations.

Grant us faith and understanding to cherish all those who fight for freedom as if they were our brothers. Grant us brotherhood in hope and union, not only for the space of this bitter war, but for the days to come which shall and must unite all the children of the earth.

Our earth is but a small star in the great universe. Yet of it we can make, if we choose, a planet unvexed by war, untroubled by hunger or fear, undivided by senseless distinctions of race, color, or theory. Grant us that courage and foreseeing to begin this task today that our children and our children's children may be proud of the name of man.

The spirit of man has awakened and the soul of man has gone forth. Grant us the wisdom and the vision to comprehend the greatness of man's spirit, that suffers and endures so hugely for a goal beyond his own brief span. Grant us honor for the dead who died in faith, honor for our living who work and strive for the faith, redemption and security for all captive lands and peoples. Grant us patience for the deluded and pity for the betrayed. And grant us the skill and the valor that shall cleanse the world of oppression and the old base doctrine that the strong must eat the weak because they are strong.

Yet most of all, grant us brotherhood, not only for this day but for all our years—a brotherhood not of words but of acts and deeds. We are all of us children of earth—grant us that simple knowledge. If our brothers are oppressed, then we are oppressed. If they hunger, we hunger. If their freedom is taken away, our freedom is not secure. Grant us the common faith that man shall know bread and peace, that he shall know justice and righteousness, freedom and security, an equal chance to do his best, not only in our own lands, but throughout the world.

And in the faith let us march toward the clean world our hands can make. Amen.

June 15, 1949

April 1996, the day after Easter: For me it feels like some new beginning. The old me has died, and now I have become a transformation of my being. Yet much of who I am, I have carried with me. I have kept my treasure and let go of the things I do not need. Today I was deeply aware of my healing. I am at peace. My skills in math, organization, grounding and patience have improved vastly. Yes, I still feel sad and confused, but also deeply content and at peace. My relationship with my children has been enhanced. I am capable of being sensitive without being too pushy or controlling. I rarely feel anger at life situations; I am deeply grateful for life's blessings and the joys of the simple things. I love life. With all that's positive, there's also a deep emptiness and loneliness.

April 22, 1996: I spoke to the cosmic being of light on the way home from work. She told me that part of my preparation for the future is to alter the soul code that plugs into the DNA at birth in such a way that it can be combined with higher-frequency DNA in the next life. She said I have done that. Biochemical and biological changes have taken place in my brain and neural synapses, much of them as I slept. She said that it is my free will, whatever I pursue on my journey: whether channeling or exposing the dark secrets. I don't really have to choose; I just feel I do. Either way, I have the Midas touch this time for the highest good, never to bring harm. I have gifts I don't even know about. She said she was glad to see me in joy, my new state of peace.

CHAPTER TWENTY-NINE

The Last Thread Unravels

July 2, 1996: I move one step closer to freedom. God help me. I went to Phoenix, to the second meeting for survivors of government mind control. There I learned about a mind-control machine, remote-controlled people and people who use their minds to enter terror programming into a computer. I have had visions of this machine under the Earth, beaming energy to induce fear and control people. It seems it might not be merely my vision. I talked with other survivors, something that always gives me a lot of validation, strength and courage.

July 10, 1996: More information on the government programming started coming up.

Delta 44/33/22/11
7643
2612
Delta 4396786
X-3482
Delta Z 4687
Delta B-4232
Delta Delta
Beta D 78643
Delta-2 876-54-2681
X-alpha
D Cross 342-876-733 (combination to a secured area)

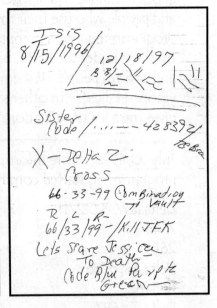

Omega findling
Cross patch
Light/7848392/B÷X-T
B/X-T
Delta cube
X73468
9265543876 Code Isis
Isis 8/15/1996 12/19/97
Sister code/428392/Zebra
X-delta Z Cross
66-33-99/kill JFK
Let's scare Jessica to death
Code Blue Purple Green

As I write this on January 24, 2002, a telepathic message from the Arcturian mothership tells me that a person who buys this book will know what these codes mean. This individual has the background, training and experience to decode this secret information. Once decoded, the results are to be passed on to a team who will deactivate the codes, which are linked to past events and plans for future events. The discrepancy you will discover in the codes is intentional to prevent the wrong people from breaking them. You will know there is a discrepancy; correct it, as you know the correct sequence. Do not contact me; it would put us both at risk. Just do the work you incarnated to do. Thank you for your service to humanity.

August 9, 1996: I was awake from 11 to 2:30 A.M. Rough night. Finally around 1:30 I meditated. I went to my safe place and to my guides. My guides sent me to a portal. I went back to the Air Force Academy. I've seen this big room with the locked vault and files before in my memories. I opened several files; then I opened a Delta file. Every time I opened a Delta file, I saw what happened. I saw planes blowing up, people in South America, leaders of peace being assassinated. I saw people injected in the middle of the night, military leaders who resisted killed in combat by their own men, terrorists in Ireland—all CIA Delta projects. When I pulled up a file, delta 32531 A O U Z, Patrick came. I went into the astral plane and with a luminescent sword, energetically deactivated some of the codes I had seen in Colorado Springs. I confronted the energy that gave power to these delta codes.

August 13, 1996: Another memory. At 5:30 A.M., I took a bath and meditated. I went to the Air Force Academy and recalled my initiation into the Delta Force. A syringe lay before the council of seven: four men and three women in a circular room. The American flag hung behind them. I stood on a circle in the center of a five-pointed star, in the center of the room with a light beaming down on me. I said the oath of allegiance with penalty of death and soul dismemberment as a consequence of disobedience. I pledged total allegiance and obedience. I went to the council and drank from a cup. I believed it was blood, but blood congeals, so it might have been something else. Then I knelt before each member. They placed their hands on my head. When I

Ode to the Wounded Mother

Oh, my child,
I call to you, to the four corners of the universe.
I, wounded woman, call my children home.
Oh, my child, I call to you, to the four corners of the universe.
My heart must heal.
My love for you, how could you know?
I call you home, to fill our dark void with love and light.
Oh, my child, I call to you, to the four corners of the universe.
We grew within the womb,
trusting, breathing, feeding, loving, as one.
We were born in joy, to be betrayed and lost to one another.
Oh, my child, I call to you, to the four corners of the universe.
Come home, to heal, so that our people may live.
Oh, my child, I call to you, to the four corners of the universe.
Mitakyue Oyasin.

reached the sixth one, he grabbed me by the hair, yelled "Liar!" and dragged me from the room. He said he had read my mind and knew I was lying. Then I was thrown in a sound chamber and bombarded with energy and beams. I screamed in agony—no place to go, no place to die, no way out. Finally, I vomited and collapsed. I was awakened; they rubbed my face in the vomit and made me clean it up. Another session: light beams, sound beams, energies. I couldn't see or hear; I just felt it rip through me. At last Delores came—the woman who had taken care of me when they brought me out of the environmental deprivation chamber I called the can. She told me I had another chance; she cleaned me up and put me in a new gown. I returned to complete the initiation. Oh, I knew in my heart that first I belonged to God, the divine God of Christ, not to them. Never to them.

September 2, 1996: I had a very powerful vision. I was taken to the galaxies, traveled beyond light and sound, to a temple on the mount. Within was a fountain, a garden and unconditional love. In the center was a tube like a centrifuge. I stepped within the cylinder of light and began to spin. As I did, I became a bubble of pure light energy; I floated casually, at ease, like a child in the womb. I floated through time and saw all the wounded mothers holding their children to their breasts. In love I came home and wrote the poem, "Ode to the Wounded Mother."

September 16, 1996: These past weeks I have been working with a Delta memory. It started on the 13 of August. I woke early and meditated, had the memory of being tied on a bed and being raped. Later in the week I went to my safe place and went through the portal to the Air Force Academy. I was at the committee—of nine this time—

who approved me before I signed the Delta contract. I was
to kneel before each of them and be asked a question. I got
to number nine. He made the sign of the cut throat. They
dragged me to the can and showed me where I'd been and
where I'd be put. I never knew what I had done "wrong."
They threw me into a tiny room and began an intense,
erratic frequency vibration. It drove me crazy. I banged my
head on the wall. Then it settled to a drone, and I blacked
out. When I came to, the one who was number nine
entered the room. Then the memory ended. I was
meditating in the bathtub. My body jolted and jumped, as
if I'd endured a cardiac resuscitation attempt. I came back in
prayer. I really suffered through this memory. At 2 A.M. I
awoke, still praying. I know I have broken the Delta
contract.

I journeyed back to Colorado Springs and retrieved the rest
of the memory, which was quite strange. The ninth
member of t he council was the alien I had seen before, the
one who turned his mind on the general and caused him to
shoot his companion. He had seemed well over six feet tall,
but now he appeared even taller, maybe seven feet in
height. Those strange Siamese cat eyes were unmistakable.
It was like meeting Satan in person. I don't remember
everything that happened. As was usual, I knelt before him,
to subject myself to his will (usually acted out by
performing fellatio, but I don't know if the creature even
had a penis). He put his fingers in my vagina and was sexual
with me. Then I was dressed in a nightgown and taken to a
room where prostitutes entertained the brass. It had a huge
circular bed. He was there. He chakra-raped me, sucking
my power from each of my chakras and my glands, leaving
me drained and empty. He tied my hands to the top of the
bed again and fingered my vagina. He said that he had put
himself in me, that I belonged to him. This is the false god,
male-perpetrator philosophy, what I had always resented in

some versions of Christian philosophy: hellfire and damnation; do as I say, or the ultimate being will destroy you, the power will be avenged and send you to hell. This was my last Delta test; then I signed the contract.

That's why I could never belong to a church that was full of damnation. My God is a living, loving God of freedom and of forgiveness—not one who would send people to hell. In my memory, I came back as a being of light and filled him, the alien, with Christ light. The next morning I woke at 3 A.M. and got up and bathed and meditated. I returned to the Delta memory as a force of lightning. I took sacred spring water and I brought the walls of Jericho down, to crumble; then I planted corn to heal the Earth.

October 1, 1996: In another vision, I went to a sweat lodge. A great Kodiak bear was running the lodge, and a wolf was the doorkeeper. I sat in the west facing the east, and they brought in these bright red stones. The lodge glowed from the lava rock being so hot. The bear leaned forward and ate me. Then he sent me down through the stones in the center of the pit of purification in the sweat lodge. I went down into the underworld. I entered into a cavern, and the claw of the beast darted out toward me. I was so frightened. I went back to my safe place, out through the sweat lodge and back to my sacred mountain. There Quanab told me no, that I had to go back. So I went back to the sweat lodge; the bear ate me again and sent me back to the underworld. This time I had my sword and shield. I touched the claw of the beast with my sword, and it turned into billions of little bits of light. I believe that within this vision lies the mythological expression of why I incarnated on this planet and who I am.

CHAPTER THIRTY

Old Man Coyote and the Ducks

October 8, 1996: No one needs another person to deceive him or her. We are our own worst enemies. How easily we humans fall prey to the illusion, how very gullible we are. The fact that we are so gullible is almost amusing. When I say we, I mean me. I am gullible. I am easily misled. I have poor discernment at times.

This journal entry reminds me of the story of Old Man Coyote and the Trickster. When I was a little girl, I would hear these stories; the Lakota people call him Ectomie, which also means the spider. From the time of creation, Old Man Coyote is the one who is sent to cause confusion and chaos, to trick us with our own gullibility and teach us our greatest lessons. Will we ever learn?

The story goes that Old Man Coyote was traveling through the forest, and he was very hungry. He always felt sorry for himself. He walked along, saying, "Oh, I'm so hungry, I don't know what I'm going to do; surely I'm going to die. I have to eat something. I haven't had anything to eat, and my stomach is shriveling."

He walked over to a rabbit hole and said, "Rabbit, would you please come out and let me eat you?" The rabbit called out, "Go away, Old Man Coyote; I'm not going to come out so you can eat me!" So Old Man Coyote kept walking, so sad, his head hanging low. Through the forest, he heard ducks. Walking closer, he saw a pond and some of the fattest and finest-looking ducks and geese he had ever seen. He said, "I don't have an arrow or a bow or a spear. I don't have any weapons. How on Earth am I going to get those ducks and geese to let me eat them? If I ask them, they will probably just tell me to get lost, like the rabbit did."

Then he came up with a plan. He put his blanket on the ground and loaded it with acorns, pinecones, sticks and leaves, until it looked as though he had a big bundle of stuff. He tied it up and slung it over his back, and he walked through the meadow where the ducks were, trying to ignore them. Since he wasn't paying attention to them, they became curious. They began following him, asking, "Old Man Coyote, what do you have in your bundle?" He said, "Oh, leave me alone; I'm busy. I'm going somewhere." The more he told them not to talk to him, the more curious they were about his bundle. Finally they said, "Oh please, Old Man Coyote, tell us what's in your bundle! Please?" He said, "Okay, dirty songs and dirty stories." At that, all of the ducks and geese got very excited: "Can we hear? Can we?" Old Man Coyote said, "No, you're too good and pure to hear these dirty songs and stories. I have to go off in the forest by myself so I can hear them." "Oh please," they begged. "Please let us hear just one dirty song, just one dirty story."

Finally, he said, "Well, I can't open up this bundle in the middle of the meadow; you have to build a lodge for me to open it. And when you build the lodge, we'll go in and I'll share one of my dirty songs and dirty stories with you." So they built the lodge, and they all went in and stood in a circle, and he placed the blanket down in the middle of the floor. Everybody was excited. Then he told them, "You have this instruction. Before I can open up this blanket, this is how we must do it. You all have to stand and close your eyes and dance around in a circle and sing a song: 'I, even I, sing and dance, it's true; I, even I, sing and dance with you.' Don't open up your eyes, whatever happens, because I have to do magic to open up this bundle, and then you'll get to see the dirty stories and dirty songs."

So the ducks, being very gullible, closed their eyes and started dancing around in a circle. He opened the blanket, quietly reached over, grabbed a duck, wrung his neck and threw him in the blanket. He thought to himself, "This is working pretty good!" He grabbed a young, tender little gosling goose, wrung her neck and threw her in the blanket. Another fat duck quickly followed. As he reached for the fourth one, she opened her eyes and squawked, "Everybody, quick! Old Man Coyote is going to kill us! Run for your life!"

All at once the whole lodge was filled with feathers, and ducks and geese were flying around making noise. Old Man Coyote jumped down in the middle of the blanket and covered up the three that he had caught and ran away. Well, they say that's why the mallard has a red eye, because she opened her eyes and warned the others that they were being tricked by Old Man Coyote. (Maybe I'm a mallard—I used to get red circles around my eyes. I'll take humor wherever I can find it.)

The story goes on: Old Man Coyote escaped during the chaos and went deep into the forest, where he dug a pit and built a big fire. He was so eager to eat the ducks and geese. When the coals were all bright, he wrapped one of the birds in clay and put it underneath the fire. He put the second one in clay and put it on the coals. Then he built a spit and put the third one over the coals so he could turn the spit and it would drip down, all juicy, and cook just like he liked it.

He was so tired from all that work that he leaned back to take a rest. The wind began to blow, and up above him, two tree branches were screeching. He said, "Oh please, tree branches, don't screech. I'm so happy, but I'm tired and need to rest." He kept begging, but they kept screeching. So he climbed up the tree to separate the branches. He put his fingers between them, and just as he did that, the wind blew really hard and caught his hand between the two branches. "Oh no! What am I to do now?" He could see his geese and ducks cooking on the fire; they smelled so good. He said, "Surely the wind will blow and set me free so that I can go down and claim my feast."

He sat in the tree for a long, long time. The birds were almost done when suddenly he saw, coming across the meadow, Old Man Coyote. (The coyote figure in myth has a lot to do with mirroring or doubling, so Old Man Coyote can be perceived as being in more than one place at once.) "Oh no, what am I going to do? If he smells these ducks and geese, he's going to come and eat them!" He thought and thought, and finally he came up with a plan. He called out, "Old Man Coyote, have a good journey! I hope you go wherever you're going fast and safe! But please don't come over and eat the duck I'm cooking on top of the fire!" Old Man Coyote hadn't even noticed until he heard that; then he smelled the aroma of cooking duck. He came over and obliged by eating the duck on top of the fire.

He burped and wiped his mouth and was getting ready to leave, when Old Man Coyote up in the tree said, "Oh thank you, my brother. You've left me the duck in clay on the coals." "You have another duck in clay on the coals?" Instantly, Old Man Coyote turned around and made a feast of the second duck. By now, Old Man Coyote in the tree was crying. He said, "Oh no! What am I to do? All that I have left is the goose under the fire. That's all you've left me, and I've worked so hard for my feast!" Of course, Old Man Coyote came back and ate the goose underneath the fire. Old Man Coyote spent the whole night in the tree, hungry and cold, before the wind came the next morning and set him free.

This is a myth that's proper for mankind. We call our own worst fears to us. We enter the lodge with the one who would destroy us, and we are curious to bring things to us that are sick and harmful. Through our own gullibility, we bring our own destruction to us. We mirror all those who would eat our feast. The secret government is working right under our noses, and we are blind to it. We do not choose to believe the truth, because we have been seduced into believing the lie. I pray that our society can wake up before Old Man Coyote wrings all of our necks for his greedy feast.

CHAPTER THIRTY-ONE

Crossing the Final Threshold

November 9, 1996: I have had an incredible healing from a Huichol shaman named Priciliano. He was directed by his spiritual elders, the guardians, to come to Santa Fe to do healing. Three people were supposed to receive healings, and I was the only one who showed up. I had never gone to a shaman for healing before, but I was guided that this was important. Well, the night before, an elder came to me in my dreams and interviewed me. Who was I? What did I want? Why had I come? Was I totally truthful? I was humbled by his presence, but it was so intense. He went over me with a fine-tooth comb.

I told him I never went to a shaman before, because I wouldn't work with one who violated women. I had heard warnings about shamans who take women's power, and I wanted to make sure I could trust him. I told him I wanted to speak the truth and had been doing so. I told him what the government had done to me. I said I knew their poison was like a magnet, attracting them to me and weakening me. I wanted to give my gift in clarity and safety—both for myself and others. I've had glimpses of the spirit world and am very respectful of the dangers; I don't take it lightly. I also knew I needed help to clear this, because it was in another dimension. I needed help from the other side.

The next morning, Friday, I woke up exhausted; fear was on the surface. I spent the day alone and in prayer. That night

I went to the shaman. The people there presented a documentary film that described the shaman as a nephew of the real Don Juan in the Carlos Castaneda books. According to their report, Castaneda had been with the Huichols, not the Yaquis. He put the Yaquis in the book to protect the family he had studied under. When Priciliano's uncle crossed over, he passed his medicine bundle to him. His uncle worked on the other side with people in dreamtime the night before their meeting (which is just what happened to me).

I learned a lot about Huichols, and I felt very good about this medicine man. The only way I can describe him is as a walking rainbow. He did a healing for me, and when he finished, he staggered a little. He said that he had lifted something from me, that it wasn't mine, but it had been put on me. He called it "mucho trabajo," much work.

I knew that this was an enormous step for me. Afterward, I rested and began to integrate what had happened. The elder who had come the night before appeared again. He thanked me and blessed me. He said he would help me and would always be there for me.

January 30, 1997: I had a vision where I was taken to the Cave of the Great Cobra. She showed me that the sky was spinning. She showed me that under the Earth, in caverns with crystals, lightbeings were aligning and transmitting with crystal devices. Then I saw the caverns where the fearmongers were, in distress. The fear energy they needed was not so available; their world of fear was collapsing in on itself. I saw all the other planet people waking up. I was told, "We have reached critical mass; there is a vast awakening." I saw the people of my cosmic being of light, the Arcturians; their alliance had come with huge ships, motherships, and placed them at the four corners of our solar system, beaming light energy into the core of Mother

Earth. It was projected back onto the surface. Lightworkers were transmitters of energy. An enormous energy shift was happening. This is the battle we are certain to complete in victory, because it is time—in the timeless sense. The numbers of the awakened ones are vast. Each one is a transmitter for high vibrational energy.

In February, I finally deprogrammed the chakra raping by the alien. Interestingly enough, in the journal I call this ET, Kahn.

February 1997: Mark this day in history—freedom is the permission to flow with the divine. Today I embrace the divine in totality, letting go of all that would bind me. I have deprogrammed Kahn's implant at the base of my tailbone; it looks like a grid, blocking the base chakra, implanted when I was coerced into signing the Delta contract. Kahn was the alien on the council, the heartless being to whom I could not give the right answer. After that incident, after being drugged and put into environmental deprivation, I was thrust into his bedchamber to please him. Afterward he called me "Earth girl." He rolled me over and blew into the base chakra, implanting the grid. He was confident that I would sign the contract and not be a risk, for the grid was electromagnetically related to his god, the intelligent life source at the heart (heartlessness) of his planet. He thought that with a certain frequency protection, I would once more be a robot. He felt smug and aloof.

Wrong! I dissolved that sucker. Then I sent his force back to him and soul-retrieved the spark of soul light he had taken from me. I brought it back to my sacred, safe place. I called for healing and redemption of the Air Force Academy. Then I integrated the entire experience with my therapist and balanced my energetics. It feels so good.

At the end of the session, I opened up my little red Bible and turned to a picture of Mary Magdalene washing Jesus'

The Lost Children

Children isolated, trapped in the silence of secret night torment,

gazing at one another with wide,

fearful eyes in the wordless promise of another world.

Permitted not the joys of comforting speech,

silently we waited in that cold, dark room,

never knowing who would be chosen to be taken to the place of pain or

when the footsteps would come to take us away.

When children are permitted, they will comfort one another,

yet this we were not permitted.

Silently we spent our nights awake or fretfully asleep,

to waken to the night cry of a child somewhere in the room or

the sound of the hard soles coming up the halls with echoing footsteps,

leaving an empty bed behind—

thankful this time it was not me.

How long the night?

An eternity to wait for the light of day.

No mother here to pat our weary faces,

no comfort but a bunk, sheet, army blanket and fear.

Then I saw you across the room from me,

your bunk below the wire-caged window,

a boy nearly my size.

You gazed at me with love radiating from your soul,

filling my dark night with hope.

My eyes returned the love, the gaze of hope.

Silently our eyes promised one another never, never to give up hope.

Silently our eyes promised to someday fly free as eagles do.

This promise made with silent eyes,

enduring forty years,

until by chance or what is fate,

our paths crossed once more,

to stand this night beneath the evening sky and

drum the Moon to rise above the gleaming peaks.

Our drums of freedom,

sending resonance of loving light to open the skies and lofty mountains.

We two eagles in free flight,

rejoicing in the failure of their plan to cage our hearts in fear.

feet. Today I wash my own feet, and I wash the feet of
Kahn. I forgive him; I embrace total compassion and
forgiveness. Hopefully, he will go to the Wizard of Oz and
get a heart!

This was a major step, because once I forgave him, I was free. I had fi-
nally gotten to the very root, the very core of the worst perpetration, be-
cause he had told me that he had some kind of power over me, the power
of the god of fear, and some part of me believed him. Once this illusion
was deprogrammed and I reached forgiveness on such a deep level, for-
giveness on every level became easier. I began coming into compassion.

At the age of fifty-two, I have done so much work in forgiveness that I
am not threatened by people who are still lost in fear. I know they have no
power over me. I have compassion for them, being stuck. I have forgiven
all my past perpetrators. Who do you think was the most important per-
son to forgive? Myself, of course. At one point, I was even angry with
God. I had to forgive him, because I knew I had agreed to do this. I am
part of God, and God is within my heart. To forgive God is to forgive my-
self. So the cycle of forgiveness—the key to freedom—began.

That summer, a friend came to visit, and something about her com-
panion triggered me. I processed through it and discovered that we had
been together at the Colorado Springs campus. I had flashbacks to the
dorm where the other children and I were kept during the experiments.

August 1997: We were forbidden to speak, punished if we
did. We would just look at one another, so lonely and
isolated, forbidden the grace of human comfort, never
knowing what would happen next. When people share a
common experience, there is a comradeship; ours was one
of silence and pain. His eyes and mine, silently promising
that someday our souls would be free. He does not
remember as I do. But the intensity of my feelings led to
the poem "The Lost Children" to try to capture this
enormous experience. I did a soul retrieval, bringing him to
a safe place.

September 5, 1997: Today Mother Teresa passed over; last
week, Princess Diana. I feel the cosmos shift. What has
been prophesied has come to be. We teeter on the very

> edge of the abyss. As a planet, a universe, a galaxy, we reach
> out for the ropes of the divine life to catch us, to swing us
> across the abyss to safety.

I became magnetized to sacred ceremonies. I kept hearing of some holy person who had come to give initiations—a Buddhist monk, a lama. I took the 21 Tara initiation and the Buddhist Five Precepts. I received initiations by a Tao priest and went to Native American ceremonies.

As I go through my journals, I find page after page relating visionary experiences and spiritual initiations, but no more recovered memories. There *is* one more, although I cannot find it in my journal. When I was working with the last memories of the Air Force Academy, I had a memory of a group of us teenagers who were dressed in gowns, like choir gowns. We were in trance, as if we were zombies, and walking down a ramp into a basement where there was an auditorium. An incredibly ugly being appeared on the stage. It was fat and disgusting—picture Jabba the Hutt. Children from the audience were being fed to him.

From the dark in the back of the room came lizard-looking people. They reminded me of the people I had seen during my rites of passage when I went into the demonic underworld. These were hunchbacked mutant creatures, Reptilian in nature. We had to have sexual contact with them, which was horrifying. Later I picked up David Icke's books *And the Truth Shall Set You Free* and *I Am Me I Am Free: The Robots' Guide to Freedom*, in which he speaks of the lizard people. Information began coming to me from other sources about the lizard people, or Reptilians. I learned from the Arcturians that the major underground Reptilian bases have left the planet. The years 1995 and 1996 correspond to the Mayan emergence from the nine hells to the thirteen heavens.

CHAPTER   THIRTY-TWO

The Past and Future Meet in the Now

In January of 1998, I went up to the Southern Ute Indians for a sweat lodge. I was reading one of David Icke's books on the way. I told my husband that I would meet David Icke. I wanted to meet him because he had said he wanted to talk to anybody who had experienced the kind of things that Kathy O'Brien had experienced. I tried to read her book, *Trance: Formation of America*, but found that it triggered me. (Remember, back in the introduction, when I warned you that information in this book might cause strong reactions that you would need to take seriously? Well, Kathy O'Brien's book had exactly that effect on me.) I did skim through it, however.

On the way up to Ignacio, my husband and I saw a white eagle. We sat beside the road and watched it for quite a while as it sat up in a tree. When I got back home, I called the number printed in the book and spoke to some people at Truth Seekers. I told them I had certain memories and wanted to discuss them with David Icke. They said that, being from the United Kingdom, he wasn't always in this country. I said, "Well, let me know when he is, because I want an appointment with him. I'll fly out to San Diego if I need to."

I did not have to do that, because he was coming to Santa Fe in March to speak at a Star Knowledge Conference. I volunteered to work at David's booth as a bookseller in order to have time with him and to get into the conference. I met several people who understood the level of work I was doing by that time: transmuting fear energy, neutralizing negative energy and clearing out vortexes and opening them up to heal.

I did get to talk with David at the gathering and found that I liked him. Even though I do not endorse all of his material, he has done an important job of getting the public to believe the unbelievable. I also met a psychologist I will just call Dr. Richard. The moment I met this man, I felt totally safe with him. I spoke of my experiences in the covert government. I even told him about Patrick. I was guided to have a session with him and recovered some sensitive information by accessing Patrick. I was told at the time that it was very top-secret information. At the time, in March of

1998, Laiolin said that she couldn't protect my life if I spoke to anyone about it. Now I'm being guided that it's all right to talk about it, because the danger has passed.

I recovered two pieces of information. One was a plan for what was called the Delta Dawn. It was supposed to be in June of 1999 (as I realized later, triggered by the Columbine High School incident). I figured that out later, because in 1998, I knew the Delta Dawn was supposed to be in June of 1999 and then the Columbine event happened in April of that year. All over the country, there were Deltas programmed with subconscious contracts with the government. The Deltas were to be triggered for a massive uprising, including events like Columbine, the Oklahoma City bombing, shootings in restaurants and schools and other acts of domestic terrorism. These first ones were intended to terror-program the psyche of the masses.

This shows how vital the work we are doing is to come to a state of unconditional love and compassion and to ascend into a love vibration. Gregg Braden says in his book, *Awakening to Zero Point*, that the megahertz of fear are lower than the megahertz of love. All these awakened people who are joining together with Gregg Braden and James Twyman for global peace prayers are influencing the frequencies on the planet, counterbalancing low-vibrational frequency emanations.

Negative-vibration generators are weakened by people awakening to a higher state of consciousness and emanating the pure love and joy vibration. Some people know how to deactivate the frequency generators, the psychotronic weaponry. A frequency was planned to activate the programs electromagnetically in the Deltas. This made sense to me, because it reflected my own experience. I recalled electromagnetic programming and altering my brain through electromagnetic programming. Once I changed my own frequencies and ascended from the fear vibration into a higher-vibrational energy, which is the Christ consciousness, I was no longer accessible to them. That's how simple it is. As long as I was afraid, the fear vibration could be linked with the low-density frequencies that were being put out. As I emanated into the Christ vibration, I was no longer available.

I believe that the vibrations of our planet are shifting and that the fear grid placed around our planet is deteriorating. I recently said during a radio interview that the planet is receiving a massive amount of cosmic energy. The interviewer said that thirty-five years ago, scientists discovered that the Earth was indeed receiving massive amounts of energy, possibly from the center of the universe. No one had a clue how this would affect humanity. Now we can see that one effect was to wake us up. Another was to provide the energy for a critical mass of individuals to make significant changes in the vibrations of the planet. Give Mother Earth credit here, too; her little heart is pumping away. She is tired of the fear and deception and is ready for a change.

I see from my visions that the Second Coming of Christ is the awakening of the Christ consciousness within the hearts of humanity. I've been told that prophets will be on the street corner and in the marketplace, that we will no longer look only to spiritual leaders for wisdom and guidance, but that we will establish a connection from our hearts directly to the Creator.

The plan to trigger the Delta Dawn backfired, because people all over the country came together in love. Columbine High School became a gathering of souls for the cause of love, to protect our children. A great deal of fear surrounded that event, but people didn't let themselves surrender to the fear. Their strength and resolve, in combination with the vibrational enhancement of the whole planet, sabotaged the plan.

On August 12 of 2001, I retrieved information about the second wave of the Delta Dawn, involving major acts of terrorism all over the world. I was given the date of September 10. I was told that much of the program was defrequencied. I was relieved when September 10 passed without incident. Then came September 11. Strange as it might sound, I gave thanks that it wasn't worse. The intent of the covert government was to cause massive panic, giving the excuse to implement martial law. Martial law *was* enforced in Florida. The national patriotism propaganda was planned well in advance. Think about it: How did all that patriotic merchandise appear so quickly? The intent was to flood the market with false patriotism, have a nuclear war and implement martial law—all in one sweep. The good news is it didn't happen. What did happen? The heart chakra of America—of the whole world—was opened up. One hundred thousand people held a spontaneous peace vigil in Berlin. You have heard story after story of bravery, love and compassion following the attacks. Why did that not happen when thousands of people were being massacred in Cambodia? Or countless other times when people were numb to human suffering? But we all felt the pain of September 11. Could it be that we are waking up?

Another piece of information I recovered from the session with Dr. Richard in 1998 was the plan to release an Armageddon virus in August of that year. Sarin nerve gas in the Tokyo subway, hunta virus in the Southwest, legionnaires' disease, the chemtrails and AIDS are all experiments in the Armageddon virus—part of the plan for the New World Order that is not going to succeed. The release of these viruses, including spraying via chemtrails, was planned as early as the 1960s. This can now be revealed, because the major threat has been deactivated with the assistance of the Arcturians and Earth-based scientists. The AIDS epidemic has taken a horrid toll, but the Armageddon plan was much more massive, viruses that would make the bubonic plague look like a simple cold. The master plan was to weaken people's psyches for complete control of the masses. The surviving population would be terrified and willing to accept complete governmental control.

But it didn't work. It is too late; we are bound for freedom. Mother Earth is birthing a new world of peace. There's still a lot of work to be done; so much suffering exists on this planet. The ones who would hold this planet in fear are still doing their best. We have entered point zero; the time of the shift of the ages is at hand.

Although the fear grid is breaking down, it is still strong in many areas, held in place by war, poverty, famine and genocide. The fear is left imprinted on the Earth's grid system. One of the ways this is done is by trapping souls. Through death-fear-sex ceremonies, the Dark Lord acquires the energy to manipulate the dimensions, creating a tear in the etheric and astral planes, opening a portal between the worlds. Souls are trapped not only in Satanic ceremonies, but in every instance of horror or mass extinction. Enough trapped souls in a certain area create a dense vibrational field, making other people in the vicinity more prone to crime, depression, suicide and racial hatred—all caused by extreme fear.

The souls must be released and the fear energy transmuted in these areas. You might know of lightworkers pursuing this work. When one of these energy fields is cleared, the Earth can produce resonating frequencies of rejuvenation. Where I live, this work has been so successful that crime rates have dropped fifty percent, according to news reports. The change is noticeable. As more areas are cleared, vortexes are opened and the vibration of the planet increases. As the love—or Christ—vibration increases, people naturally begin making better choices. They are attracted to activities, places and people of a higher vibration. I predict that we will see a marked change within the next decade. The popularity of violent movies will decline, crime rates will drop and industries that support violence will fail. Satanic cults will lose their grip on the psyches of those they now control.

The transformation of this planet, the prophecies say, will happen in the next seven generations. We are in the times of purification, the times referred to in the book of Revelation. The Hopi prophecy tells us we can choose a gentle path or severe purification. Every single person is important to critical mass. As a Hopi elder recently said, "We are the ones we have been waiting for." We are now planting the seeds, laying the groundwork for that transformation. The psyche of the planet is evolving; we are awakening to a higher state of consciousness.

I thank God that not everybody has to make the journey I made. I believe that I am part of a soul group who agreed to make this journey to shift the paradigm. If I had to do it all over again, I would—in a minute. I made the journey into the darkest part of society. I lived to recover, become strong, awaken spiritually and tell my story. I knew this several years ago, that I had to struggle, step by step, through these grueling body memories and troubles, defying terror at every turn of the road. I felt that I was making the journey for others, and I predicted several years ago that new techniques would emerge to help people clear this energy without having to go through the terror of remembering. Now there are. I do not believe that remembering is what makes people well. I have seen too many survivors who start remembering and get trapped in fear. No, the secret to healing is in vibration, in clearing dense energy blockages and allowing the aura, the soul, the essence of self to move into freedom. Freedom comes from a change of the vibrational field to the vibration of pure Christ light or enlightenment. I am not saying that we all have to become enlightened to be free, but rather that the path of enlightenment and the path of soul freedom are one and the same.

Just as I knew years ago that new techniques would help people move through this process more gently, now I'm being shown this incredible healing in my visions. There are new healing modalities: sound/vibration, angelic music, essential oils, flower essences, dolphin essences. When I first found an implant in myself and learned to deactivate it, nobody was talking about that; now lots of people are suddenly clearing implants. Not all these modalities are readily available to the general public, but they will be. Herbs are now sold at Wal-Mart. We are entering a renaissance of healing and awakening.

CHAPTER   THIRTY-THREE

Sun Dance Visions of World Healing

In July of 1998, I attended the Southern Ute Sun dance in Ignacio, Colorado. The Southern Ute do not pierce like the northern tribes; the men dance for days without food or water as they pray for a vision. My former husband was dancing; I was there to support his pledge. I served in the camp of Grandma Bertha and Grandpa Vincent. I had just returned from a vision quest with a Mayan priest myself and had slept very little.

Grandma Bertha had asked me to sing with the Ute women, and I was with them when one of the dancers went to the pole and I had a vision. The Sun dancer went up a golden set of steps. At the top was a golden doorway. Christ stood in the doorway with his hand outstretched. The Sun dancer walked into Christ.

Christ turned around, walked over to a throne and became a white eagle, which spread its wings and flew across what is called Turtle Island, this continent. As it flew, from its belly there came a stream of little white birds—small eagles or doves. They flew to the four directions in four streams, almost like ribbons. At each corner of the four directions, they did indeed bring back a ribbon of each color of the four races: red, black, white and yellow. They made a ball and flew underneath, at the eagle's talons, into the belly of the eagle. The eagle then flew to Hawaii, across a volcano, across a spring. It came at last to a great cave and spiraled down into the Cave of the Great Cobra.

Two weeks before that Sun dance, I had been with Ammachi, the beloved Hindu saint, receiving darshan. I had a vision of the emergence of the fountain of life of the divine feminine in the center of the Cave of the Great Cobra. The heart and trust and faith of all the women on this planet emerged from that fountain. Afterward, there was a spring in the center of the Cave of the Great Cobra. As the white eagle flew into the Great Cobra's cave, it dropped that ball into the spring. I looked around and saw many people of many clans. Everybody was celebrating, and as we watched, a great tree of peace emerged from that spring.

I was filled with prayer and wonder. Before our very eyes, the Earth split and the tree rose to the surface. I found myself with my husband, standing beneath that great tree of peace. The people stood in a circle around the tree; they stood in quadrants, forming a circle and a cross. The Asian people stood between the east and the south; the red people, the Native Americans, were standing between the south and the west; the African-Americans stood between the west and the north; the Caucasians between the north and the east. So it was yellow, red, black and white, all standing separate but in one circle. Then my husband and I began a snake dance, and as we wound between the people and they followed us, we kept dancing until the people stood together as a rainbow nation, in unity through diversity, all as a family of man. Then we led a traditional Hispanic wedding dance called the Marcha, and then we went into a spiral dance. As we all spiraled in, we touched the Great Tree of the White Roots of Peace. Then I opened up my eyes.

Every morning at the Sun dance, people gather before sunrise and the Sun dancers blow their eagle-bone whistles. Everyone faces the east and waits for the Sun to rise. When the Sun first crests the mountain, we bless ourselves with the first rays of the morning Sun. On the last day, I faced the east, and the eagle-bone whistles blew. I closed my eyes and saw all the victims of genocide on the planet rise from their graves of sorrow. They rose up, and as they rose, they transformed from the degradation of death and sorrow to an assembly of their cultures, standing in their traditional dress. They brought their grandmothers and grandchildren, the grandfathers, mothers and sons, the daughters and the fathers. They came dressed as Scots and as Greeks, as Africans and South Americans and Hawaiians. They were all coming to that Sun dance to celebrate the resurrection, to celebrate Mother Earth's resurrection from a place of great despair to be birthed into a new world of freedom, peace and healing.

The last ones came from the Middle East, all dressed in white and carrying flowers. Beloved Gandhi and his wife, Ba, led them. They were so beautiful. As Gandhi and his wife were right in front of me, I saw their smiling faces.

Just as the Sun began to crest the mountain, I opened my eyes and greeted a new day. I blessed myself with the rays of our Sun Father. My heart is filled with prayers of thanksgiving and praise for this beautiful vision.

WELLS FARGO

Date:	08/14/16
Time:	11:22 AM
Location:	BALLARD
ATM:	6901E

Customer Card:	XXXXXXX0534
Transaction #:	5545
Transaction:	Deposit To Checking
Amount:	$565.00
To:	Checking X-8751
Deposit Credit Date:	08/15/16

Available Balance:	$4,336.32

Deposit will be available:

Date	Amount
08/14/16	$400.00
08/16/16	$165.00
Total Deposit	$565.00

Deposited Checks:

1.	Check No.:1415	$125.00
2.	Check No.:7538	$145.00
3.	Check No.:6458	$215.00
4.	Check No.:7534	$80.00

Thank you for banking with Wells Fargo.
For questions, call 1-800-869-3557
Business customers call 1-800-225-5935

business. We are grateful you
have chosen us.

Go to *wellsfargo.com/locator* to find
ATMs and retail banking stores near you

24/7 Customer Service
1-800-TO-WELLS (1-800-869-3557)

Thank you for using our ATM.
We appreciate your business.

NSM-210WW-0715

EPILOGUE

A Final Thought

People have risen up at many times in history, in revolutions too numerous to count, only to be put back into bondage because they rose up through fighting, through war, through destruction. I do believe the rule of the universe is that when evil fights evil, when there is violence against violence, more evil is born. The final freedom will be won when an army of people rises up and refuses to be controlled by fear. These rainbow warriors will refuse to fight the dirty wars, refuse to hate one another. These warriors will embrace peace, love and brotherhood, carrying the sword of truth and the shield of unconditional love. They will enter into the new vibration, into a state of consciousness where individuals no longer participate in the destruction of our planet. When that change happens on the grass-roots level, our world will change.

Recent visions have shown me that we will have peace in the Holy Land when the Holy Mother brings the warring brothers to the table to feast. News reports tell of some soldiers in the Mideast who laid down their weapons and refused to fight. This is a good start.

One of the steps toward that change is to open up our minds to the truth. You must know that I'm sharing an intimate part of myself, and I'm taking a risk when I do that. I know most survivors would never bare their souls to people the way I am doing to you, my readers. My prayer is that you'll open up your hearts to me. I pray that you'll feel my story, that you'll hear my song of freedom, that you will know deep in your hearts I speak the truth. And as we all know, the truth will set us free.

I pray that someday the truth about the secret government mind-control experiments will come to light, that I will have an opportunity to stand before Congress, the UN, the world court, and testify— and be heard. I pray for the consciousness of our society to rise to the point where these atrocities are no longer tolerated. My freedom is not enough.

Thank you for having the courage to journey with me to the abyss, the courage to enter a place of such dark despair. Thank you for journeying with me to the place of healing. I know this book has not been easy to read. Nor has it been easy for me to go back and relive those experiences. When I first opened up those journals, I felt a sense of shock and terror. I didn't want to go back and look at it all again. But in my heart was a resolve: my story needed to be told. And my story is our story. Blessed be.

Wakan Tanka, Great Mystery,
I offer this song of my soul,
my story, as a prayer.
I pray for healing
for my people,
all of the children of Mother Earth.
I pray that a day comes
when we "the people"
no longer live under
the shadow of fear.
I pray that I might
be an instrument of your peace,
that in some way, Creator God,
my truth is carried
by the wings of eagles
to be received in
the hearts of humanity.
Lord, help us to free ourselves
from this ancient bondage.
Help us to awaken a new world
of peace and freedom—that the children
shall suffer no more.
Oh! Mitakyue Oyasin,
we are all related.

A P P E N D I X   A

The Advisory Committee
on Human Radiation Experiments

Included in this appendix is pertinent information associated with the Advisory Committee on Human Radiation Experiments. All of this information is public record.

These documents should be available on the Internet by searching the title of the Advisory Committee and typing in the date March 15, 1995. I testified under the name Suzzanne Starr. I have a copy of a video of my testimony, which can be made available for educational purposes.

[Editor's Note: The information contained in Appendix A has been reprinted directly from original documents and therefore has not been edited.]

APPENDIX A

PART 1
The Advisory Committee's
Official Statement

ADVISORY COMMITTEE ON HUMAN RADIATION EXPERIMENTS
1726 M STREET, N.W., SUITE 600
WASHINGTON, D.C. 20036

The Advisory Committee on Human Radiation Experiments is a 14-member committee of nationally recognized experts in the areas of bioethics, history of science, radiation biology and oncology, epidemiology, law and nuclear medicine. The Committee also includes a public representative. Appointed by the President in April 1994, the members are to prepare a report, due in 1995, about the use of human beings as subjects of federally funded research using ionizing radiation. Ruth Faden, Ph.D., M.P.H., a bioethicist at Johns Hopkins University, chairs the Advisory Committee.

The Committee's report will be issued to an Interagency Working Group composed of the secretaries of the departments of Defense, Energy, Health and Human Services, Justice, and Veterans Affairs, and the directors of the Central Intelligence Agency and the Office of .Management and Budget, and the administrator of the National Aeronautics and Space Administration.

The Committee's charter includes the investigation of experiments conducted since 1944 with ionizing radiation, the investigation of specific intentional releases of radiation into the environment, and the recommendation to the working group of remedies for abuses of human subjects in past experiments, and of policies to improve ethical practices in today's research.

The Committee held its first meeting in April 1994 and has met approximately monthly since. A staff of professionals in history, bioethics, nuclear medicine and epidemiology works in Washington, D.C., under the Committee's direction. The staff is headed by Executive Director Dan Guttman. Stephen Klaidman is spokesman for the Committee.

The Advisory Committee's meetings are public and materials presented to members of the Committee at its meetings become public record. The Committee's schedule includes at least one meeting on the West Coast and also includes meetings of panels to hear testimony at other sites in the United States.

ADVISORY COMMITTEE ON HUMAN RADIATION EXPERIMENTS
1726 M STREET, N.W., SUITE 600
WASHINGTON, D.C. 20036

Why was the Advisory Committee formed?

The President of the United States appointed the Committee to analyze these questions: What is the federal government's responsibility for wrongs and harms to human subjects as a result of experiments with ionizing radiation? What remedies are appropriate for those wronged or harmed? And what lessons learned from studying research standards and practices in the past and present can be applied to the future?

Who are members of the Advisory Committee?

The 14 members are nationally recognized experts in bioethics, epidemiology, radiation oncology and biology, history of science, law and nuclear medicine. The Committee also includes a citizen representative. Ruth Faden, a bioethicist at Johns Hopkins University, chairs the Advisory Committee.

What is the Committee authorized to review?

The Committee's charter includes the review of experiments conducted since the 1940s with ionizing radiation and the investigation of specific intentional releases of radiation into the environment.

The Committee's mandate does not include common and routine clinical practices, such as established diagnosis and treatment methods. An important question is how to define the difference between ordinary practice and experimental procedures.

Another important question is whether accidental exposures gave agencies or researchers a chance to conduct "experiments of opportunity."

What will the Advisory Committee do?

The members will prepare a report designed to answer the three questions posed above. The report will be issued in 1995 to an Interagency Working Group composed of the secretaries of the departments of Defense, Energy, Health and Human Services, Justice, and Veterans Affairs, and the directors of the Central Intelligence Agency and the Office of Management and Budget, and the administrator of the National Aeronautics and Space Administration.

How will the Advisory Committee evaluate today's practices?

A sample of research protocols funded by federal agencies in fiscal year 1993 is being used to assess ethical standards and procedures in today's environment. Researchers and subjects of research will be interviewed.

How has the Committee looked into past practices?

The President directed federal agencies to search their files for information about research on human subjects in the past. This process has been revised and expanded under the Committee's direction. Literally thousands of documents, many previously unreported and some of them only declassified this year, have been made available to the public as a result of this effort.

Many documents are, of course, fragmentary accounts of experiments. Recreating the ethics policies, standards and practices of 40 or 50 years ago is difficult, much less recreating the conversations between subjects and researchers.

The Advisory Committee has reviewed many private collections left by subjects of experiments and by researchers.

How has the Committee responded to public concern about these experiments?

The Committee recognizes the importance of hearing directly from people throughout the country and including them in its activities. The Committee seeks out participants in past experiments to hear about their experiences and use their recollections to guide its research and inform its judgments.

In addition to soliciting the views of subjects and other interested parties at its Washington meetings, the Committee has scheduled public meetings around the country to hear first-hand from persons involved in research. The Committee has gained valuable documents and insights from working with subjects or their families, as well as researchers, and that process will continue throughout the life of the Committee's work.

What are key questions about experimentation?

The Committee must define the boundaries of experimentation. What is an experiment? How does it differ from innovative treatment? How does it differ from training, as in the case of military units participating in atomic weapons tests in the 1950s? When is an experiment over? Each question bears on the scope of the Committee's endeavors and the way it evaluates the evidence before it.

What are the ethical questions in research?

The issues to be weighed by the Committee are many and complex. These include the risks or harm to the subject, and the benefit to the subject or to society as a whole; whether subject populations have been chosen fairly and appropriately; whether subjects have been fully informed and have fully consented to participate in research.

The Committee has discovered more extensive ethical codes and policies in the government than had previously been known. It's not always clear whether they were applied, or how they were interpreted in different circumstances. These codes and policies, however, are critical to the determination of whether experiment subjects were appropriately informed of risks or harms, and selected fairly for the purposes of experimentation.

How can people contact the Committee?

The Committee staff can be reached by telephone at 202/254-9795 or in writing at 1726 M Street NW, Suite 600, Washington, D.C. 20036.

A P P E N D I X   A

PART 2
Excerpts from Testimonies
to the Advisory Committee

ADVISORY COMMITTEE ON HUMAN RADIATION EXPERIMENTS
1726 M STREET, N.W., SUITE 600
WASHINGTON, D.C. 20036

Public Comment Participants

March 15, 1995
1:00 p.m. - 3:15 p.m.

1. Dr. Ernest J. Sternglass, University of Pittsburgh

2. Mrs. Elmerine Whitfield Bell, Dallas, TX

3. Mr. Steve Schwartz, Washington, D.C.

4. Mr. Cooper Brown, National Association
   of Radiation Victims

5. Dr. Oscar Rosen, National Association
   of Atomic Veterans

6. Mr. Glenn Alcalay, New York, NY

7. Ms. Denise Nelson, Bethesda, MD

8. Ms. Chris DeNicola. Ms. Valerie Wolf,
   and Ms. Claudia Mullen, New Orleans, LA

9. Ms. Suzzanne Starr. Chimayo, NM

Excerpts
from

United States of America
Advisory Committee on Human Radiation Experiments

Wednesday
March 15, 1998

Subject: MKULTRA and Radiation Experiments

Testimonies by:

Chris DeNicola
Valerie Wolf
Claudia Mullen
Suzzanne Starr

Also includes a letter dated December 19, 1995 from President Clinton
concerning the Task Force on Radiation and Human Rights

UNITED STATES OF AMERICA
ADVISORY COMMITTEE ON HUMAN RADIATION EXPERIMENTS

(PUBLIC MEETING)

Executive Chambers
The Madison Hotel
15th and M Streets, NW
Washington, D.C.

Wednesday,
March 15, 1995

1:00 p.m.

Advisory Committee Members:

RUTH R. FADEN, PH.D., M.P.H. - CHAIR
KENNETH R. FEINBERG, J.D.
ELI GLATSTEIN, M.D.
DR. JAY KATZ
PATRICIA A. KING, J.D.
SUSAN E. LEDERER, PH.D.
RUTH MACKLIN, PH.D.
LOIS L. NORRIS
NANCY L. OLEINICK, PH.D.
HENRY D. ROYAL, M.D.
DUNCAN C. THOMAS, PH.D.
REED V. TUCKSON, M.D.

Staff Members:

DAN GUTTMAN
ANNA MASTROIANNI

A G E N D A

P R O C E E D I N G S

1:00 p.m.

Opening Remarks

DR. FADEN: Good morning. Excuse me. I'm used to the meeting starting in the morning. Good afternoon.

We have Phil Caplan from the White House to open the meeting, please, officially.

MR. CAPLAN: Good afternoon. As the designated federal official for the Advisory Committee, I declare this meeting open.

DR. FADEN: Thank you. Thank you, Phil.

I can't decide if we're happier to see him in the beginning, when the meeting starts, or at the end when he closes it. When is he more welcomed.

Well, welcome to everyone here. This is the 12th meeting. Is it the 12th meeting? Yes, the 12th meeting. Okay. Scary thought. This is the 12th meeting of the Advisory Committee on Human Radiation Experiments. Welcome, everyone here. We've had a change of venue. So, I trust everybody could find The Madison. We were almost getting to feel at home in the last hotel we were in, and we're now here.

We have a very packed agenda. The meeting begins this afternoon and goes through all day Thursday and all day Friday. It's been typical for me to start the meetings with a kind of quick overview of what we were hoping to accomplish in this particular meeting, and let me just do that, run down and go straight to our important subject for today, which is Public Comment.

One objective of today's meeting, as is true for all our meetings and for our small panel meetings throughout the country, is to hear from members of the public, anyone who wishes

DR. THOMAS: I've heard reference to this document before, and I haven't seen it either. I don't know whether the staff has.

I have the vague recollection that --

MS. NELSON: I would like to find it out myself. I'd like to see the original.

DR. THOMAS: Yes. Me, too, because I --

MS. NELSON: Yes.

DR. THOMAS: -- have heard reference to an earlier discussion, where someone, and I don't recall whom, was saying that that statement was referring to the land and not to the people, and I think it's really important to get to the bottom of that.

MS. NELSON: Well, there are actually two statements: One was a low-use segment of the population, and another one was virtually uninhabited.

DR. THOMAS: Well, if anyone, yourself or any of the other members of the audience, can point us in the direction of the original documents, it would --

MS. NELSON: Okay. I will make a note of it.

DR. THOMAS: -- be very important for us.

MS. NELSON: I will make a note of that, to look those up for you.

DR. FADEN: Thank you very much, Ms. Nelson.

MS. NELSON: Thank you.

DR. FADEN: We appreciate it.

We next have a panel of people who have asked to present, and again please forgive me if I'm not pronouncing people's names correctly, but we have Ms. Chris DeNicola, Ms. Valerie Wolf, and Ms. Claudia Mullen. Are you all of New Orleans, is that correct?

MS. WOLF: Yes, that is correct.

DR. FADEN: Thank you for making the effort to come up to speak to us today.

Statement of Chris DeNicola, Valerie Wolf and

Claudia Mullen, New Orleans, Louisiana

MS. WOLF: Okay. I'm going to start. My name is Valerie Wolf.

In listening to the testimony today, it all sounds really familiar. I am here to talk about a possible link between radiation and mind-control experimentation that began in the late 1940s.

The main reason that mind-control research is being mentioned is because people are alleging that they were exposed as children to mind-control radiation drugs and chemical experimentation, which were administered by the same doctors who are known to have been involved in conducting both radiation and mind-control research.

Written documentation has been provided revealing the names of people and the names of research projects in statements from people across the country.

It is also important to understand that mind-control techniques and follow-ups into adulthood may have been used to intimidate these particular research subjects into not talking about their victimization in government research.

As a therapist for the past 22 years, I have specialized in treating victims and perpetrators of trauma and their families. When word got out that I was appearing at this hearing, nearly 40 therapists across the country, and I had about a week and a half to prepare, contacted me to talk about clients who had reported being subjects in radiation and mind-control experiments.

The consistency of people's stories about the purpose of the mind-control and pain-induction techniques, such as electric shock, use of hallucinogens, sensory deprivation, hypnosis, dislocation of limbs and sexual abuse, is remarkable.

There is almost nothing published on this aspect of mind-control used with children, and these clients come from all over the country, having had no contact with each other.

What was startlingly was that therapists reported many of these clients were also physically ill with auto-immune problems, thyroid problems, multiple sclerosis, and other muscle and connective tissue diseases as well as mysterious ailments for which a diagnosis cannot be found.

While somatization disorder is commonly found in these clients, many of the clients who have been involved in the human experimentation with the government have multiple medically-documented physical ailments, and I was really shocked today to hear one of the speakers talk about the cysts and the teeth breaking off, because I have a client that that's happening to.

Many people are afraid to tell their doctors their histories as mind-control subjects for fear of being considered to be crazy. These clients have named some of the same people, particularly a Dr. Green, who was associated with clients' reports of childhood induction of pain, mind-control techniques, and childhood sexual abuse.

One of my clients, who had seen him with a name tag, identified him as Dr. L. Wilson Green. A person with this same name was the scientific director of the Chemical and Radiological Laboratories at the Army Chemical Center, and that he was engaged in doing research for the Army and other intelligence agencies.

Other names that have come to light are Dr. Sidney Gottlieb and Dr. Martin Orne, who, it is reported, were also involved in radiation research.

It needs to be made clear that people have remembered these names and events spontaneously with free recall and without the use of any memory-retrievable techniques, such as hypnosis. As much as possible, we have tried to verify the memories with family members, records and experts in the field.

Many attempts have been made through Freedom of Information Act filings to gain access to the mind-control research documentation. These requests have generally been slowed down or denied, although some information has been obtained, which suggests that at least some of the information supplied by these clients is true.

It is important that we obtain all of the information contained in the CIA and military files to verify or deny our clients' memories. Although many of the files for MK Ultra may have been destroyed, whatever is left, along with the files for other projects, such as Bluebird and Artichoke, to name only two, contain valuable information.

Furthermore, if, as the evidence suggests, some of these people were used in radiation experiments, there might be information in the mind-control experiment file on radiation experiments.

We need this information to help in the rehabilitation and treatment of many people who have severe psychological and medical problems which interfere with their social, emotional and financial well-being.

Finally, I urge you to recommend an investigation into these matters. Although there was a commission on mind-control, it did not include experiments on children because most of them were too young or still involved in the research in the late 1970s to come forward.

The only way to end the harassment and suffering of these people is to make public what has happened to them in the mind-control experiments. Please recommend that there be an investigation and that the files be opened on the mind-control experiments as they related to children.

Thank you.

DR. FADEN: Thank you.

MS. DeNICOLA: Good afternoon. I'm Christine DeNicola, born July 1962, rendering me 32 years of age.

I was a subject in radiation as well as mind-control and drug experiments performed by a man I knew as Dr. Green.

My parents were divorced around 1966, and Donald Richard Ebner, my natural father, was involved with Dr. Green in the experiments. I was a subject from 1966 to 1976. Dr. Green performed radiation experiments on me in 1970, focusing on my neck, throat and chest in 1972, focusing on my chest and my uterus in 1975.

Each time I became dizzy, nauseous and threw up. All these experiments were performed on me in conjunction with mind-control techniques and drugs in Tucson, Arizona.

Dr. Green was using me mostly as a mind-control subject from 1966 to 1973. His objective was to gain control of my mind and train me to be a spy assassin. The first significant memory took place at Kansas City University in 1966. Don Ebner took me there by plane when my mom was out of town. I was in what looked like a laboratory, and there seemed to be other children. I was strapped down, naked, spread-eagle on a table, on my back.

Dr. Green had electrodes on my body, including my head. He used what looked like an overhead projector and repeatedly said he was burning different images into my brain while a red light flashed aimed at my forehead.

In between each sequence, he used electric shock on my body and told me to go deeper and deeper, while repeating each image would go deeper into my brain, and I would do whatever he told me to do.

I felt drugged because he had given me a shot before he started the procedure. When it was over, he gave me another shot. The next thing I remember, I was with my grandparents again in Tucson, Arizona. I was four years old.

You can see from this experiment that Dr. Green used trauma, drugs, post-hypnotic suggestion and more trauma in an effort to gain total control of my mind. He used me in radiation experiments, both for the purposes of determining the effects of radiation on various parts of my body and to terrorize me as an additional trauma in the mind-control experiments.

The rest of the experiments took place in Tucson, Arizona, out in the desert. I was taught how to pick locks, be secretive, use my photographic memory, and a technique to withhold information by repeating numbers to myself.

Dr. Green moved on to wanting me to kill dolls that looked like real children. I stabbed a doll with a spear once after being severely traumatized, but the next time, I refused. He used many pain-induction techniques, but as I got older, I resisted more and more.

He often tied me down in a cage, which was near his office. Between 1972 and 1976, he and his assistants were sometimes careless and left the cage unlocked. Whenever physically possible, I snuck into his office and found files with reports and memos addressed to CIA and military personnel.

Included in these files were project, sub-project, subject and experiment names with some code numbers for radiation and mind-control experiments, which I have submitted in your written documentation.

I was caught twice, and Dr. Green ruthlessly used electric shock, drugs, spun me on a table, put shots in my stomach and my back, dislocated my joints, and hypnotic techniques to make me feel crazy and suicidal.

Because of my rebellion and growing lack of cooperation, they gave up on me as a spy assassin. Consequently, the last two years, 1974 to 1976, Dr. Green used various mind-control techniques to reverse the spy assassin messages, to self-destruct and death messages.

His purpose. He wanted me dead, and I have struggled to stay alive all of my adult life, all of my adult life. I believe it is by the grace of God that I am still alive.

These horrible experiments have profoundly affected my life. I developed multiple personality disorder because Dr. Green's goal was to split my mind into as many parts as possible so he could control me totally. He failed. But I've had to endure years of constant physical, mental and emotional pain even to this day.

I've been in therapy consistently for 12 years, and it wasn't until I found my current therapist two and a half years ago, who had knowledge of the mind-control experiments, that I finally have been able to make real progress and begin to heal.

In closing, I ask that you keep in mind that the memories I have described are but a glimpse of the countless others that took place over the 10 years between 1966 and 1976, that they weren't just radiation but mind-control and drug experiments as well.

I have included more detailed information of what I remember in your written documentation. Please help us by recommending an investigation and making the information available so that therapists and other mental health professionals can help more people like myself.

I know I can get better. I am getting better, and I know others can, too, with the proper help. Please help us in an effort to prevent these heinous acts from continuing in the future.

Thank you very much.

DR. FADEN: Thank you.

(Applause)

MS. MULLEN: Good afternoon.

Between the years of 1957 and 1974, I became a pawn in the government's game, whose ultimate goal was mind-control and to create the perfect spy, all through the use of chemicals, radiation, drugs, hypnosis, electric shock, isolation in tubs of water, sleep deprivation, brain-washing, verbal, physical, emotional and sexual abuse.

I was exploited unwittingly for nearly three decades of my life, and the only explanations given to me were that "the end justifies the means", and "I was serving my country in their bold effort to fight communism".

I can only summarize my circumstances by saying they took an already-abused seven-year old child and compounded my suffering beyond belief. The saddest part is I know for a fact that I was not alone. There were countless other children in my same situation, and there was no one to help us until now.

I've already submitted as much information as possible, including conversations overheard of the agencies responsible. I'm able to report all this to you in such detail because of my photographic memory and the arrogance of the doctors -- the arrogance of the people involved. They were certain they would always control my mind.

Although the process of recalling these atrocities is not an easy one, nor is it without some danger to myself and my family, I feel the risk is worth taking.

Dr. L. Wilson Green, who claimed to have received $50 million from the Edgewood Chemical and Radiology Laboratory as part of a TSD or technical science division of the CIA, once described to Dr. Charles Brown that "children were used as subjects because they were more fun to work and cheaper, too." They needed lower profile subjects than soldiers or government people.

So, only young willing females would do. Besides, he said, "I like scaring them. They and the agency think I'm a god, creating subjects experiments for whatever deviant purposes Sid and James could think up." Sid being Dr. Sidney Gottlieb, James, Dr. James Hamilton.

In 1958, I was to be tested, they told me, by some important doctors from the society or the Human Ecology Society, and I was instructed to cooperate. I was told not to look at anyone's faces, and not -- try hard not to ignore -- to try hard not to ignore any names as this was a very secret project, but I was told that all these things would help me forget.

Naturally, as most children do, I did the opposite, and I remembered as much as I could, but Dr. John Gittinger tested me, Dr. Cameron gave me the shots, and Dr. Green the x-rays.

Then I was told by Sid Gottlieb that "I was ripe for the big A" meaning Artichoke. By the time I left to go home, just like every time from then on, I would remember only whatever explanations Dr. Robert G. Heath of Tulane Medical University gave me for the odd bruises, needle marks, burns on my head, fingers, and even the genital soreness. I had no reason to believe otherwise. They had already begun to control my mind.

The next year, I was sent to a lodge in Maryland called Deep Creek Cabins to learn how to sexually please men. I was taught how to coerce them into talking about themselves, and it was Richard Helms, who was deputy director of the CIA, Dr. Gottlieb, George White, Morris Allen, were all planning on filming as many high government agency officials and heads of academic institutions and foundations as possible, so that later, when the funding for mind-control and radiation started to dwindle, projects would continue.

I was used to entrap many unwitting men, including themselves, all with the use of a hidden camera. I was only nine years old when this sexual humiliation began. I overheard conversations about a part of the agency called Ord, which I found out was Office of Research and Development. It was run by Dr. Green, Dr. Steven Aldridge, Martin Orne, and Morris Allen.

Once a crude remark was made by Dr. Gottlieb about a certain possible leak over New Orleans involving a large group of retarded children who were being given massive doses of radiation. He asked why was Wilson so worried about a few retarded kids, after all, they would be the least likely to spill the beans.

Another time, I heard Dr. Martin Orne, who was the director then of the scientific office, and later head of the Institute for Experimental Research state that, "In order to keep more funding coming from different sources for radiation and mind-control projects, he suggested stepping up the amounts of stressors used and also the blackmail portion of the experiments". He said it needed to be done faster and to get rid of the subjects or they were asking for us to come back later and haunt them with our remembrances.

There's much more I could tell you about government-sponsored research, including project names, cell project numbers, people involved, facilities used, tests and other forms of pain induction, but I think I've given more than enough information to recommend further investigation of all the mind-control projects, especially as they involve so much abuse of the radiation.

I would love nothing more than to say that I had dreamed the whole thing up and need just to forget it, but that would be a tragic mistake. It would also be a lie.

All these atrocities did occur to me and to countless other children, and all under the guise of defending our country. It is because of the cumulative effects of exposure to radiation, chemicals, drugs, pain and subsequent mental and physical distress that I've been robbed of the ability to work and even to bear any children of my own.

It is blatantly obvious that none of this was needed nor should it ever have been allowed to take place at all, and the only means we have to seek out the awful truth and bring it to light is by opening whatever files remain on all the projects and through another presidential commission on mind-control.

I believe that every citizen of this nation has the right to know just what is fact and what is fiction. It is our greatest protection against the possibility of this ever happening again.

In conclusion, I can offer you no more than what I've given you today, the truth, and I thank you for your time.

(Applause)

DR. FADEN: Thank you for your presentations. We appreciate that this is not an easy thing to do.

Are there comments or questions from the committee? Duncan?

DR. THOMAS: Could I ask either of you, where were your parents through all this? Do you have any idea how you were recruited in the first place? Did they -- do you have parents, and did your parents know anything about what was going on?

MS. DeNICOLA: I can make a brief statement on that. It was my father who was involved with Dr. Green. My mother was not aware because they were divorced when I was four years old. Well, maybe before that, separated, and what would happen, how he gained access to me is these experiments took place actually in the middle of the night, and he would sneak in while my mom was asleep and take me out, and she had absolutely no knowledge of what happened.

However, when these memories did surface, and I began to tell her about them, she -- there was no question in her mind that he was capable. He had been in the military, in the Air Force. He had access to meet Dr. Green.

So, in answer to your question, it was my father. He groomed me from the very beginning, started sexually abusing me from the very beginning, and it was just something that he wanted to do, and he was closely involved with Dr. Green, but my mom had no knowledge.

The only thing she knew was that she wanted to get away from him. She didn't know why. She just knew she had to get away from him because of my reaction to him. I'm sorry. I didn't mean to go on. Thank you.

MS. MULLEN: Do you want an answer from me, also?

DR. THOMAS: It's up to you.

MS. MULLEN: If you want. The way I got involved was I was adopted when I was two and a half by a woman who sexually abused me, and then she was a friend of the chairman of the board of Tulane University at the time, and as a favor to him, she -- I began to show symptoms of, you know, typical of childhood abuse, when I was very, very young, and she asked him to recommend a psychiatrist, and he recommended Dr. Heath, who was involved with the project already, and, so, when he discovered that I already had been abused from the time I was practically born, and that I was -- had the ability to associate and that I had almost perfect recall, and I passed all the personality tests that they gave me, he suggested me for the project, and, so, that's how I got involved into it.

My father had no idea, and he died when I was very young, but I don't know if my mother knew or not. I don't think she really cared, to tell you the truth, and then she died when I was teenager. So, after that, they had access to me.

DR. FADEN: Lois?

MS. NORRIS: You mentioned that there are others across the country who are coming -- who are recalling similar things. Do they all cover the same time span, generally, or do you have a feel for that?

MS. WOLF: Yeah. Generally, they cover the same time span from about the late 1940s until -- see, one of the things that we're hearing about is people that were assigned to monitor them in case they should start to remember because it's so horrible what was done, so we're not exactly sure when the actual experimentation took place and when it got into just the monitoring to make sure that they were still under control, and not everybody is being monitored.

So, but, yeah, pretty much, I think, from the late '40s through the 1970s, and maybe even into 1984.

MS. MULLEN: Later than that, I found out, because after my parents died, then there was no one to protect me, to . monitor that she spoke of. My particular monitor was a physician at Tulane University, and, so, he was a family friend, also, of my mother's,, and he just kept on making sure that I kept going back and forgetting.

MS. WOLF: So, it's kind of unclear as to when -- whether it stopped or whether it -- you know, where the --

MS. MULLEN: They still monitor you, though. That's why I am taking some danger in coming here today, because I'm still being watched.

MS. WOLF: I know this sounds unbelievable, but I mean there's actual -- she gets stuff in the mail. She gets phone calls. People have been writing things on her house, using the pseudonym that they used when she was at Tulane, and only they have knowledge of that name.

MS. MULLEN: My real name was never used, ever, in anything. So.

MS. NORRIS: Were they all children at the time?

MS. WOLF: Yeah. All children. And the thing is, is as therapists, we are trying really hard to figure this out, and to get as much information as we can.

Claudia's memories have been verified, a lot of them, because the way I have approached this is as I don't read in the field. I don't -- and, so, as people give me information, I send them to experts, like Alan Scheflin, who has a lot of information, and then he'll get back to me to confirm or deny. He has never denied any information that I've sent him.

Some of it can't be because we don't have all the information, but a lot of Claudia's memories have been validated, and they're not in any published source. The only way she would know the things she knows is if she filed Freedom of Information Act information, and this is what Alan Scheflin is telling me.

So, I have every -- and then I have been very careful not to know a whole lot, so if someone tells me something, I don't even cue them that -- because I don't know either.

DR. THOMAS: It seems to me that documentary evidence is going to be key to establishing the truth of these cases.

MS. WOLF: Yes, absolutely.

DR. THOMAS: It's hard for me to imagine that a program as large and as complex as you people have described could have gone on for so long without a great deal of documentation.

The question is where is this documentation now? It becomes a Catch-22 if it is said that all of the documentation resides within the CIA files, and all of it's secret, and they won't give it to us. But what you've described is a pattern of very complex organization which involves plenty of people outside of the CIA as well.

Therefore, there must be a substantial amount of documentation which could be discovered. You just mentioned about the letters that some of you are still receiving. There is a lead to documentation.

Can you describe for me what efforts have been made, either by yourselves or by other people who are working on this story, to try to track down some of this documentation, and what you meant a moment ago when you said that some of these memories have been verified or validated?

MS. WOLF: Okay. Dr. Alan Scheflin, and you have his resume in the documentation and a statement from him about Claudia in your documentation, he has been for the past 20 years filing Freedom of Information Act filings to get this information, has been piecing it all together.

Other people across the country have been doing the same, going back to the government files, getting what they can, and what they've also been doing is writing books, sharing information. So, he has actual Freedom of Information Act information.

The problem is that it's -- when the requests are going in now, they're being slowed down or denied or just kind of lost in the shuffle, and the information is very difficult to get.

DR. THOMAS: I'm sorry. I don't see the documentation in the package that was provided to me. Is there something missing?

MS. MULLEN: I have -- I supplied --

MS. WOLF: I sent a --

MS. MULLEN: -- project numbers, names.

MS. WOLF: -- packet of documentation overnight mail, should have been here Monday, and some more yesterday. So, maybe it isn't --

DR. FADEN: If we haven't received it, we'll let you know.

MS. WOLF: Okay. I sent the first one to Steve Klaidman, and the second one to Kristen Crotty. You have it?

COMMITTEE MEMBER: Yes, we have some of this material.

MS. WOLF: Okay. And, again, it was, you know, what I could pull together in about a week and a half from across the country, but the consistency of the stories, and the thing is, we want to verify it.

So, Alan has amassed over 20 years from Freedom of Information Act, from memos other people give him or sharing information, a lot of information, but we don't have the complete story. There's still a lot of stuff that we don't know, and that's what we're trying to find out because --

DR. THOMAS: Does any of this documentation specifically refer to radiation experiments? Because we are told by CIA that they never did any radiation experiments. So, what we need is documentation in order to pursue that.

MS. MULLEN: All you have to do is look up anything on Ord, the one that I mentioned that I overheard them speaking about. That was almost strictly radiation, and that was run by Dr. Steven Aldridge, Martin Orne.

DR. THOMAS: And that's appeared in the package which you sent Steve Klaidman?

MS. MULLEN: Yes, and I gave you project numbers, project names, sub-project numbers, even the subjects. We were given numbers ourselves for each specific experiment, and I overheard my number because they would -- they would assume that -- they would use techniques so that you would forget. You know, when you go home, you wouldn't remember what happened. So, they just talked freely in front of me. That's why no one ever hid their face or wore a mask or anything, because they knew that I would not remember, and I didn't. I didn't remember until two years ago.

MS. WOLF: And, also, I think you can follow up on Dr. L. Wilson Green. I don't know if you've come across him, but he seems to have been involved in both, and I think realistically, in terms of the mind-controls, some of the subjects were used in mind-control radiation. Some, as you've been hearing, have been strictly radiation, and some were strictly mind-control.

I think the reason it's coming up now is because in some of the stuff people are remembering, they knew that it would break down. They really worked hard to induce amnesia, and they knew it would break down, and I think in the last couple of years, that that's what's been happening, because we're hearing more and more, and, you know, -- so, we're just trying to find out what's happening here. That's -- so, we'd appreciate any help you could give us on that.

DR. FADEN: Thank you. Did you want to make --

MS. DeNICOLA: Yes, I did. I just wanted to address you for a moment. The question you asked about the documentation on radiation specifically. Included in my packet, and I don't know if you have that or not, there is - it's entitled, "Radiation File Information". There are names of subjects names, experiment names, and some code numbers that I remembered, and the problem is we have no way of verifying this without opening the files.

I mean I --

MS. WOLF: You have them.

MS. DeNICOLA: Yeah.

MS. WOLF: You have what she remembers, and you have what Claudia remembers.

MS. DeNICOLA: Do you have the documentation?

DR. THOMAS: All I have from you is your three-page -- four-page -- three-page document.

MS. WOLF: There is a whole packet of information.

DR. FADEN: We can clarify that.

DR. THOMAS: I gather the staff has it. So, we can get that.

DR. FADEN: We can clarify what we don't have, what we do have, and whatever it is we can put together, and we thank you very much --

MS. WOLF: Okay. Thank you.

DR. FADEN: -- for your traveling from New Orleans to present to us.

A P P E N D I X   A

PART 3
Written Testimonies for Public Record
Submitted to Advisory Committee by
Therapist Valerie Wolf on Behalf of
Therapists, Researchers and Clients
Across the Nation. Clients' Names
Have Been Omitted.

March 9, 1995

To Whom It May Concern:

My name is Alan W. Scheflin. I am a Professor of Law at Santa Clara University Law School, and a judicially recognized expert in mind and behavior control. I co-authored a nonfiction book about government mind control programs entitled "The Mind Manipulators," which was published in a dozen countries.

I am writing in support of the testimony of Claudia S. Mullen and for the purpose of encouraging the opening of secret government files on radiation and on mind control. I have been studying these secret programs since 1975 and it is my conclusion that there are at minimum hundreds, and most likely thousands, of American citizens who could benefit from learning that they were used as experimental guinea pigs in government research projects.

Claudia's therapist has been kind enough to send me, with her patient's informed consent, some of the pertinent records reflecting Claudia's memories of her experiences as an unwitting subject in these experiments. I have been able to confirm that some of the information Claudia has provided is absolutely true and could not have been derived from any published source. I am persuaded that Claudia is proof that secret government mind control experimentation is on-going and vastly more expansive than government authorities are willing to admit.

I know that many of the stories that will be told by witnesses will sound unbelievable. Please do not dismiss them out of hand. I learned the hard way that, although there is much disinformation about mind control experiments, there is also much truth in the least likely stories.

Release of remaining documents on secret government experiments is in the public interest and would not threaten national security. It is time for citizens to again trust their government. Public disclosure would be the act of good faith to encourage that trust. Furthermore, and most important, there remain victims of these programs who deserve to have that victimization come to an end. Let the truth set them free.

It would be my pleasure to supply any additional information requested.

John D. Boyd, Ph.D.

March 9, 1995

Valerie Wolfe

New Orleans, LA 70118

CITIZEN'S REPORT TO THE PRESIDENT'S ADVISORY COMMITTEE ON HUMAN RADIATION EXPERIMENTS

As a licensed clinical psychologist in private practice, I have treated three patients whose memories of childhood abuse include the detailed recall of sophisticated mind control technology being inflicted upon them by "experts" in collusion with the patients' mentally disturbed parents. The independent reports of these individuals contained similar information of an esoteric and intricate nature concerning mind control technology which in my opinion could be gained only through personal experience. I am submitting their letters to you because the non-familial perpetrators of their abuse may fall within the purview of the Commission's investigation, i.e., individuals who began mind control experimentation on citizens of the United States of America during the 1940's.

Having practiced psychotherapy for twenty-five years, and served on the faculties of Ohio State University and the University of Virginia, I am well aware of the controversial nature of these patients' allegations. As a Diplomate of the American Board of Psychological Hypnosis I am knowledgeable in the area of human memory. My scientific training has led me to thoroughly scrutinize these patients' memories and conclude that the recollections are based upon actual experience.

Letters from Renee Bright and Christine Gentry (pseudonyms) refer to mind control abuse originating in the 1940's. Their dissociative material appeared to me to have major experimental or programming flaws, while the dissociated effects in John Smith were relatively precise, having been administered in the 1960's. I wonder if 15-20 years of practice yielded greater efficiency, the technology being refined as it was utilized by successive perpetrators?

I am available for testimony or other forms of input to the Commission. Please give this information your most serious investigation.

John D. Boyd, Ph.D.

John D. Boyd

Licensed Clinical Psychologist

To: The President's Advisory Commission On Human Radiation
Experiments
Via: Dr. John Boyd.

I entered treatment for depression with my original therapist in
1974, after eliciting a promise from her never to hypnotize or hospitalize
me without my permission. When she asked the reason for my request, I
answered that I could not trust doctors not to manipulate my mind, drug
and/or kill me. I did not, however, know the basis of my mistrust.

Shortly after beginning therapy, I experienced the first of many
"flashbacks" through which I was to recover memories. These memories
seemed "stranger than fiction", since my family had always been socially
prominent. I grew up in eastern Pennsylvania and the New York suburbs,
my stepfather an executive board member of several national
corporations. Yet, over the years, many of these memories were validated
to a reasonable extent.

My first memories, in 1974, were of sexual abuse by my mother
which began in early childhood. In late 1978, I began to recover
memories of similar abuse by my stepfather. The memories regarding my
stepfather, however, involved group sex, bright lights, electroshock, cattle
prods, drugs, pornography, torture. My diagnosis until this time had
been vague; I began to insist that I must be schizophrenic. My therapist
revealed to me, in 1980, that I was MPD.

In 1986, I testified before *The Attorney General's Commission On
Pornography* under a different pseudonym. In that testimony, I spoke of
my stepfather's involvement in some type of national organization or
network. I remembered being used by my stepfather as a specimen, or
guinea pig, in some type of experiment in which my stepfather was
involved, the purpose of which was to perfect efficient techniques *to be
utilized in preparing people* for some type of directed behaviors, one of
which was pornography. He, then, taught these procedures in different
areas around the county.

Beginning when I was eleven, in 1951, I was periodically drugged in
my sleep, then taken to the basement of our house where I was placed,
naked, on a table. I would be surrounded by, approximately, five to eight
people[1] and my stepfather would demonstrate different torture
techniques which would leave no residual marks as evidence. These
included inserting increasingly larger dildos into my rectum for periods
of time in order to stretch me without any tears; demonstrations of how a
sharp knife pressed on strategic sensitive areas, ie. nipples, vaginal
points, neck points, etc. would reduce resistance—the manner in which
the knife should be held for greatest effectiveness, how to determine the

---

[1] I approximated this number from the voices I heard and the bodies I sensed to be present.

pressure point at which laceration would occur; demonstrations with
electroshock pulses of increasing intensity, or a cattle prod inserted into
various orifices, to accomplish the same. These "sessions" occurred
approximately once every few months until I was fourteen, in 1954. I am
able to recount this, even though I was drugged, do to my ability to
dissociate. I had always slept with "one eye open", since I never knew
when I would be taken out at night to be *terrorized*. I had learned at an
early age that disclosure would prompt a worse situation and that no
escape was possible. These "sessions" were only one type of many
indoctrination "sessions" which I have remembered.

While I worked very hard in therapy to integrate my experiences
and personalities, I was unable to make any permenant progress, a
frustration and a puzzle for both my therapist and me. I remained barely
functional for a number of years, battling periodic homicidal and suicidal
urges with the help of prescribed tranquilizers and continual therapeutic
support. Thus, in April 1991, I checked myself into a hospital in northern
Virginia which had developed a specialized unit for the treatment of
Dissociative Disorders. Here, I met my second therapist.

He, too, was puzzled by my inability to progress in treatment, since
I had begun seventeen years before and had been able to recover my
memories without the benefit of hypnosis.

One day, at the end of a session in March 1992, he asked me if the
name "Dr. Green" meant anything to me. I answered—no, I didn't think
so—, then asked him who Dr. Green was. He said that a colleague had
called him that week to report that this doctor's name was coming up, in
association with ritual abuse, by survivors in different parts of the
country. I, then, heard myself say—that his name was not really
"Green", but Greenberg, Greenbaum or something like that; that I was
not sure, but did not think that he was a medical doctor, rather some
other type of scientist; that he was a German Jew, who, because he did not
look Jewish, passed as a Gentile (my stepfather referred to him as an
"Aryan Jew"); that he had learned mind-control techniques in Nazi
Germany, then was brought to this country to teach these techniques;
that he was the man who taught my stepfather, who, in turn, taught
others—nationally.

I cannot identify "Dr. Green" physically, as I was always either
blindfolded or facing into a bright light during indoctrination sessions.
"Dr. Green" was present at many of the initial "sessions" referred to
above, as well as others at different sites. I do remember that he spoke
German (as did my stepfather) and had an accent. I learned that he was
actually Jewish (with a number tattooed somewhere on his body) from
overhearing a heated conversation between my stepfather and another
man involved, when they discovered this fact.

I do not remember the specifics of any programming. However, I
do remember the techniques by which they were instilled: hypnosis,

electroshock, sensory deprivation (by isolation in closets, in underground dirt "rooms", in "graves", under water, etc); death threats to self, others and animals; use of drugs (ie. varying doses of sodium penythol, peyote or other hallucinoginic drugs, some drug which was an intense sexual stimulant); torture by any and all means imaginable; promises of organizational promotion, success and security; seduction and blackmail. The physical and psychological trauma would produce dissociation, at which point specific indoctrination and programmed responses would be introduced, ie. *alters* which performed specific duties or responded to particular cues. At the same time, "natural" alters would form as isolated parts of the original personality in response to the trauma. If one was not aware of *created alters*, one could not address them.

After our initial discussion regarding "Dr. Green", my therapist informed me that specific programs had been instilled in MPD systems as a means of mind-control. In July 1992, I began "Deprogramming Treatment" with Dr. Boyd. As a result, I have been able to terminate therapy and am now free from any need of medication. I do, however, live with some residual fear. It is my fervant hope that this Commission will be able to contribute some understanding of the above circumstances.

Thank you for your efforts.

March 8, 1995.

March 7, 1995

To: The President's Advisory Commission on Human Radiation Experimentation

Dear Commissioners:

This letter is being written and forwarded to your committee through the office of Dr. John Boyd. I am most willing to express to the Commission my involvement, memories and "experiences" of the man I came to know as *Dr. Green.* I believe appropriate to advise you that Dr. Boyd is not my personal therapist, but I am requesting, at this point, that any information I am willing to share be communicated through Dr. Boyd for personal reasons.

As a ritual abuse survivor, much of my recovery has been contingent upon my willingness to re-examine my childhood. I believe that a tenacious will and a basic emotional stability has helped me to perceive more clearly, and even to understand the horrifying abuses to which I was subjected. Painful as the experiences of my past have been, it is through them that I have learned why I have become who I am. Unfortunately, the abuses perpetrated against me have robbed me of much of who I was, and perhaps . . . who I might have been.

My parents are of well-educated, economically and socially well-established New Jersey families. My father has been prominent in state politics, Masonic organizations and statewide business ventures. My mother is an accomplished artist, and businesswoman in her own right. My parents, who are still living, were my initial abusers, but much of my abuse was in the form of mind-control techniques and radical behavioral experimentation.

I remember, when I was about four or five, a man came to our house for dinner. He was introduced as Dr. Green, and saw him many times after that evening, both at our house and at another location to which we traveled. Dr. Green was very reserved, yet very polite, but formal. He always seemed to stand very straight, and his movements appeared to be very purposed, almost military-like. I remember being told that he was an important person, and somehow it was very important to my parents that I behaved well in his company. His bearing and presence made an immediate impression on me, and I vividly remember that he seemed to have foreign characteristics to his speech. This recollection was emphasized by the memory that one time I made him angry, and he spoke in a language that I did not understand. I somehow think it might have been German.

My parents were involved in an ideologically unique, intergenerational sect, and a part of the activity of the sect involved the abuse of others, generally children. It was deemed necessary to methodically control members behaviors and thought processes to fully participate in the cultic goals. Certain of the children were selected, those considered to be the *best and the brightest*, for future leadership within the organization. At about the age of four or five (1949-1950), I was selected for future leadership, and was thus *trained* by Dr. Green.

As a result of the extreme abuse, I was taught, and learned well, how to *dissociate*; thus creating *alters* (or sub-persona) to accomplish certain deeds or tasks for myself and others. The techniques of dissociation, and the creation of alters were purposefully taught to me by and with the frequent use of various drugs ("truth" serum and what were called "dream drugs", which I now believe to be hallucinatories of some kind) and sensory deprivations. The methods of mind control, for which I became a subject, were actuated by Dr. Green and an accomplice friend of his, another doctor.

I understand that the creation, or *programing*, of specific *alters* was a part of the abuse plan to allow me to behave in certain ways; and while my learned dissociation may have saved my life then, I believe that there have been times that these created "toxic alters" might have allowed, or even encouraged my demise. I also know that the creation of alters took place over a long period of time and many abuses. I know now too that the creation or evolution of these alters covers a period of time of approximately *nine* years. I also realize that the manipulation of my mind was a planned, organized and purposeful action carried out by a skilled man whose eyes demanded my concentration and obedient response.

Initially, I remember that I was put in a very dark, damp, basement closet-like place (I think an herb cellar) by myself, with no light for a long period of time, only to be *rescued* by the doctor, who I was told I must trust. I came to depend upon him and believed that he was the only person that could save me. I learned to trust and depend upon his every word. I later came to accept that any unwillingness on my part to obey, would result in my incarceration either in the "herb cellar" or in some dark, cold place (once it was in some kind of cave, another time in a dirt hole in a barn floor with a trap door).

Sometimes, especially when I had to memorize something, they used bright lights, of different colors. At times the lights would flash very rapidly, sometimes more slowly. Frequently the light effect was enhanced with the use of drugs. When I successfully related to my inquisitors the appropriate answers to their questions, or responded with the ideal feedback, the lights would be discontinued. Then there were times that only one light was used, a very bright, very large light that stayed on during our entire "session". It was during this time that I learned to focus clearly on him. It was as though I could see only him, only his eyes, with an aura around the dark outline of his body.

There have been many times that I have tried to dispel these memories as childhood fantasies, but they do not go away. Even after I have remembered them, the horrors do not subside and the memories do not fade. It has been some time now, yet I still remember people (Dr. Green and others), places (traveling at night, almost always at night, to a place near some body of water, for *training*), and the training itself (the memorization of certain words and symbols, and the creation of other *persons* who could be "called out" by the use of specific words for some potential task, or to protect that training and *programmed* behavior desired by the creators).

The memories are real, horrible and incredulous as they may sound. They are the emotionally painful bruises that I carry daily. They are a reality of scientific experimentation gone too far, by demented people who believe that people can be sacrificed for research and children will not remember; or perhaps the expectation or hope was that children would remember, and be called back at some future time to accomplish some unknown "*task*".

TO: President's Advisory Commission on Human Radiation
Experiments

I am a 36 year old white male married with three
children. At the age of 30, I went into a spiraling
depression with suicidal tendencies. At the age of 31,
I was hospitalized and released in about four weeks. I
was on antidepressants and in therapy with a
psychiatrist. I went to work and things went well for
about six months, and then things started happening all
over again. I was suffering from depression, cutting
myself, domestic violence, anger, and traffic
violations. I was accused of embezzlement, lying and
stealing. I remembered none of these things, but there
was evidence, so I took the blame. I left home
intending to kill myself. If it had not been for my
wife, I would have. I was hospitalized again, six
weeks this time. I was scared to tell the doctors I
didn't remember the things I was accused of. I was
looking at jail. My wife and her family managed to pay
off my embezzlement and make deals with the law. In
the hospital, I met a patient that gave me Dr. John D.
Boyd's name. She thought he might could help me.

Dr. Boyd did some tests on me, and he said that I was
highly dissociative. Over the next few weeks, he gave
me the diagnosis of MULTIPLE PERSONALITY DISORDER. I
was aware of nine personalities at that time. Memories
were coming back to me in flashes and dreams. At times
I would just keep seeing the same picture over and over
in my mind. I would draw them and give them to Dr.
Boyd. Sometimes these pictures made no sense
whatsoever, but in time they did. These memories were
so horrible that most of the time I couldn't believe
them. I was seeing Dr. Boyd twice a week just to
survive and understand what was happening. After six
months, I checked myself into a hospital for MPD. My
anger was so out-of-control that I was in fear of
hurting my wife and children. I was there for three
weeks and went back home. I still saw Dr. Boyd twice a
week for the next one and a half years, and even now,
still see him once a week.

I have remembered many abuses by my parents and
brother. The worst thing my parents did was to send me

to live with my uncle on a tobacco farm during the
summers. My uncle was a member of a religious cult
with an evil ideology. In the name of his religion, I
was tortured in many ways. He would frequently take me
to a big "church" in Greensboro, NC. There I was
meticulously tortured in order to split my mind and
control me. I met a man there by the name of DR.
GREEN. This man and others strapped me to a metal
table, electrodes were placed on my temples, chest, and
ankles. I was shocked at intermittent intervals while
strobe lights were being flashed and instructions were
being yelled at me about my internal workings and my
future. This began when I was eight years old. There
were times they would wrap my up like a mummy in ice
cold sheets, pouring cold water over me, yelling and
screaming things at me while they were sticking me with
needles. I was drugged at time, and they made me
believe I did things that I now know I didn't do, but
as a child I was sure I had done.

They would keep me awake hours on end with no food or
water. They enjoyed seeing children beg for food and
cry to go to sleep. During times of torture they had
tape recorded messages playing, videos playing, all with
instructions for me to follow. I was to lead a normal
life and at the age of 33 return. The last few times I
was taken to Greensboro I was introduced to a DR.
LOWENSTEIN and DR ROSENBURG. I was strapped in a chair,
and the electrodes were put on me. They would call out
alters, and if they didn't answer, I would get shocked.
Personalities would be called forth to recall their
programming (instructions) in explicit detail, and any
wrong answers always ended in being shocked. These are
only a part of my memories. My life was almost ruined
by these people. Reliving these memories was the
hardest thing I've ever had to do.

At that time, I had over 400 alters. Now, Dr. Boyd and
I have integrated all but about 30. I live a fairly
normal life with my wife and children. I've been lucky
they stuck by me. I am in a community college now, and
I have two more semesters to complete before I graduate.
I have done well with a 3.8 GPA.

I can still recall these memories, and I will assure
you that they are not hallucinations or dreams. The

abuse I suffered under these people was very systematic and deliberate in order to split my mind creating alter personalities to achieve total mind control over me. There was an elaborate setup used to torture us. It reminds me of an operating room.

My mother and brother have confirmed some of my memories, and I have many body scars and conditions that coincide with my memories. My wife and I secretly visited my uncle's farm to confirm my memories of the placement of barns, smokehouses, cabins, ponds, etc. where abuse took place. My map was almost identical to their placement and it has been almost 20 years since I've seen it. I wrote a letter to my uncle denouncing what he did to me and tell him that I no longer wanted anything to do with his religion. I have received a couple of messages from my uncle directly and about four messages indirectly from other family members.

My brother, now at the age of 41, has begun having memories for the past year. I am certain that he has suffered from the same abuse I did. He has just now, as of December 1994 started receiving therapy.

Thank you for listening to my story, and I hope that you can put some conclusion to this abuse that many of us suffer from.

March 5, 1995
Valerie Wolf
New Orleans, LA 70118

[note: a copy of this letter will be mailed tomorrow]

Dear Ms. Wolf,

Re: CIA and Military Mind Control

Further to our recent telephone conversation, I am writing to support your presentation to the Presidential radiation committee and your request that an inquiry be made into the overlapping subject of CIA and military mind control.

I am a psychiatrist with over 100 publications in professional journals. My area of specialty is dissociative identity disorder (DID) (formerly called multiple personality disorder), a topic on which I have published two books, one with John Wiley and Sons, and one with the University of Toronto Press. I have another book on the subject in press with the University of Toronto Press. Another book recently published by Wiley, of which I wrote about one third, deals partly with DID. I was the 1994 President of the International Society for the study of Dissociation, which has about 3000 members.

I became interested in CIA and military mind control when patients with DID began describing involvement in mind control research occurring on military bases and in hospital settings. Since there is no way to tell clinically whether these memories are real, I began to do background reading and research on mind control in 1992. I enclose a reading list of the materials I have read.

In an article in the April 1971 issue of *Science Digest* G.H. Estabrooks describes using hypnosis to create artificial DID in military personnel during World War II. The purpose of the DID was for infiltration and courier operations—the amnesia involved created a layer of security from defection and interrogation inside the subject's mind. Estabrooks describes inserting specific code phrases used to call out the alter personality holding the classified information, of which the main part of the person was unaware. Estabrooks also wrote a textbook on hypnosis that went through a series of editions.

Declassified materials describe a large mind control research program conducted by the CIA and the military from 1951–1973 under cryptonyms including MKNAOMI, BLUEBIRD, ARTICHOKE, MKULTRA, and

MKSEARCH. I have in my possession about 80 of the 149 MKULTRA Subproject files, which I obtained through the Freedom of Information Act. I am conducting ongoing research identifying the investigators on these projects, obtaining their publications from my medical school library, and filing Freedom of Information Act requests with the CIA on each deceased investigator of interest. Through this process I have amassed thousands of pages of published papers. I am able to tie together specific MKULTRA and MKSEARCH Subprojects with the principal investigators, the funding fronts used by the CIA, and the publications resulting from the projects—the funding was classified, yet much of the research was published in regular journals in sanitized form without the CIA involvement being acknowledged.

Some of the MKULTRA and MKSEARCH investigators did not realize that their grants were really from the CIA but others are verified as being witting of CIA involvement and having TOP SECRET clearance from the CIA in the Subproject files. Such cleared investigators include Carl Rogers, Martin Orne, and Louis Jolyon West.

Drs. Orne and West are still alive. Their C.V.'s list funding from many different military intelligence sources. They and many other still living individuals could be called to testify at hearings.

The techniques of experimental mind control reported by DID patients include use of hallucinogens, sensory deprivation and isolation, physical spinning, hypnosis, and other methods, each of which is described in published reports arising from military and CIA projects run from 1951–1973. Published articles in my files include descriptions of administration of 150 mcg of LSD to children age 5-10 years on a daily basis for days, weeks, months, and in a few cases even years. Neurosurgeons at Tulane, Yale, and Harvard did extensive research on brain electrode implants with intelligence funding, and combined brain implants with large numbers of drugs including hallucinogens. In a paper I have, Dr. Jose Delgado at Yale describes implanting electrodes in the brain of an 11-year-old boy and stimulating the boy's brain with a remote transmitter that had a range of up to 100 feet (this research was done in the 1960's). When a button was pushed on the transmitter, a specific electrode fired, and the boy would state that he was unsure whether he was male or female, and that he wanted to marry Dr. Delgado. This behavior occurred only when a specific brain electrode was stimulated.

I mention this research to underline how sophisticated and destructive much of the documented mind control has been. MKULTRA alone included four Subprojects on children—one was conducted at the International Children's Summer Camp in Maine by an unwitting investigator. The MKULTRA Subproject file in my possession for this project states that the CIA's interest in this research was in establishing contact with foreign nationals of potential future operational use by the CIA—the children who served as subjects in the project were as young as 11 years old.

DID patients in treatment throughout the United States and Canada are describing involvement in mind control research that is much more sophisticated than MKULTRA and MKSEARCH. It includes deliberate sexual abuse of children to make them more dissociative. Although the reality of this research is not documented, the possibility that it is real is so serious that a formal investigation is warranted. Although some or many of the DID patients' memories may be distorted or inaccurate, it is not plausible that the CIA and military intelligence agencies simply stopped this research in 1973, as they claim. If it continues to the present, it must have become much more sophisticated.

I would be pleased to testify at length at any hearings on CIA and military mind control.

Sincerely,

Colin A. Ross, M.D.

TO THE PRESIDENTIAL COMMISSION
ON RADIATION EXPERIMENTATION
BY GOVERNMENTAL AGENCIES

    I am a licensed clinical social worker in
private practice in New Mexico and I have been
treating victims of government mind control
programming for over five years. In that time
period, I have come in contact, through my own
practice and in consultation with other
therapists and facilities in my community, with
up to 100 individuals (conservative estimate)
with evidence of mind control programming. I
have worked directly with four psychiatric
hospitals and treatment centers, two with
programs for dissociative disorders, and up to
two or three dozen local therapists, giving me
some sense of the overall survivor community
here. This community is appallingly large for
such a small state, perhaps due the
considerable military presence here.

    In my own practice, I have treated or
consulted with up to forty individuals with
histories and symptoms typical of mind control
victims. Of the fifteen individuals who have
been in therapy with me over the past five and
a half years for a minimum of two to four years
each, 6 have clear and explicit recall of mind
control programming which took place on
military bases and in government labs; 6 others
had alter personalities who reported memories
of same. (Because the programmers dissociate
these individuals, recall typically is a
progressive process with one part of the person
remembering before the rest does.) Of the six
with clear recall, one also received radiation.
Another is herself a trained programmer of
children who has detailed information of how
some of the programming is done.

    All of my patients report receiving
programming from early childhood. Frequently a
family member was involved in the military or
worked for a government laboratory.
Additionally, I have had a sixth patient who
was a licensed therapist herself and left the
state to work with another therapist with
expertise in this area when she realized she
had been unconsciously involved with government
mind control effecting her own patients.

Patients have reported being experimented upon in laboratories and on military bases and university campuses here in New Mexico (Sandia Labs - numerous reports, Kirtland Air Force Base, Los Alamos Labs, Roswell - numerous reports, White Sands Missile Base, University of New Mexico laboratories), in Illinois (Chicago, Argon Labs), in Colorado (Colorado Springs - numerous reports), Texas (Amarillo and other numerous locations near military bases), California (Edwards Air Force Base, Berkeley Labs, and other locations.) Much of the programming reported has gone on since the 1960's (some as early as the 40's and 50's) up to and including the present. Most of my current patients continue to be programmed even while they are in treatment in what appears to be efforts to sabotage the treatment process (especially recall) and redissociate the patient. Underground facilities where programming is done have been reported at Sandia Labs by four patients and in Colorado Springs (NORAD) by two patients, while numerous patients have referred to Colorado Springs generally.

Current programming of my patients appears to be ongoing at Sandia Labs (bunkers), Kirtland Airforce Base, Roswell, N.M. Other locations may be involved as well.

All programming is based on creating dissociated ego states in the individual and is diverse and particularized to the individual. Certain types of base programs, as well as secondary programs, exist which can be identified in most individuals even though the details of the programs vary.

Universally, patients report the following mind control experiences from infancy (involvement of the immediate family is commonly the case):

Use of drugs, electroshock, sexual molestation and rape, various physical tortures (drowning and resuscitation, burning, starvation, physical isolation, physical abuse of various types). Also used are computer screens, flotation tanks, isolation booths, gurneys, IV's, restraints, video screens, audio technology, virtual reality, etc.

All who have been involved in mind control experimentation and programming in government labs or on military bases are convinced of government involvement. Government agencies referred to are the CIA, Department of Defense, NASA among others. These individuals are convinced by their programmers they risk death or harm to their loved ones if they talk and that there is nowhere to turn for help in our society. They are subjected to programming to doubt their own reality and told no one will ever believe them. Care is taken to protect the anonymity of the programmers. Multiple programmers are used, usually dressed alike with similar haircuts, etc. Often a therapist look-alike is evoked in the laboratory setting to further confuse the victim, although most survivors can usually tell the difference afterwards if not during the actual programming session. The programmers appear to have achieved a level of considerable sophistication in their technology and practice.

While it is not possible at this time to verify all of the accounts that we receive of mind control tortures, there is enough underlying consistency to these reports from unconnected sources to merit our investigation of them. It is imperative that a Presidential Commission be appointed to investigate the potential for crimes against American citizens who, if they are in fact being tortured and abused, are being ruthlessly exploited and who have no recourse for protection or validation.

March 8, 1995, New Mexico

**PRESIDENTIAL COMMISSION
WRITTEN ON MARCH 9TH, 1995 BY A PHD LICENSED
PSYCHOLOGIST**

**REPORT ON BEHAVIOR AND ACTIVITIES REPORTED BY MY
PATIENTS FROM 1988 TO THE PRESENT:**

Personal statement:

Although I am well qualified in the correct use of hypnosis, the information I am describing in this document was told to me by my patients without the use of hypnosis. Hypnosis was used later to help my patients process these horrendous memories and rebuild their sense of self. The patients, as they processed their memories, would describe how they had been fooled or tricked with the use of goggles, virtual reality types of experiences, viewing of videotapes, drugs, hypnosis, etc. After I met Nazi alters, I read about Nazi thinking. Only recently have I read about the CIA experiments in publicly accessible books, particularly the Cameron experiments, and was shocked at the similarities and also the updates that my patients reported that appeared to consistently follow from what I was able to read.

These patients journaled these memories first. Some were "repressed memories" that came up for these patients through flashbacks, but the vast majority of what was reported to me were the memories of alter personalities that had never forgotten. What happened to them had not been allowed to be shared with the host. Amnesia was very successful in most of these patients until they felt they were in a safe environment and could begin to tell. All of these patients felt that they would not be believed and had been told that by their perpetrators. At first, I had all of the normal disbelief in this information, but over time as patients reported the same information time and time again in detail (and I also had corroboration such as an item left at someones home to scare them into silence, the black shock box, described below, a written warning found on my car,) I personally began to believe in the overall reality of this. I never knew whether the individual memories of my patients were true or not true. My role was to work with them to come to their own conclusions. What I did know is that these patients presented with all of the symptoms of individuals who had been terribly traumatized, tortured and humiliated to the point that alter personalities were formed, the symptoms of severe post traumatic stress disorder and other severe psychiatric disorders were found. These patients were very frightened in the telling of what had happened to them.

Personally, I never wanted to know this information and it was never a part of my clinical or personal world. I did not know what humans were capable of doing to humans. I have recently read the works of de Sade and have more of an understanding that humans are the only species on this earth that purposely torture their own kind. I was naive not to have known this, but I had sheltered myself and my children from horror films and violence and did not grow up knowing about anything violent other than that the Holocaust had taken place. It is with fear that I share this information. I am afraid it will fall into the wrong hands, that I will somehow be identified and harmed more than I already have been. My life has been threatened many times, patients have attacked me, patients have told me they were sent to attack me, kill me or discredit me. I have been accused of implanting all of this in my patients. I did not nor do I think it is possible for me to have implanted these ideas. Working with these patients, I heard things that truly shocked and horrified me and that I wish that I had never heard. I feel that I accidentally walked into a world that I was not supposed to ever know about.

Clinically, I am fully aware that patients are suggestible, that I have a responsibility to be careful and not lead my patients to conclusions about their experiences. I used their words to describe their experiences and that is one reason why it took me time to figure out that they might be talking about mind control techniques but using different words like "cult" or "programming." I feel that I abided by this during my care of these patients.

This is only an outline. Details of the forms of abuse would take pages. More was reported to me and I have lists of names, dates, locations, but am reluctant to share more than this unless at least this much information is taken seriously by someone that I can trust.

General Overview and Common Traits:

1. Approximately 100 patients have been referred or have self referred for psychotherapy of varying time lengths or for consultation over the last 6 years.
2. At first I saw patients that resided in and around a major southern city. Later, patients were referred from all over the United States. I have also seen many patients in consultations that other therapists have brought to my office with specific therapeutic questions.
3. Regardless of where these patients lived, they reported the same basic information. Common traits were found in most of the patients who reported or described participating in what appear to fall into the classification of radiation or mind control experiments.
4. Patients reported that the list of experiences below were among the ways that multiple personalities, operatives and amnesia were produced within their personality structure.
         ECT was used on various parts of the body, usually the physical places that do not readily show or in tissue that heals quickly. Patients told me no scars were to be found. This included the head, teeth, ears, the nipples,

vagina, rectum and other parts of the body. A cattle prod type instrument was used to train patients to behave in certain ways.

Most patients described a helmet they wore that was related to both ECT and to sounds, such as taped messages in their ears, intense pain, disorientation, isolation, etc.

Goggles were often described that show colors or complete blackness as a part of sensory deprivation.

Goggles that gave the impression of "virtual reality" were described by my patients long before that concept was on the market. They reported that these goggles were used for them to view images that terrified them, made them think they had done horrendous things, including committing crimes such as murder, cannibalism, and also the images were used for blackmail purposes. ("You did this and we will send you to prison if you ever tell.")

Sensory deprivation in the home included closets, laundry hampers, drawers, and being locked in car trunks. Outside the home, this deprivation included totally soundproofed rooms and no light. They reported a sense of being left for hours or days in isolation with no human contact. They were left in a room on LSD and other drugs or used sexually while on these drugs. Patients report being held upside down in what is described as a black hole as a means of sensory deprivation.

Some patients described a hyperbaric chamber where the pressure changed and was very painful to them.

Immersion in water was used including being shackled in a cage, with a helmet, goggles, and a sense of being able to feel pain and then eventually not feeling anything at all.

All patients described black "shock" boxes that were a source of electroshock and used by perpetrators on them or that they used at home on themselves. Two of them have been turned in by patients of another therapist in my area. So far, one has been examined and was traced back to the CIA. Most patients were trained to torture themselves in places that do not show. (Inside the ear, nose, mouth, vagina, rectum.) The black box that was turned in to a therapist was a source of voltage. It included two attachments that could be connected, one was a long cord with a two pronged end that could be placed anywhere in the body and the other was a converted curling iron. I personally saw this equipment. There is a videotape of the patient describing the use of this apparatus, her explanation as to why it is that she used it on herself regularly and an analysis by a certified electrician in regard to the complexity of the internal mechanisms. The electrician felt the patient could not have made the devices herself. Patients have turned in other devices to therapists that they report that they use for self-torture that are usually normal house hold items such as curling irons, and other ordinary easily purchased items. The patients reported that they were programmed to hurt themselves and had to do it.

All of the patients said that the ECT and other forms of torture mentioned above were used to create multiple personalities that have specific jobs. Lipton's concept of "doubling" enters in here. The patients reported that they have a group of alter personalities that lead their normal life. They have other parts that are trained or programmed to be prostitutes, be involved in pornography, run drugs and money within cities and across borders and internationally. Some patients reported that they had "operatives" with separate identities, social security numbers, passports, etc and had jobs in other countries. They refer to specific people they have to kill, bombs to be planted in certain places and how they will not be suspected because they are usually young or middle aged, white and female and not the profile looked for in these types of crimes.

Most of the patients reported that they were forced to be active perpetrators from a young age, to do to others what had been done to them. They were then told that they were just like those who had harmed them and that they would go to prison if anyone found out.

5. Clinically:

Most of these patients had pseudo grand mal seizures with full tonic, clonic movement and apnea, up to 125 of them in one psychotherapy session and they attributed it to being shocked through ECT by their perpetrators to create alter personalities. Those that were tested had normal EEGs. One patient was tested while having a pseudo grand mal seizure and nothing showed up on the EEG. It appeared to be a body memory.

They had automatic behavior from very robotically trying to kill themselves in various ways, to trying to kill the therapist, to trying to leave the office to kill somebody else.

Most of these patients responded to certain sounds such as clickers, metronomes or just clicking the tongue or hand clapping. Patients would vacillate from calm to robotically asking: "who do you want me to kill?" depending upon the sound that was heard.

Most of them were programmed to resist therapy, create cognitive confusion and to later recant their memories.

Most of the patients had multiple layers of alter personalities with strong amnesia between certain layers, particularly the layers that had specific antisocial jobs.

The patients are terrified that if this information known they will be killed or have to kill themselves, their therapist, or their loved ones.

Those that have children are expected to start conditioning them at birth on the same plan so that most of the children of these severe patients, if allowed to be in treatment, were found to be MPD and described the same experiences as their parents.

The patients described torture from very early in childhood that persisted even during therapy since the programming does not permit them to stop what appear to be conditioned responses to act sado-maschocistically.

Almost all of them describe a doctor or hospital setting, being strapped to a bed or table to have various experiments done to them including ECT, drugs, helmets, tapes to listen to, sexual assault of all types.

These patients described terribly demeaning, humiliating acts with the psychology being that nobody wants them, loves them and that their only hope is that their perpetrators will care for them.

Most patients described Neo-Nazi alter personalities who believed in the coming of the next Reich, had Nazi thinking, had alters named after concentration camps, Hitler, Adolph, other Nazi leaders and had a belief system of Aryan Supremacy. The thinking was clearly not something obtained except through intense brainwashing and not available to the general public.

6. More specific experiences that one or more patients reported:

A patient described situations where everyone wore the protection used by X-ray technicians except the patient. The patient thinks radiation of some sort occurred.

Patients reported being hung in a harness around the waist, straps around the upper body with straps in the area of the vagina and rectum. These were used to use ECT on the head, nipples, insert objects and ECT devices in the vagina and rectum. Depending upon the age of the patient, this was originally described as used for torture and complete control of the patient. Then, the patient reported that she was trained to be the perfect prostitute and to react in certain ways with certain men. Depending upon what was needed either as a prostitute or in a pornographic film, the patient was trained to react in certain ways, play particular roles and alter personalities were made to play those roles. This was described as starting at around 5 years of age and being used throughout their life for training or punishment purposes. Patients reported that, in retrospect, this made the prostitution and pornography go more smoothly.

Many patients reported being trained to be "programmers" by the "Dr. Green" which included starting with young children and using various quite involved techniques to mind control their subjects. The purpose was to create operatives, multiplicity and amnesia about all that happened. Any deviations in behavior were to be corrected by "adjustments" or further torture with ECT and other very painful tortures.

Most described routine use of a torture table where they were strapped down and then a variety of the above tortures were used depending upon what was needed.

Recruiting of children and adults into this situation was also reported by my patients. They described going to malls and other places and seeking out vulnerable people. If appropriate, they acted as a prostitute and also gave free drugs to get them locally involved. Others, especially the homeless or out of work, were promised jobs, given bus or airplane money and put on a bus or airplane. Usually from this city, relocation was reported to be to the Colorado Springs, Denver area.

Almost all patients reported being chained or shackled so that the patient had to remain on hands and knees and then made to have sex with specially trained dogs. After the training, this was used in both activities involving prostitution and pornography.

Almost all patients described being kept naked in cages while waiting for many of the above activities to occur to them while watching it happen to others.

Patients described enemas, being made to eat their feces, drink their urine and have their mouth used as the toilet for others in totally breaking down the person. This was also reported to be used during prostitution and pornography.

Many described mandatory family participation at home and particularly in front of others and in pornographic films. It was reported that sibling acts and parent child acts were especially valued by the perpetrators.

Some patients described an "arena" where spectators observed combinations of sexual perversion. This was always reported as very important, with important people there including foreign dignitaries. This was followed by individual prostitution in well decorated rooms. The patients believed this happened in this city and in Denver or Colorado Springs.

A few described planned murders by operatives and discussed future murders and bomb sites picked.

Many named military bases as locations for these experiments, especially in the area between Austin and San Antonio and Colorado Springs. They also named medical centers and hospitals and universities.

Full family involvement was expected where the parent was expected to include the children and take them to be programmed at a very early age.

Some patients provided a long list of names of people involved in these activities. These were often the same names from patients that to my knowledge had never met. This list included doctors, both local and in other cities that were the "Dr. Green" and described as specializing in torture.

Other doctors aborted fetuses that were used for various purposes or took care of any problems involved with the torture to make sure the patient was well, could go home and not have to visit another physician.

Some patients lists of people involved included government officials, important people locally as well as ordinary citizens and many children. Many patients reported that they had to report in to a "Master" on a regular basis to make sure everything was correctly followed. All patients with a master talked with great reluctance and fear of their master and few identified them by name. Patients reported that people involved often did not use their real name or went by their maiden name or middle name.

Many patients reported an organized system placed inside them by "Dr. Green" so that they reported themselves as being programmed or mind controlled. They reported that sounds, hand signals, messages and sounds over the phone, certain dates, etc., would cause involuntary behaviors to occur. Usually the host or presenting personality was amnestic to this programming and the activities done were contrary to what the host ever wanted to do.

I hope this is helpful to you in serving to help victims of these forms of abuse.

March 10, 1995

After working with Disassociative Disorder clients for five years, it became apparent that there were some differences in the recovery process, the feel of their energy, and difference in layers/ dividisions of altered states within their system.

When I began this work in January 1990, I had heard little of Satanic cults and/or medical experimentation or even systemic and sadistic abuse. Clients with Satanic cult/KKK/ witchcraft organized crimes connections seemed to be able to break through the programming, once safe in a hospital or away from the groups and to be able to move through memories and find a spirituality that helped them in the process of healing. When clients talked about computers, cold sterile rooms, hospitals, doctors, military procedures and training; the memories were more difficult to access. These clients had a much more flat affect, more depersonalized and had a more difficult time finding a spirituality to help them in the process.

Repeatedly, I kept hearing some of the same procedures: spinal taps, experiments in water and other flotation tanks, EKG, EEGs, drugs (especially nicotine and hallcunigentons, electrical shock treatments, including putting tubes down the throat and shocking to stop the heart and other functions). Many talked of needles and medication being put in the brain cavity and other parts of the brain cortex to be stimulated to ascertain pain tolerance, disassociatve tolerance and other functions or lack of functions. Experiments with colors and lights were used a great deal as were mirrors to distort reality and to test clients' ability to repeat numbers and words. As in the cult activities, extreme sensory deprivation and sensory overload were used to distort reality and to confuse the senses. Every mind control technique known has mentioned by the clients and others not known before by this therapist.

Repeatedly information about being in intelligence and/or warfare became a common theme. Clients have had memories of going to Boy/Girl Scout camps to learn warfare techniques and being in government underground facilities.

One client told me that they were made to believe they had been abducted by UFOs, so that if memories were retrieved, they would be discredited by the community.

Each one with the military mind control/ experimentation had been trained for specific purposes . . . scanning computer information, accessing secret codes from computers, assassination of whoever they were told, couriers, prostitution/escort services to seduce government/political officials for information and blackmail purposes.

Several talked about "glowing in the dark", being given something . . . drug or radiation and watched by medical personnel to assess their reaction. Several talked of genetic experimentation . . . one miscarried in her early 20's and wasn't allowed to have a D & C until the doctors attempted to save the fetus that they had genetically engineered.

It also became clear that there were some common backgrounds of these clients . . . their caretakers/parents had connection with the Masons (money, influence and political connections) and all branches of the military . . . Navy, Army and Air Force. A couple of clients have memories of hearing their parents being paid to utilize the children or they were given free medical care.

Intricate programming codes included Greek Alphabet, Kabalistic terms, colors, numerology

and semiprecious stones. Many of the codes
were common terms to keep the clients
programmed and confused in everyday life and
basically amnestic to the mind control
information.

After the client has presented dreams and
memories of medical mind control/
experimentation, to verify their being
programmed, I have put them under a deep trance
and asked anything about "Alpha". It becomes
clear very quickly if they have this
background. Usually, an alter appears
angrily/fearfully about being discovered.
Because of the danger of flooding them with
memories and overwhelming them with
programming, I have not used hypnosis after
that and have allowed the client to take their
own process time to access information and
memories at the speed and rate that they can
handle it. That has seemed to work better than
using a systemactic approach to hypnosis,
especially for outpatient work.

After working extensively with thirty five (35)
clients and six children with systematic and
sadistic abuse and disassociatve disorders,
thirteen adult survivors are known to have the
mind control/medical experimentation.

For the purpose of this report and the
hearings, I will list the clients with memories
of radiation poisoning/injections. I will list
the doctors and locations as the clients have
given. Because I want to protect their
identity and mine, because we are all well
aware that I am being watched and monitored
about who and when I see the survivors. I will
attempt to list the salient facts in a concise
way, to be used for the hearings.

CA, 39 year old female, born in 1955 in
Oakland, Cal at the Naval Station. She grew up
in Colo. where they moved immediately after the
birth and her father, in the AirForce moved

them between Gunnison, Colo., Pampa, Texas and
Amarillo, Texas. She has memories of being the
underground facility in C. Springs, NORAD, as
well as her AirForce uncle took her to the
underground facilities in Nev. Information
that she has secured includes that both parents
were hypnotized and told that she would be made
available to them at any time, in return for
the government leaving the other children
alone. Her father was also used as an
experimental subject and was periodically in
and out of state hospitals for mental
breakdowns. He subsequently committed suicide.
The family was drawn into this by her paternal
grandfather in Pampa, Texas, who had been in
trouble with the government and was immunity
for the use of his son and the children. She
had information that she was poisoned by
radiation as an infant in 1956 and subsequently
by Dr. Volkenstein from Pampa between 1958–1961.
She was told she had an extra kidney and had
surgery as an infant. Subsequently it has been
found that her kidney was destroyed by
radiation and had to be removed within the
first 18 months. Presently her ANA (Anti
Nuclear Antibioties) are positive and she had
ongoing health problems. She also knows that
her uncle took her to Nevada every summer
vacation and she was subjected to radiation
poisoning from 1970 to 1974. The doctors who
are mentioned frequently by her include: Dr.
Rosenbaum, Dr. Greenbaum, Dr. Volkenstein, DR.
William Mullens and Dr. Woolsworth Russell.
She was also given hormone shots yearly and had
a complete hysterectomy by the time she was in
her mid twenties. She has had repeated
occurrances of breast cysts over the years.

CWS, 42 year old female, born in 1952 in Waco,
Texas. She had experimentation done as late as
1975 in Baylor University Hospital in Waco,
when she was miscarrying and the doctor refused
to allow D&C to heal, and insisted she be
transported to the hospital where she has
memories of them trying to save the fetus which

had been genetically engineered and was
supposed to become available to them when the
child was three years old. It was the wisdom
of the Universe that allowed that baby to be
miscarried and the client was finally able to
grieve that baby and why it miscarried, after
all these years. She has memories of
strychnine being used for heart experiments
(she remembers the taste of bitter almonds).
She remembers that the doctor made several
mistakes . . . clotted her blood and she had
damage of the pancreas and had another heart
stoppage. She had radiation poisoning done
repeatedly and cancer of the vulva was
diagnosed in 1994 and she is currently in
remission for that cancer. She remember spinal
taps with radiation and many experiments done
in hypberchambers and water containers. She
has memories of experiments being done on the
brain and to see how far she would disassociate
before coming back. She remembers being a part
of experiments with several children and being
used as examples in a classroom of the
University Hospital. The doctors that she
mentions are Dr. Avant, Dr. Greenbaum, Dr.
Green and Dr. Cochran. A doctor Pastrel tried
to make the kids more comfortable but seemed
unable to get them away from the experiments at
the University Hospital.

CS- 41 year old female born in 1953, where many
of the experiments occurred in Lufkin Memorial
Hospital and Crocket Hospital in Texas. The
child was given cobalt and radiation treatments
for a skin disorder for the first six years of
her life. As a four year old, she remembers
her father telling her that the radiation was
like "radio waves". By the time she was 13
years old, she had a ulcerated uterus and
continues to have abnormal pap smears. She
also had a great deal of gum and teeth
experimentation and was told that a microphone
was put in her molar area. Trauma done to her
upper teeth and gums have been validated by
subsequent xrays and the current dentist cannot

figure out how the trauma could have occurred.
She also has memories of her pituary gland
being injected with radiation. She has been
told that she cannot have children, but no
explanation.
She has memories of a nurse putting a needle in
her neck and upper right shoulder in 1960 and
not wanting the doctor to know what she was
doing.
The doctors that she talks about are: Dr.
Charles Evans, Dr. Trout, Dr. Temple, Dr.
Kerth, Dr. Lupertz and Dr. Goldshe in Crockett,
Texas.
Her father traveled all the time and the memory
is that her mother thought she was helping
medical science by making the client available
for experiments. She also has a memory that
the experiments stopped because they were
considered a faillure.

CK, 38 year old female, born 1956 in Athens,
Texas. The experiments were done at Tyler
Memorial Hospital in Tyler, Texas. Her father
was a veteran of WWII and had PTSD and was
involved with KKK and the Masons. She has
memories of the experiments occurring between
August, 1961 and 1967, although she had was
told she was born with 4 kidneys and one was
removed at age 18 months. She feels that the
radiation poisoning killed one kidney. The
experiments that she remembers included seeing
how much pain she could endure. She also has
memories of learning how to memorize numbers,
shapes and other codes. Much of her
programming was done with food, so she has an
ongoing issue with an eating disorder,
fluctuating between not eating and overeating.
The doctors that she talks about are: Dr.
Claywater, Dr. Green and Dr. Holt. She also
mentioned that the hospital was all green.

CKM, 30 year old male, born in 1965 in New York
and spent time in Cleveland, Ohio and Dallas,
Texas. He is beginning to have memories of
being underground with large doors, huge

computers and a hospital setting. He knows he has been poisoned by radiation but does not have the clear memories yet and has not mentioned the doctors or specific places yet.

CL, 47 year old female, born in Ohio, in 1947. Father worked for Manhatten project and when she was diagnosed with Disassociative Disorder, appeared to be relieved about a great secret but died very quickly and unusually of Altzhiemer's Disease. She believes that he could have had radiation poisoning, because of the progress of the disease did not make medical sense. She has flashes of underground labs, sterile rooms, halls and being trained as a solider in the Navy. She has just began retrieving memories.

All of the aforementioned clients also had a history of a great deal of systematic and sadistic abuse from incestual parents and other relatives, history of witchcraft, Satanic cult, KKK, NeoNazi and other torture and abuse. One client feels that her father was abusive to her so that he couldn't become too attached since he had been forced to take her to the hospitals. That seems to have some merit to it. It also appears that if parents were blackmailed to just did it for "God and Country", it was a part of the whole picture where their child was dehumanized and treated like an object and served the parents' needs.

Several of the clients are just now getting the memories and so they are incomplete, but I have included the ones that have definite memories of medical/mind control abuse. Only two of the thirty five, did not have other systematic abuse . . . one's mother was schizophrenic and thought she was helping the country and the other person was sexually abused by various members of the extended family over a long period of time.

March 12, 1995

I have first hand knowledge of the radiation experiments and other experiments conducted on human subjects, without informed consent, by U.S. government officials and at U.S. government facilities (as well as other facilities) during the 1950's and 1960's.

The experiments on me began when I was about three years old and the experiments continued for about a twenty year period. The experiments and related activities included the following:

o   use of radiation on my body and inserting radioactive material into me;

o   administration of various mind-altering drugs including LSD;

o   physical torture including 1) pulling my knees out of their sockets repeatedly; and 2) insertion of various painful objects in various parts of my body;

o   sexual experiments, rituals and torture of many kinds;

o   mind control experiments utilizing extensive electroshock, hypnosis and drug administration combined with various kinds of intense mind programming;

o   administration of blood products and other chemicals through transfusions and other modes of delivery; and

o   child pornography photographing of me (alone and with others).

This experimentation was extensive and the experiments occurred repeatedly and frequently. The experiments were often accompanied by terrible death threats and torture to convince me not to tell anyone what was going on. One of the most extensive means of torture and mind control, which began at an early age and continued throughout all the years, was the use of snakes to terrify me.

The group involved in these experiments was primarily composed of people in U.S. intelligence agencies and various branches of the military, although some civilian government officials were also involved. Many of the governmental officials were in high level positions. Some activities related to the experiments involved private citizens. My own father was involved with Naval Intelligence in World War II and that was mainly how my family and I were linked to the intelligence and military officials that were involved for so many years in the radiation and mind control experiments conducted in this country.

The locale for the experimentation done on me from 1947-1962 included principally Utah, Nevada, Arizona and California, but some experiments occurred in other Western states. Most experiments occurred in U.S. government facilities or on U.S. property.

Starting in 1962, the nightmare of experiments and related activities continued for me for several more years when I was relocated to the Washington, D.C. area. Again, the experimentation, torture and abuse occurred in many U.S. government facilities including in: 1) high level intelligence and military facilities in Northern Virginia; 2) CIA safe houses in the area; 3) private homes of some government officials in the metropolitan area including Alexandria, Falls Church and Arlington; 4) Ft. Detrick in Frederick, Maryland; and 5) in the Fort Meade/NSA area in Maryland.

There are a number of names of government officials who were involved in the radiation and mind control experiments and related activities that I can supply, but among the key individuals were Dr. Sidney Gottlieb of the CIA and Dr. White, Dr. Green and Dr. Hamilton who were working for Gottlieb in some capacity. There was a Nazi doctor who played a key role in some of the physical and other sadistic experiments done to me.

There is more information that I can supply about some of the government and non-government facilities that were used. For example, I have drawings of the layouts of some of the property and places where products of some of the experiments were disposed of. In order to protect myself, I have placed this material, along with other more extensive documentation, in several safe and secure places.

The personal consequences of the nightmare of these experiments, torture and abuse have been devastating—physically, mentally, emotionally and spiritually. I had significant physical health problems as a child and even more significant medical problems for over twenty years of my adult life. I have had many years of psychotherapy to cope with the effects of these radiation and mind control experiments and my professional career and my relationships have suffered as well. But perhaps the greatest burden for me now has been the emotional and physical pain caused by these experiments, combined with the knowledge that my country's government allowed such experiments and other activities to take place—that there was insufficient oversight to curb the excesses and atrocities that occurred.

I believe that it is only with the full revelation of what occurred in these experiments that the safeguards that are supposed to operate in our democracy can be put in place so as to avoid such tragedies in the future. Despite all that has happened to me, I believe in the wisdom of our democracy, but I know better than most citizens of the terrible excesses of governmental power, especially when secrecy and national security are used by the government as a cover for human evil and an attitude that the ends justify the means.

Despite my fear of the consequences, I am willing to publicly testify if this can be worked-out in a satisfactory manner. I would be willing to face the potential significant consequences of this public testimony because I believe so strongly in the need for the public to know what happened and for the government to be forced to take extensive action in response to these revelations to avoid such atrocities in the future.

March 12, 1995

March 08, 1995

Affidavit of -----------

    I, ---------- would like to swear to and
state the following:

1. I was physically abused and my mind
programmed at V.A. hospitals during the years
1950 to 1954. I was between the ages of 11-14
at the time. My father, Ralph A. Matson was a
Major or Lt. Colonel in the U.S. Army. I
specifically remember being abused in the Salt
Lake City, Utah, V.A. Hospital at Fort Douglas.
It was the old V.A. Hospital.

    The methods used to program my mind were
pain and torture, repetitive sounds in my ears,
flashing lights, sleep deprivation, drugs etc.
My father was often present during these
sessions. The torture and programing was done
by doctors and/or orderlies. Sometimes there
were other men in business suits present. The
names Green Room, Greenbaum or Greentree are
associated with these sessions.

I remember being taken to other V.A. hospitals
around the country by my father when he went to
"camp". I am not sure of their localities.
The program methods used were similar.

2. Between 1975 and 1980 I was in the care of a
psychiatrist Dr. Tom Fox MD, in Logan, Utah. He
continued to program, sexually and physically
abuse me. He used his private office as well as
the old Logan Hospital and other localities. At
times he was joined by a Dr. Black from Southern
Utah. The last incident I recall was in 1985 at
St. Marks Hospital in Salt Lake City, Utah,
where I had been hospitalized for depression and
ECT treatments. Although he was not my
attending physician, Dr. Black visited me
several times to check if the mind programming
was still intact.

3. I have had a 30 year history of mental
illness with various diagnoses. Since my
memories have emerged and I have received
proper treatment, I am finally getting well.

March 8, 1995

The statements herein contained are allegations asserted to have been committed by the Central Intelligence Agency of the United States of America from January 1964 through July 1976. This is a first-hand account written by the recipient of these actions, who will pseudonymically be referred to as "--------" to reduce the risk of retribution from the actors involved.

I (-------) wish only to document these happenings, and have no intention of personally pursuing these matters legally. The following reflects events as I witnessed them, and is in no way, an attempt to slander any representative individual or group of any government or organization.

PROGRAMMING

I was three years and four months (3yrs 4mo) old when I was taken to what would later become known to me as the "Station." Located underground near Amarillo, Texas, the Station was a large, sterile facility I was taken to many times throughout the course of my training. I am unable to identify the exact location, as I was placed in a burlap sack, tucked in the back floorboard of my parents' 1957 Comet, and driven to a location known only to them to be turned over to my "teachers," (government agents who programmed me). Most often, these trips occurred between 3:00-4:00 am, and I was not allowed to see anything until the "teachers" had me in the Station. I was given a mild, oral short-acting, sedative to assist my parents in delivering me quietly.

For the first six (6) months, I was "taught my lessons" in a closet-like space painted white. Its dimensions were approximately 3' X 3' X 10'. There was a door making one panel of the closet where myself and my "teachers" entered and exited. The door was knobbed only on the outside so that once inside, I had no way of letting myself out. The panel across from the door had a small square cut out and approximately 5' up where light from a photo projector shown through. There were also holes in the same panel, where later, electroshock implements would be wired through.

During each programming session, I was placed in the closet, facing the door panel. I was completely naked. After a period of about ten (10) minutes of total darkness, the light projector would shine through the small opening, making a large light square on the door panel. Elementary, cut-out figures of bunnies, kittens, squares, circles, and boxes were attached to wooden tongue depressors and placed in front of the projector, creating a large shadow of themselves on the door panel. Some of these figures were constructed of transparent materials, making an outlined shadow, while others were made out of black materials (construction paper), forming a completely filled shadow on the panel. The temperature of the closet was kept cool enough to just be uncomfortable to bare skin. A women's voice accompanied the shadow figures. Most of what the woman said was about good and bad, with "good" associated with the black figures, and "bad" coupled with the opaque shadows (exactly opposite of Western culture's binary pairings). Many states of deprivation were used in addition to the visual stimulation like hunger, cold, heat, too much auditory stimuli, too little auditory stimuli, etc. The woman referred to me as "it" (i.e. "Does it know what this is?" "Does it want out of the box?"). I was not allowed to move onto other programming until I created a dissociative ego state separate from the rest of my psyche. They gave the ego state a name of their choosing and called me that name when they wanted her to present.

In addition to the Station, I was taken by my mother to an ophthalmologist's office in the city of Amarillo a number of times. I was five years (5 yrs.) old the first time I can recall (although my mother reports that I was "treated" by this doctor from age two). My mother turned me over to the "nurse" calling patients back. The "nurse" took me to a small ophthalmology office located right in the center of the building, with an administrative office off to the right of the room. The "nurse" sat me in a chair in the administrative office, across from an empty physician's desk. After about ten (10) minutes, a large-framed, middle-aged, red-haired woman in a green two-piece suite and light stockings entered the office, introduced herself as "Mrs. Simms," and took a seat opposite me. She was smiling and calling me yet another name. She explained that we would be doing a number of "fun" things together throughout the course of the day. She praised me for being well-mannered, and led me to a black examination chair in the exam room. The "nurse" administered stinging eye drops in each of my eyes and the room went completely black. I heard the "nurse" call my new name and asked if I was "here yet." She then projected english words and letters on the wall across from me. My eyes were out of focus. The "nurse" became more and more irritated with my silence and told me she was going to get the doctor to make me speak. "Mrs. Simms" came in was not friendly this time. For what seemed like many hours, I was forced to repeat letter and number sequences that had no meaning to me. Most of the sequences were nonsense pairs, or things that are not typically grouped together. Some of the letters were upside-down. There was a break in the day, when I was given back to my mother for a short period of time, but none of my physical needs were attended to like my need for food, liquid, or to be taken to the bathroom. We had come in the morning, and were not released until the sun was going down. There were about ten (10) days intermittently spent this way over the next year, and an additional ten (10) days at age 11.

When I turned eight years (8 yrs) old, the torture aspect of the programming became much worse. I was accompanied by "teachers" at the Station to a tank holding a large amount of water and between one and three dolphins. All the "teachers" were dressed exactly the same: plain, gray suite, white long-sleeved shirt, black leather shoes, black plastic-rimmed glasses, gold-colored watchband, and crew haircut. They were indistinguishable from one another. Very few women were present, but the ones I saw wore grey, two-pieced suite skirts with light stockings. Their hair was pinned in a bun and they wore black low-heeled shoes. Again, I was naked when all the "teachers" in the room were clothed. I was told that I was going to learn to "speak to the dolphins." A number of these sessions were used to familiarize me with the dolphins and the dolphins with me. I was given a set of headphones and was able to hear the sounds the dolphins were making underwater. I was instructed to imitate those sounds. I remained silent. When I was noncompliant, I was placed in the closet described at the first of this section and electrically shocked at terminal points on my temples, wrists, thighs, and ankles. Before each shock, I heard a woman's voice say, "We are very unhappy with you." My eyes and teeth hurt from the electricity. I was taken out of the closet and back to the water tank over and over, but I refused to imitate the dolphins. By this time, I was being used to program younger children in the same manner as I had been programmed at the beginning. I was angry that I was being used for the "teachers'" means, and not obeying was the only way I could think to protest. I was told if I continued to refuse, my little sister would be slain in front of me, that some of my programming subjects would be killed, that I would be forced to kill my sister or my subjects, etc. I was drown in the tank on three (3) occasions, and resuscitated in a pool of water and vomit. I was forced to eat a fetal puppy, hind legs first. I became more and more resistant. The final act of torture occurred when I was eight years, 2 months old. I was electroshocked in the closet and taken to the tank. One of the teachers was holding a three month old baby girl by the back of the neck. She was making no noise. There was a man in a diving suit in the tank with one of the dolphins. He was holding a large, serrated knife in his hand. The teacher on the platform told me I was to decide which of these, the baby or the dolphin, would live. After remaining silent for four or five minutes, I softly said, "Save the baby." The diver stabbed the dolphin in the middle of its chest and made a slit down the length of its body. Blood and enterals flooded the water. I was pushed into the water from behind. When I came up for air, I saw that the platform teacher had dropped the baby in the water anyway and she was floating face-down on the surface, dead.

I lost consciousness, and woke up nine (9) days later in a free-standing surgical center in Amarillo. The center was abandoned and silent, except for the sound of the respirator I was connected to. A doctor came in several hours later to disconnect the respirator. I was taken back to my parents, residing in a small town in the Texas Panhandle. Not a word was spoken of the event, but when I returned to my third grade class after Christmas break 1968, I was unable to recall anything I had learned in school previously (multiplication tables, social studies lessons, etc.). I was not taken to the Station for a number of months after the coma.

At some point between ages 9 and 11, instructions were coupled with a series of chess moves. I made many flights to Europe (Germany and England mostly) for "finishing," where I was versed in political issues (i.e. the Cuban Missile Crisis), classic literary works, and other matters of world interest. I was instructed (mostly by elderly women) on the differences in types of wine, entrees, clothing, manners, etc. I was taught by younger women how to maneuver sexually to "take a man's mind off anything." After much training, I was used in the United States to assist the C.I.A. in covert operations, mostly as a sexual escort to distract government officials that were later assassinated by other players in the operation. All of these assignments were initiated over the phone by a male voice saying a specific, pre-laid chess move in a certain order, which would bring a dissociated part of me to the forefront for further instructions at a designated meeting place. Each assignment was delivered with the explicit warning that death would be sure should I deviate from the instructions in any way.

In 1976, the government stopped using me. Contact was reestablished in January 1994, when I was placed on "stand-by" status for an assignment in North Vietnam. Details of the job were never relayed to me and I never went to Vietnam. I was abducted from a college campus in New Mexico in August of 1994, and taken to an underground facility I believe now to be associated with a prominent lab in Albuquerque, New Mexico. I had begun work on a project involving "computer hacking" data off the InterNet of demographic information on elementary school-aged children entered on classroom computers, when I became aware of the dissociated part of me that was participating, and discontinued any activity around that. I have received telephone calls, verbal threats, and was even physically assaulted, for refusing to continue the project. Before each of the three (3) abductions, a stranger would approach me and speak a chess move, altering out a compliant ego state. I would regain consciousness in the surroundings of my own home, unaware that I had been anywhere or done anything. Once I realized what was happening, I refused to go with the abductor the fourth time and have not been to the facility since.

These events have caused a great deal of difficulty for me, and remain a formidable obstacle I face each day. The painful part is that I was harmed by an agency of my own government, in direct violation of rights I am guaranteed as a citizen of the United States. No one in our country should be subject to such mistreatment yet, I believe these activities are still going on today. Any action leading to the protection of our nation's children (and adults) from such damaging abuse is worth the time and money it will cost to carry it out.

Thank you for your consideration of the above. God bless you in the days ahead.

Connecticut
March 3, 1995

The Presidential Committee on Radiation

Dear Sirs:

This is my personal witness of victimization by radiation and a progression of mind control techniques. The following knowledge has come to me outside the benefit of a therapeutic relationship. I look forward to being able to support my personal truth with published material. It is written anonymously in accordance with my understanding of the spirit of its presentation. I have attempted to outline extensively documented recall contained in audiotaped and written material shared with both law enforcement and therapeutic communities since 1988. Names of people mentioned here are those I commonly knew them by and may not represent their legal identities. I have drawn many of them and would welcome the opportunity to view photographs with the purpose of identifying them. Names of places mentioned were overheard in conversation at times when the person responsible for me seemed to think I was too drugged or dissociated to remember. I have drawn some of these places and I would welcome the opportunity to validate my memories by visiting them.

I was born in 1944 into a family which had consistently had emotionally, physically and sexually traumatized all offspring for generations. My legal father was in the Air Force. A young physician I knew as Dr. Korim (spelling?) instructed my mother in the beginning of mind control techniques at the age of 6 months until my middle teens. A friend of my mother's with Navy survival training named Joe Montalbueno (spelling?) assisted by a boyhood friend of my father's named Henry Blessing have continued to carry out mind control techniques on me all of my life.

At the age of 18 months I met a person I knew as Herr Doctor. My mother spoke to him in German. I was taken to New York City where I was subjected to what I believe to be radiation to my head. The machines resembled older styled X-Ray units and produced the generator whirring sound peculiar to them. I was also given electric shock.

At two I was enrolled in a class of 10 other girls who were being taught dissociative techniques by

Prune, a school in New Britain. The rest of the group seemed to range in age to 10 years old. I was sexually abused routinely after class to curb my rebellious nature. My mother broke my left arm across the top when I was 3 so that I would not use my left hand. They used water, lights, hypnosis, sexual abuse, electric shock to train me to pass messages form person to person. There were often men in military uniforms who participated in this training.

I learned how to handle weapons, particularly how an ice pick left as neat hole. A hole that allowed so little blood to escape that the victim could remain in public view for hours before they would be discovered to not be napping. With each stage of the training I split inside my mind, more and more. Joe tested my reaction to centrifugal force and what restraints I could escape from in laboratories in the Quantico, VA area. I was taken on planes to Germany and Egypt to assist Joe with arson, to Israel alone with messages, to Mexico for terrorist activities. I remember a small laboratory in a partially exposed basement of a large building I visited many times, starting at age 4, south of Washington, D.C. I was taken to Connecticut to a building connected with the Compensating Reservoir in Barkhamsted. Some of my training took place at a camp in Amston, CT. At the age of 14, I was drugged and woke up on a stretcher where I heard men outside my door discussing how they had "gotten me past the guards at Langley" that night.

At the age of 15 Joe introduced me to an elderly man he referred to as the "Senator". At the Mayflower Hotel in Washington, D.C., the portly gentleman was brought to a room adjoining ours. Our closet space was filled with photographic equipment viewing the senator scene. I refused to participate. I was severely punished.

Joe has continued to influence my life and has tried to intimidate me to this day. He has interfered with my relationship with my husband and my children. He still tries to get me to do jobs for him as I had been trained to do so long ago.

I thank you for listening to this witness. Because of my extensive exposure to mind control techniques, the darkness of my relationship with Joe and his associates as touched my husband, my children, other family members, employers and friends. It threatens now to touch a third generation! Maybe my eventual freedom and complete healing will forever remain beyond my reach. With every breath I take, I pray that it is not so. I am vulnerable to anyone who knows my cues and triggers better than I do. I am vulnerable to anyone who is threatened by what may still lay buried deep in my memory. There is no law prohibiting anyone from attempting to kill me by activating my own mind against me.

I physically struggle with the accumulated affects of my accumulated trauma daily. Ligaments were stretched when vertebra, hip, elbow and knee joints were dislocated. Nerves were damaged by electrical impact. Muscles contract, trying to adapt to compensating positional changes. I have no idea what possible consequences my future holds for me due to my exposure to radiation. Our system of justice does not protect me from the people who have attempted to steal my entire life.

The group of my personal perpetrators is relatively small. But, I wonder what national policy lays behind this type of child abuse and why? I wonder who sanctioned and developed it. I wonder who attempts to conceal the truth of its existence and extent from the American people now?

I request from the members of the committee a thoroughly complete investigation of this type of severe child abuse. You must prevent future generations from being victimized by those who are elected and chosen to protect them. I believe this is a matter of utmost importance and demands the full resources of your office.

APPENDIX A

PART 4
White House Correspondence

THE WHITE HOUSE

WASHINGTON

December 19, 1995

Mr. Cooper Brown
Task Force on Radiation and Human Rights
6935 Laurel Avenue
Takoma Park, Maryland 20912

Dear Mr. Brown:

Thank you for your letter of October 12. I am glad you were able to be at the White House when I received the Advisory Committee on Human Radiation Experiment's final report.

The Advisory Committee's report was an indispensable part of our effort to restore the confidence of the American people in the integrity of their government. From the declassification of thousands of pages of documents to the public hearings and the many revelations the Advisory Committee made about decision-making in the Cold War-era, I hope you feel, as I do, that the government has kept its commitment to tell the truth about this chapter in our history.

The progress we have made in medicine and science are due in large part to our commitment to research, but we must remain vigilant when that research involves human subjects. That is why I directed each agency of our government that conducts, supports, or regulates research involving human subjects to review its procedures. An interim report is due back to me by Christmas and a final report is due early next year. The new National Bioethics Advisory Committee will supervise this process and ensure that our research protections are adequate and failsafe.

I have asked Secretary O'Leary and Dr. Tara O'Toole, Assistant Secretary of Energy for Environment, Safety and Health; and Attorney General Janet Reno and Eva M. Plaza, Deputy Attorney General, Torts Branch, to look more closely at the other issues you have raised in your letter.

Thank you for your support, and I look forward to your continued involvement.

Sincerely,

Bill Clinton

THE WHITE HOUSE

Office of the Press Secretary

For Immediate Release   February 17, 1994

February 17, 1994

MEMORANDUM FOR THE VICE PRESIDENT
               THE HEADS OF EXECUTIVE DEPARTMENTS
               AND AGENCIES

SUBJECT: Review of Federal Policy for the Protection of
              Human Subjects

Federally funded biomedical and behavioral research has resulted
in major advances in health care and improved the quality of
life for all Americans. The pursuit of new knowledge in these
fields of research often requires experiments that involve human
subjects. Although human subjects research is an essential
element of biomedical and behavioral research, bioethical
considerations must influence the design and conduct of
such research.

Since 1947, when guidelines for research with human subjects
were promulgated, there has been increasingly widespread
recognition of the need for voluntary and informed consent
and a scientifically valid design of experiments involving
human subjects.

Over time, this recognition has evolved into a rigorous and
formalized system of regulations and guidelines, which were
codified in governmental policies on human subject research,
and were included in the former Department of Health, Education
and Welfare's regulations in 1974, 45 C.F.R. 46. In 1991,
16 agencies formally adopted the core of these regulations in
a common Federal Policy for the Protection of Human Subjects.
This Policy requires that all research protocols involving human
subjects be reviewed by an Institutional Review Board. This
review ensures that (1) risks are minimized and reasonable in
relation to anticipated benefits; (2) there is informed consent;
and (3) the rights and welfare of the subjects are maintained
(56 Fed. Reg. 28003 (June 18, 1991)).

Although these regulations provide the framework for protecting
human subjects in research, we must exercise constant care
and ensure that these regulations are strictly enforced by
departments and agencies. Therefore, I direct each department
and agency of Government to review present practices to assure
compliance with the Federal Policy for the Protection of Human
Subjects and to cease immediately sponsoring or conducting any
experiments involving humans that do not fully comply with the
Federal Policy.

                         WILLIAM J. CLINTON

A P P E N D I X   A

PART 5
The Advisory Committee's
Final Report

Executive Summary and Guide to Final Report

Advisory Committee on Human Radiation Experiments

Advisory Committee on Human Radiation Experiments

The Final Report of the Advisory Committee on Human Radiation Experiments (stock number 061-000-00-848-9), the supplemental volumes to the Final Report (stock numbers 061-000-00850-1, 061-000-00851-9, and 061-000-00852-7), and additional copies of this Executive Summary (stock number 061-000-00849-7) may be purchased from the Superintendent of Documents, U.S. Government Printing Office.

All telephone orders should be directed to:
Superintendent of Documents
U.S. Government Printing Office
Washington, D.C. 20402
(202) 512-1800
FAX (202) 512-2250
8 a.m. to 4 p.m., Eastern time, M-F

All mail orders should be directed to:
U.S. Government Printing Office
P.O. Box 371954
Pittsburgh, PA 15250-7954

An Internet site containing ACHRE information (replicating the Advisory Committee's original gopher) will be available at George Washington University. The site contains complete records of Advisory Committee actions as approved; complete descriptions of the primary research materials discovered and analyzed; complete descriptions of the print and non-print secondary resources used by the Advisory Committee; a copy of the Interim Report of October 21, 1994, and a copy of the Final Report; and other information. The address is http://www.seas.gwu.edu/nsarchive/radiation. The site will be maintained by the National Security Archive at GWU.

Printed in the United States of America

Advisory Committee on Human Radiation Experiments

FINAL REPORT

EXECUTIVE SUMMARY

AND

GUIDE TO FINAL REPORT

THE CREATION OF THE ADVISORY COMMITTEE

On January 15, 1994, President Clinton appointed the Advisory Committee on Human Radiation Experiments. The President created the Committee to investigate reports of possibly unethical experiments funded by the government decades ago.

The members of the Advisory Committee were fourteen private citizens from around the country: a representative of the general public and thirteen experts in bioethics, radiation oncology and biology, nuclear medicine, epidemiology and biostatistics, public health, history of science and medicine, and law.

President Clinton asked us to deliver our recommendations to a Cabinet-level group, the Human Radiation Interagency Working Group, whose members are the Secretaries of Defense, Energy, Health and Human Services, and Veterans Affairs; the Attorney General; the Administrator of the National Aeronautics and Space Administration; the Director of Central Intelligence; and the Director of the Office of Management and Budget. Some of the experiments the Committee was asked to investigate, and particularly a series that included the injection of plutonium into unsuspecting hospital patients, were of special concern to Secretary of Energy Hazel O'Leary. Her department had its origins in the federal agencies that had sponsored the plutonium experiments. These agencies were responsible for the development of nuclear weapons and during the Cold War their

3

activities had been shrouded in secrecy. But now the Cold War was over.

The controversy surrounding the plutonium experiments and others like them brought basic questions to the fore: How many experiments were conducted or sponsored by the government, and why? How many were secret? Was anyone harmed? What was disclosed to those subjected to risk, and what opportunity did they have for consent? By what rules should the past be judged? What remedies are due those who were wronged or harmed by the government in the past? How well do federal rules that today govern human experimentation work? What lessons can be learned for application to the future? Our Final Report provides the details of the Committee's answers to these questions. This Executive Summary presents an overview of the work done by the Committee, our findings and recommendations, and the contents of the Final Report.

THE PRESIDENT'S CHARGE

The President directed the Advisory Committee to uncover the history of human radiation experiments during the period 1944 through 1974. It was in 1944 that the first known human radiation experiment of interest was planned, and in 1974 that the Department of Health, Education and Welfare adopted regulations governing the conduct of human research, a watershed event in the history of federal protections for human subjects.

In addition to asking us to investigate human radiation experiments, the President directed us to examine cases in which the government had intentionally released radiation into the

4

environment for research purposes. He further charged us with identifying the ethical and scientific standards for evaluating these events, and with making recommendations to ensure that whatever wrongdoing may have occurred in the past cannot be repeated.

We were asked to address human experiments and intentional releases that involved radiation. The ethical issues we addressed and the moral framework we developed are, however, applicable to all research involving human subjects.

The breadth of the Committee's charge was remarkable. We were called on to review government programs that spanned administrations from Franklin Roosevelt to Gerald Ford. As an independent advisory committee, we were free to pursue our charge as we saw fit. The decisions we reached regarding the course of our inquiry and the nature of our findings and recommendations were entirely our own.

THE COMMITTEE'S APPROACH

At our first meeting, we immediately realized that we were embarking on an intense and challenging investigation of an important aspect of our nation's past and present, a task that required new insights and difficult judgments about ethical questions that persist even today.

Between April 1994 and July 1995, the Advisory Committee held sixteen public meetings, most in Washington, D.C. In addition, subsets of Committee members presided over public forums in cities throughout the country. The Committee heard from more than 200 witnesses and interviewed dozens of

professionals who were familiar with experiments involving radiation. A special effort, called the Ethics Oral History Project, was undertaken to learn from eminent physicians about how research with human subjects was conducted in the 1940s and 1950s.

We were granted unprecedented access to government documents. The President directed all the federal agencies involved to make available to the Committee any documents that might further our inquiry, wherever they might be located and whether or not they were still secret.

As we began our search into the past, we quickly discovered that it was going to be extremely difficult to piece together a coherent picture. Many critical documents had long since been forgotten and were stored in obscure locations throughout the country. Often they were buried in collections that bore no obvious connection to human radiation experiments. There was no easy way to identify how many experiments had been conducted, where they took place, and which government agencies had sponsored them. Nor was there a quick way to learn what rules applied to these experiments for the period prior to the mid-1960s. With the assistance of hundreds of federal officials and agency staff, the Committee retrieved and reviewed hundreds of thousands of government documents. Some of the most important documents were secret and were declassified at our request. Even after this extraordinary effort, the historical record remains incomplete. Some potentially important collections could not be located and were evidently lost or destroyed years ago.

Nevertheless, the documents that were recovered enabled us to identify nearly 4,000 human radiation experiments sponsored by the federal government between 1944 and 1974. In the great majority of cases, only fragmentary data was locatable; the identity of subjects and the specific radiation exposures involved were typically unavailable. Given the constraints of information, even more so than time, it was impossible for the Committee to review all these experiments, nor could we evaluate the experiences of countless individual subjects. We thus decided to focus our investigation on representative case studies reflecting eight different categories of experiments that together addressed our charge and priorities. These case studies included:

- experiments with plutonium and other atomic bomb materials
- the Atomic Energy Commission's program of radioisotope distribution
- nontherapeutic research on children
- total body irradiation
- research on prisoners
- human experimentation in connection with nuclear weapons testing
- intentional environmental releases of radiation
- observational research involving uranium miners and residents of the Marshall Islands

In addition to assessing the ethics of human radiation experiments conducted decades ago, it was also important to explore the current conduct of human radiation research. Insofar as wrongdoing may have occurred in the past, we needed to examine the likelihood that such things could happen today. We therefore undertook three projects:

- A review of how each agency of the federal government that currently conducts or funds research involving human subjects regulates this activity and oversees it.

- An examination of the documents and consent forms of research projects that are today sponsored by the federal government in order to develop insight into the current status of protections for the rights and interests of human subjects.

- Interviews of nearly 1,900 patients receiving out-patient medical care in private hospitals and federal facilities throughout the country. We asked them whether they were currently, or had been, subjects of research, and why they had agreed to participate in research or had refused.

THE HISTORICAL CONTEXT

Since its discovery 100 years ago, radioactivity has been a basic tool of medical research and diagnosis. In addition to the many uses of the x ray, it was soon discovered that radiation could be used to treat cancer and that the introduction of "tracer" amounts of radioisotopes into the human body could help to diagnose disease and understand bodily processes. At the same time, the perils of overexposure to radiation were becoming apparent.

During World War II the new field of radiation science was at the center of one of the most ambitious and secret research efforts the world has known--the Manhattan Project. Human radiation experiments were undertaken in secret to help under stand radiation risks to workers engaged in the development of the atomic bomb.

Following the war, the new Atomic Energy Commission used facilities built to make the atomic bomb to produce radioisotopes for medical research and other peacetime uses. This highly publicized program provided the radioisotopes that were used in thousands of human experiments conducted in research facilities throughout the country and the world. This research, in turn, was part of a larger postwar transformation of biomedical research through the infusion of substantial government monies and technical support.

The intersection of government and biomedical research brought with it new roles and new ethical questions for medical researchers. Many of these researchers were also physicians who operated within a tradition of medical ethics that enjoined them to put the interests of their patients first. When the doctor also was a researcher, however, the potential for conflict emerged between the advancement of science and the advancement of the patient's well-being.

Other ethical issues were posed as medical researchers were called on by government officials to play new roles in the development and testing of nuclear weapons. For example, as advisers they were asked to provide human research data that could reassure officials about the effects of radiation, but as scientists they were not always convinced that human research could provide scientifically useful data. Similarly, as scientists, they came from a tradition in which research results were freely debated. In their capacity as advisers to and officials of the government, however, these researchers found that the openness of science now needed to be constrained.

None of these tensions were unique to radiation research. Radiation represents just one of several examples of the tension of the weapons potential of new scientific discoveries during and after World War II. Similarly, the tensions between clinical research and the treatment of patients were emerging throughout medical science, and were not found only in research involving radiation. Not only were these issues not unique to the 1940s and 1950s. Today society still struggles with conflicts between the openness of science and the preservation of national security, as well as with conflicts between the advancement of medical science and the rights and interests of patients.

KEY FINDINGS

Human Radiation Experiments

- Between 1944 and 1974 the federal government sponsored several thousand human radiation experiments. In the great majority of cases, the experiments were conducted to advance biomedical science; some experiments were conducted to advance national interests in defense or space exploration; and some experiments served both biomedical and defense or space exploration purposes. As noted, in the great majority of cases only fragmentary data are available.

- The majority of human radiation experiments identified by the Advisory Committee involved radioactive tracers administered in amounts that are likely to be similar to those used in research today. Most of these tracer studies involved adult subjects and are unlikely to have caused physical harm. However, in some nontherapeutic tracer studies involving children, radioisotope exposures were associated with increases in the potential lifetime risk for developing thyroid cancer that would be considered unacceptable today. The Advisory Committee also identified several studies in which patients died soon after receiving external radiation or radioisotope doses in the therapeutic range that were associated with acute radiation effects.

• Although the AEC, the Defense Department and the National Institutes of Health recognized at an early date that research should proceed only with the consent of the human subject, there is little evidence of rules or practices of consent in research with healthy subjects. It was commonplace during the 1940s and 1950s for physicians to use patients as subjects of research without their awareness or consent. By contrast, the government and its researchers focused with substantial success on the minimization of risk in the conduct of experiments, particularly with respect to research involving radioisotopes. But little attention was paid during this period to issues of fairness in the selection of subjects.

• Government officials and investigators are blameworthy for not having had policies and practices in place to protect the rights and interests of human subjects who were used in research from which the subjects could not possibly derive direct medical benefit. To the extent that there was reason to believe that research might provide a direct medical benefit to subjects, government officials and biomedical professionals are less blameworthy for not having had such protections and practices in place.

11

Intentional Releases

• During the 1944-1974 period, the government conducted several hundred intentional releases of radiation into the environment for research purposes. Generally, these releases were not conducted for the purpose of studying the effects of radiation on humans. Instead they were usually conducted to test the operation of weapons, the safety of equipment, or the dispersal of radiation into the environment.

• For those intentional releases where dose reconstructions have been undertaken, it is unlikely that members of the public were directly harmed solely as a consequence of these tests. However, these releases were conducted in secret and despite continued requests from the public that stretch back well over a decade, some information about them was made public only during the life of the Advisory Committee.

Uranium Miners

• As a consequence of exposure to radon and its daughter products in underground uranium mines, at least several hundred miners died of lung cancer and surviving miners remain at elevated risk. These men, who were the subject of government study as they mined uranium for use in weapons manufacturing, were subject to radon exposures well in excess of levels known to be hazardous. The government failed to act to require the reduction of the hazard by ventilating the mines, and it failed to adequately warn the miners of the hazard to which they were being exposed.

12

Secrecy and the Public Trust

- The greatest harm from past experiments and intentional releases may be the legacy of distrust they created. Hundreds of intentional releases took place in secret, and remained secret for decades. Important discussion of the policies to govern human experimentation also took place in secret. Information about human experiments was kept secret out of concern for embarrassment to the government, potential legal liability, and worry that public misunderstanding would jeopardize government programs.

- In a few instances, people used as experimental subjects and their families were denied the opportunity to pursue redress for possible wrongdoing because of actions taken by the government to keep the truth from them. Where programs were legitimately kept secret for national security reasons, the government often did not create or maintain adequate records, thereby preventing the public, and those most at risk, from learning the facts in a timely and complete fashion.

Contemporary Human Subjects Research

- Human research involving radioisotopes is currently subjected to more safeguards and levels of review than most other areas of research involving human subjects. There are no apparent differences between the treatment of human subjects of radiation research and human subjects of other biomedical research.

- Based on the Advisory Committee's review, it appears that much of human subjects research poses only minimal risk

13

of harm to subjects. In our review of research documents that bear on human subjects issues, we found no problems or only minor problems in most of the minimal-risk studies we examined.

- Our review of documents identified examples of complicated, higher-risk studies in which human subjects issues were carefully and adequately addressed and that included excellent consent forms. In our interview project, there was little evidence that patient-subjects felt coerced or pressured by investigators to participate in research. We interviewed patients who had declined offers to become research subjects, reinforcing the impression that there are often contexts in which potential research subjects have a genuine choice.

- At the same time, however, we also found evidence suggesting serious deficiencies in aspects of the current system for the protection of the rights and interests of human subjects. For example, consent forms do not always provide adequate information and may be misleading about the impact of research participation on people's lives. Some patients with serious illnesses appear to have unrealistic expectations about the benefits of being subjects in research.

Current Regulations on Secrecy in Human Research and Environmental Releases

- Human research can still be conducted in secret today, and under some conditions informed consent in secret research can be waived.

14

Events that raise the same concerns as the intentional releases in the Committee's charter could take place in secret today under current environmental laws.

Other Findings

The Committee's complete findings, including findings regarding experiments conducted in conjunction with atmospheric atomic testing and other population exposures, appear in chapter 17 of the Final Report.

KEY RECOMMENDATIONS

Apologies and Compensation

The government should deliver a personal, individualized apology and provide financial compensation to those subjects of human radiation experiments, or their next of kin, in cases where:

• efforts were made by the government to keep information secret from these individuals or their families, or the public, for the purpose of avoiding embarrassment or potential legal liability, and where this secrecy had the effect of denying individuals the opportunity to pursue potential grievances.

• there was no prospect of direct medical benefit to the subjects, or interventions considered controversial at the time were presented as standard practice, and physical injury attributable to the experiment resulted.

Uranium Miners

• The Interagency Working Group, together with Congress, should give serious consideration to amending the provisions of the Radiation Exposure Compensation Act of 1990 relating to uranium miners in order to provide compensation to *all* miners who develop lung cancer after some minimal duration of employment underground (such as one year), without requiring a specific level of exposure. The act should also be reviewed to determine whether the documentation standards for compensation should be liberalized.

Improved Protection for Human Subjects

- The Committee found no differences between human radiation research and other areas of research with respect to human subjects issues, either in the past or the present. In comparison to the practices and policies of the 1940s and 1950s, there have been significant advances in the federal government's system for the protection of the rights and interests of human subjects. But deficiencies remain. Efforts should be undertaken on a national scale to ensure the centrality of ethics in the conduct of scientists whose research involves human subjects.

- One problem in need of immediate attention by the government and the biomedical research community is unrealistic expectations among some patients with serious illnesses about the prospect of direct medical benefit from participating in research. Also, among the consent forms we reviewed, some appear to be overly optimistic in portraying the likely benefits of research, to inadequately explain the impact of research procedures on quality of life and personal finances, and to be incomprehensible to lay people.

- A mechanism should be established to provide for continuing interpretation and application in an open and public forum of ethics rules and principles for the conduct of human subjects research. Three examples of policy issues in need of public resolution that the Advisory Committee confronted in our work are: (1) Clarification of the meaning of minimal risk in research with healthy children; (2) regulations to cover the conduct of research with institutionalized children; and (3) guidelines for research with adults

17

of questionable competence, particularly for research in which subjects are placed at more than minimal risk but are offered no prospect of direct medical benefit.

Secrecy: Balancing National Security and the Public Trust

Current policies do not adequately safeguard against the recurrence of the kinds of events we studied that fostered distrust. The Advisory Committee concludes that there may be special circumstances in which it may be necessary to conduct human research or intentional releases in secret. However, to the extent that the government conducts such activities with elements of secrecy, special protections of the rights and interests of individuals and the public are needed.

Research involving human subjects. The Advisory Committee recommends the adoption of federal policies requiring:

- the informed consent of all human subjects of classified research. This requirement should not be subject to exemption or waiver.

- that classified research involving human subjects be permitted only after the review and approval of an independent panel of appropriate nongovernmental experts and citizen representatives, all with the necessary security clearances.

Environmental releases. There must be independent review to assure that the action is needed, that risk is minimized, and that records will be kept to assure a proper accounting to the public at the earliest date consistent with legitimate national security concerns. Specifically, the Committee recommends that:

18

- Secret environmental releases of hazardous substances should be permitted only after the review and approval of an independent panel. This panel should consist of appropriate, nongovernmental experts and citizen representatives, all with the necessary security clearances.

- An appropriate government agency, such as the Environmental Protection Agency, should maintain a program directed at the oversight of classified programs, with suitably cleared personnel.

Other Recommendations

The Committee's complete recommendations, including recommendations regarding experiments conducted in conjunction with atmospheric atomic testing and other population exposures, appear in chapter 18 of the Final Report.

WHAT'S NEXT: THE ADVISORY COMMITTEE'S LEGACY

Interagency Working Group Review

The Interagency Working Group will review our findings and recommendations and determine the next steps to be taken.

Continued Public Right To Know

The complete records assembled by the Committee are available to the public through the National Archives. Citizens wishing to know about experiments in which they, or family members, may have taken part, will have continued access to the Committee's database of 4,000 experiments, as well as the hundreds of thousands of further documents assembled by the Committee. The Final Report contains "A Citizen's Guide to the Nation's Archives: Where the Records Are and How to Find Them." This guide explains how to find federal records, how to obtain information and services from the member agencies of the Interagency Working Group and the Nuclear Regulatory Commission, how to locate personal medical records, and how to use the Advisory Committee's collection.

Supplemental volumes to the Final Report contain supporting documents and background material as well as an exhaustive index to sources and documentation. These volumes should prove useful to citizens, scholars, and others interested in pursuing the many dimensions of this history that we could not fully explore.

Advisory Committee on Human Radiation Experiments

GUIDE TO THE REPORT

The Final Report is written in an easily accessible style, but it is of necessity long. This guide provides a roadmap and capsule descriptions of each section of the report.

Preface

The Preface explains why the Committee was created, the President's charge, and the Committee's approach.

Introduction: The Atomic Century

The Introduction describes the intersection of several developments: the birth and remarkable growth of radiation science; the parallel changes in medicine and medical research; and the intersection of these changes with government programs that called on medical researchers to play important new roles beyond that involved in the traditional doctor-patient relationship. The Introduction concludes with a section titled "The Basics of Radiation Science" for the lay reader.

Part I. Ethics of Human Subjects Research: A Historical Perspective

Chapter 1. Government Standards for Human Experiments: The 1940s and 1950s

In chapter 1 we report what we have been able to reconstruct about government rules and policies in the 1940s and 1950s regarding human experiments. We focus primarily on the Atomic Energy Commission and the Department of Defense, because their history with respect to human subjects research policy is less well known than that of the Department of Health, Education and Welfare (now the Department of Health and

Human Services). Drawing on records that were previously obscure, or only recently declassified, we reveal the perhaps surprising finding that officials and experts in the highest reaches of the AEC and DOD discussed requirements for human experiments in the first years of the Cold War. We also briefly discuss the research policies of DHEW and the Veterans Administration during these years.

Chapter 2. Postwar Professional Standards and Practices for Human Experiments

In chapter 2 we turn from a consideration of government standards to an exploration of the norms and practices of physicians and medical scientists who conducted research with human subjects during this period. We include here an analysis of the significance of the Nuremberg Code, which arose out of the international war crimes trial of German physicians in 1947. Using the results of our Ethics Oral History Project, and other sources, we also examine how scientists of the time viewed their moral responsibilities to human subjects as well as how this translated into the manner in which they conducted their research. Of particular interest are the differences in professional norms and practices between research in which patients are used as subjects and research involving so-called healthy volunteers.

Chapter 3. Government Standards for Human Experiments: The 1960s and 1970s

In chapter 3 we return to the question of government standards, focusing now on the 1960s and 1970s. In the first part of this chapter, we review the well-documented developments that influenced and led up to two landmark events in the history

of government policy on research involving human subjects: the promulgation by DHEW of comprehensive regulations for oversight of human subjects research and passage by Congress of the National Research Act. In the latter part of the chapter we review developments and policies governing human research in agencies other than DHEW, a history that has received comparatively little scholarly attention. We also discuss scandals in human research conducted by the DOD and the CIA that came to light in the 1970s and that influenced subsequent agency policies.

Chapter 4. Ethics Standards in Retrospect

With the historical context established in chapters 1 through 3, we turn in chapter 4 to the core of our charge. Here we put forward and defend three kinds of ethical standards for evaluating human radiation experiments conducted from 1944 to 1974. These are (1) basic ethical principles that are widely accepted and generally regarded as so fundamental as to be applicable to the past as well as the present; (2) the policies of government departments and agencies at the time; and (3) rules of professional ethics that were widely accepted at the time. We embed these standards in a moral framework intended to clarify and facilitate the difficult task of making judgments about the past.

Part II. Case Studies

Chapter 5. Experiments with Plutonium, Uranium, and Polonium

In chapter 5, we look at the Manhattan Project plutonium-injection experiments and related experimentation. Sick patients were used in sometimes secret experimentation to develop data needed to protect the health and safety of nuclear weapons workers. The experiments raise questions of the use of sick patients for purposes that are not of benefit to them, the role of national security in permitting conduct that might not otherwise be justified, and the use of secrecy for the purpose of protecting the government from embarrassment and potential liability.

Chapter 6. The AEC Program of Radioisotope Distribution

In contrast to the plutonium injections, the vast majority of human radiation experiments were not conducted in secret. Indeed, the use of radioisotopes in biomedical research was publicly and actively promoted by the Atomic Energy Commission. Among the several thousand experiments about which little information is currently available, most fall into this category. The Committee adopted a two-pronged strategy to study this phenomenon. In chapter 6, we describe the system the AEC developed for the distribution of isotopes to be used in human research. This system was the primary provider of the source material for human experimentation in the postwar period. In studying the operation of the radioisotope distribution system, and the related "human use" committees at local institutions, we sought to learn the ground rules that governed the conduct of the majority of human radiation experiments, most of which have received little or no public attention. Also

in this chapter we review how research with radioisotopes has contributed to advances in medicine.

Chapter 7. Nontherapeutic Research on Children

The Committee then selected for particular consideration, in chapter 7, radioisotope research that used children as subjects. We determined to focus on children for several reasons. First, at low levels of radiation exposure, children are at greater risk of harm than adults. Second, children were the most appropriate group in which to pursue the Committee's mandate with respect to notification of former subjects for medical reasons. They are the group most likely to have been harmed by their participation in research, and they are more likely than other former subjects still to be alive. Third, when the Committee considered how best to study subject populations that were most likely to be exploited because of their relative dependency or powerlessness, children were the only subjects who could readily be identified in the meager documentation available. By contrast, characteristics such as gender, ethnicity, and social class were rarely noted in research reports of the day.

Chapter 8. Total-Body Irradiation: Problems When Research and Treatment are Intertwined

Moving from case studies focused on the injection or ingestion of radioisotopes, chapter 8 shifts to experimentation in which sick patients were subjected to externally administered total-body irradiation (TBI). The Committee discovered that the highly publicized TBI experiments conducted at the University of Cincinnati were only the last of a series in which the government sought to use data from patients undergoing TBI treatment to gain information for nuclear weapons development and use.

This experimentation spanned the period from World War II to the early 1970s, during which the ethics of experimentation became increasingly subject to public debate and government regulation. In contrast with the experiments that flowed from the AEC's radioisotope program, the use of external radiation such as TBI did not in its earlier years involve a government requirement of prior review for risk. The TBI experimentation raises basic questions about the responsibility of the government when it seeks to gather research data in conjunction with medical interventions of debatable benefit to sick patients.

Chapter 9. Prisoners: A Captive Research Population

In chapter 9 we examine experimentation on healthy subjects, specifically prisoners, for the purpose of learning the effects of external irradiation on the testes, such as might be experienced by astronauts in space. The prisoner experiments were studied because they received significant public attention and because a literally captive population was chosen to bear risks to which no other group of experimental subjects had been exposed or has been exposed since. This research took place during a period in which the once commonly accepted practice of nontherapeutic experimentation on prisoners was increasingly subject to public criticism and moral outrage.

Chapter 10. Atomic Veterans: Human Experimentation in Connection with Bomb Tests

Chapter 10 also explores research involving healthy subjects: human experimentation conducted in connection with atomic bomb tests. More than 200,000 service personnel--now known as atomic veterans--participated at atomic bomb test sites,

mostly for training and test-management purposes. A small number also were used as subjects of experimentation. The Committee heard from many atomic veterans and their family members who were concerned about both the long-term health effects of these exposures and the government's conduct. In seeking to reconstruct the story of human experimentation in connection with bomb tests, we found need and opportunity to examine the meaning of human experimentation in an occupational setting where risk is the norm.

Chapter 11. Intentional Releases: Lifting the Veil of Secrecy

In chapter 11 we address the thirteen intentional releases of radiation into the environment specified in the Committee's charter, as well as additional releases identified during the life of the Committee. In contrast with biomedical experimentation, individuals and communities were not typically the subject of study in these intentional releases. The secret releases were to test intelligence equipment, the potential of radiological warfare, and the mechanism of the atomic bomb. While the risk posed by intentional releases was relatively small, the releases often took place in secret and remained secret for years.

Chapter 12. Observational Data Gathering

The final case study, in chapter 12, looks at two groups that were put at risk by nuclear weapons development and testing programs and as a consequence became the subjects of observational research: workers who mined uranium for the Atomic Energy Commission in the western United States from the 1940s to 1960s and residents of the Marshall Islands, whose Pacific homeland was irradiated as a consequence of a hydrogen bomb test in 1954. While these observational studies do not fit the classic definition of an experiment, in which the investigator controls the variable under study (in this case radiation exposure), they are instances of research involving human subjects. The Committee elected to examine the experiences of the uranium miners and the Marshallese because they raise important issues in the ethics of human research not illustrated in the previous case studies and because numerous public witnesses impressed on the Committee the significance of the lessons to be learned from their histories.

Chapter 13. Secrecy, Human Radiation Experiments, and Intentional Releases

Part II concludes with an exploration of an important theme common to many of the case studies--openness and secrecy in the government's conduct concerning human radiation research and intentional releases. In chapter 13 we step back and look at what rules governed what the public was told about the topics under the Committee's purview, whether these rules were publicly known, and whether they were followed.

Part III. Contemporary Projects

Chapter 14. Current Federal Policies Governing Human Subjects Research

Chapter 14 reviews the current regulatory structure for human subjects research conducted or supported by federal departments and agencies, a structure that has been in place since 1991. This "Common Rule" has its roots in the human subject protection regulations promulgated by DHEW in 1974. The historical developments behind these regulations are described in chapter 3. Following a summary of the essential features of

the Common Rule, chapter 14 discusses several subjects of particular relevance to the Advisory Committee's work, such as special review processes for ionizing radiation research, protection for human subjects in classified research, and audit procedures of institutions performing human subjects research.

Chapter 15. Research Proposal Review Project

Chapter 15 describes the Research Proposal Review Project (RPRP), the Advisory Committee's examination of documents from research projects conducted at institutions throughout the country, including both radiation and nonradiation proposals. Documents utilized in the RPRP were those available to the local institutional review boards (IRBs) at the institutions where the research was conducted. The goals of the RPRP were to gain an understanding of the ethics of radiation research as compared with nonradiation research; how well research proposals address central ethical considerations such as risk, voluntariness, and subject selection; and whether informed consent procedures seem to be appropriate.

Chapter 16. Subject Interview Study

The RPRP discussed in chapter 15 reviewed documents prepared by investigators and institutions and submitted in IRB applications. This study was complemented by a nationwide effort to learn about research from the perspective of patients themselves, including those who were and were not research subjects. The Subject Interview Study (SIS), described in chapter 16, was conducted through interviews with nearly 1,900 patients throughout the country. The SIS aimed to learn the perspectives of former, current, and prospective research subjects by asking about their attitudes and beliefs regarding the endeavor of human subject research generally and their participation specifically.

Discussion of Part III

The RPRP tried to understand the experience of human subjects research from the standpoint of the local oversight process, while the SIS tried to understand it from the standpoint of the participant. Although the two studies related to different research projects and different groups of patients and subjects, some common tensions in the human research experience emerge in both projects, and they are described in the "Discussion" section of part III. For example, it has long been recognized that the physician who engages in research with patient-subjects assumes two roles that could conflict: that of the caregiver and that of the researcher. The goals inherent in each role are different: direct benefit of the individual patient in the first case and the acquisition of general medical knowledge in the second case. The interviews with SIS participants suggest that at least some patient-subjects are not aware of this distinction or of the potential for conflict. In our review of documents in the RPRP we found that the written information provided to potential patient-subjects sometimes obscured, rather than highlighted, the differences between research and medical care and thus likely contributed to the potential for patients to confuse the two.

Part IV. Coming to Terms with the Past, Looking Ahead to the Future: Findings and Recommendations

Chapter 17. Findings

In chapter 17, our findings are presented in two parts, first for the period 1944 through 1974 and then for the contemporary period. These parts, in turn, are divided into findings regarding biomedical experiments and those regarding population exposures.

We begin our presentation of findings for the period 1944 through 1974 with a summation of what we have learned about human radiation experiments: their number and purpose, the likelihood that they produced harm, and how human radiation experimentation contributed to advances in medicine. We then summarize what we have found concerning the nature of federal rules and policies governing research involving human subjects during this period, and the implementation of these rules in the conduct of human radiation experiments. Findings about the nature and implementation of federal rules cover issues of consent, risk, the selection of subjects, and the role of national security considerations.

Our findings about government rules are followed by a finding on the norms and practices of physicians and other biomedical scientists for the use of human subjects. We then turn to the Committee's finding on the evaluation of past experiments, in which we summarize the moral framework adopted by the Committee for this purpose. Next, we present our findings for experiments conducted in conjunction with atmospheric atomic testing, intentional releases, and other population exposures. The remaining findings for the contemporary period address issues of government secrecy and record keeping.

Our findings for the contemporary period summarize what we have learned about the rules and practices that currently govern the conduct of radiation research involving human subjects, as well as human research generally, and about the status of government regulations regarding intentional releases.

Chapter 18. Recommendations

Chapter 18 presents the Committee's recommendations to the Human Radiation Interagency Working Group and to the American people. The Committee's inquiry focused on research conducted by the government to serve the public good--the promotion and protection of national security and the advancement of science and medicine. The pursuit of these ends--today, as well as yesterday--inevitably means that some individuals are put at risk for the benefit of the greater good. The past shows us that research can bear fruits of incalculable value. Unfortunately, however, the government's conduct with respect to some research performed in the past has left a legacy of distrust. Actions must be taken to ensure that, in the future, the ends of national security and the advancement of medicine will proceed only through means that safeguard the dignity, health, and safety of the individuals and groups who may be put at risk in the process.

Many of our recommendations are directed not to the past but toward the future. The Committee calls for changes in the current federal system for the protection of the rights and interests of human subjects. These include changes in institutional review boards; in the interpretation of ethics rules and

policies; in the conduct of research involving military personnel as subjects; in oversight, accountability, and sanctions for ethics violations; and in compensation for research injuries. Unlike the 1944-1974 period, in which the Committee focused primarily on research that offered subjects no prospect of medical benefit, our recommendations for the future emphasize protections for patients who are subjects of therapeutic research, as many of the contemporary issues involving research with human subjects occur in this setting. We also call for the adoption of special protections for the conduct of human research or environmental releases in secret, protections that are not currently in place.

We realize, however, that regulations and policies are no guarantee of ethical conduct. If the events of the past are not to be repeated, it is essential that the research community come to increasingly value the ethics of research involving human subjects as central to the scientific enterprise. We harbor no illusions about the Pollyanna-ish quality of a recommendation for professional education in research ethics; we call for much more. We ask that the biomedical research community, together with the government, cause a transformation in commitment to the ethics of human research. We recognize and celebrate the progress that has occurred in the past fifty years. We recognize and honor the commitment to research ethics that currently exists among many biomedical scientists and many institutional review boards. But more needs to be done. The scientists of the future must have a clear understanding of their duties to human subjects and a clear expectation that the leaders of their fields value good ethics as much as they do good science. At stake is not only the well-being of future subjects, but also, at least in part, the future of biomedical science. To the extent that that future depends on public support, it requires the public's trust.

There can be no better guarantor of that trust than the ethics of the research community.

Finally, our examination of the history of the past half century has helped us understand that the revision of regulations that govern human research, the creation of new oversight mechanisms, and even a scrupulous professional ethics are necessary, but are not sufficient, means to needed reform. Of at least equal import is the development of a more common understanding *among the public* of research involving human subjects, its purposes, and its limitations. Furthermore, if the conduct of the government and of the professional community is to be improved, that conduct must be available for scrutiny by the American people so that they can make more informed decisions about the protection and promotion of their own health and that of the members of their family. It is toward that end that we close our report with recommendations for continued openness in government and in biomedical research. It is also toward that end and that this report is dedicated. Some of what is regrettable about the past happened, at least in part, because we as citizens let it happen. Let the lessons of history remind us all that the best safeguard for the future is an informed and active citizenry.

36

A P P E N D I X   A

PART 6

Bibliography Submitted
to the Advisory Committee
as Part of Public Record

This bibliography has been taken from testimony submitted by Collin Ross, MD, as part of the testimony submitted by Valerie Wolf to the Advisory Committee on Human Radiation Experiments. Please note that the author has not read or researched this material, with the exception of books by Robert Jay Lifton, but chose to include it for those who wish to read further on this subject.

Bibliography

Books on CIA Mind Control

William Bowart. *Operation Mind Control*. New York: W.W. Norton, 1978.

Anne Collins. *In The Sleep Room. The Story of CIA Brainwashing Experiments in Canada*. Toronto: Lester & Orpen Dennys, 1988.

Donald Bain. *The Control of Candy Jones*. Chicago: Playboy Press, 1976.

Don Gillmoor. *I Swear By Apollo*. Dr. Ewen Cameron and the CIA Brainwashing Experiments. Montreal: Eden Press, 1987.

Martin Lee and Bruce Shlain. *Acid Dreams. The Complete Social History of LSD: The CIA, the Sixties, and Beyond*. New York: Grove Weidenfeld, 1992.

John Marks. *The Search For the Manchurian Candidate*. New York: W.W. Norton, 1988.

Gordon Thomas. *Journey Into Madness. The True Story of Secret CIA Mind Control and Medical Abuse*. New York: Bantam, 1989.

Harvey Weinstein. *Psychiatry and the CIA: Victims of Mind Control*. Washington, DC: American Psychiatric Press, 1990.

Articles

Harold Abramson. *The Use of LSD in Psychotherapy. Transactions of a Conference on d-Lysergic Acid Diethylamide (LSD-25), April 22, 23 and 24, 1959, Princeton, N.J.* New York: Josiah Macy, Jr. Foundation, 1960.

Harold Abramson. *The Use of LSD in Psychotherapy and Alcoholism*. Indianapolis: Bobbs-Merrill Company, 1967.

G.H. Estabrooks. Hypnosis comes of age. *Science Digest*, April, 1971, 44-50.

Alan Sheflin. Freedom of the mind as an international human rights issue. *Human Rights Law Journal*, Volume 3, Number 1-4, 3-63, 1982.

Senate Hearings

Quality of Health Care - Human Experimentation, 1973. Hearings Before the Subcommittee on Health of the Committee on Labor and Public Welfare, United States Senate, Ninety-Third Congress, First Session.

Biomedical and Behavioral Research, 1975. Joint Hearings Before the Subcommittee on Labor and Public Welfare and the Subcommittee on Administratve Practice and Procedure of the Committee on the Judiciary, United States Senate, Ninety-Fourth Congress, First Session on Human-Use Experimentation Programs of the Department of Defense and Central Intelligence Agency.

Human Drug Testing by the CIA, 1977. Hearings before the Subcommittee on Health and Scientific Research of the Committee on Human Resources, United States Senate, Ninety-Fourth Congress, First Session.

Project MKULTRA, The CIA's Program of Research in Behavioral Modification. Hearings Before the Select Committee on Intelligence, and Subcommittee on Health and Scientific Research of the Committee on Human Resources, United States Senate, Ninety-Fourth Congress, Second Session, 1977.

Other Books

James Bamford. *The Puzzle Palace. Inside the National Security Agency, America's Most Secret Intelligence Organization.* New York: Penguin Books, 1982.

Tom Bower. *The Paperclip Conspiracy. The Hunt for the Nazi Scientists.* Boston: Little, Brown and Company, 1987.

Stephan L. Chorover. *From Genesis to Genocide. The Meaning of Human Nature and the Power of Behavioral Control.* Cambridge: The MIT Press, 1979.

G.H. Estabrooks. *Hypnotism.* New York: E.P. Dutton, 1943.

Howard Frazier. *Uncloaking the CIA.* New York: The Free Press, 1975.

William M. Gaylin, Joel S. Meister, and Robert C. Neville. *Operating on the Mind. The Psychosurgery Conflict.* New York: Basic Books, 1975.

Linda Hunt. *Secret Agenda. The United States Government, Nazi Scientists, and Project Paperclip, 1945 to 1990.* New York: St. Martin's Press, 1991.

Rhondri Jeffreys-Jones. *The CIA and American Democracy.* New York: Yale University Press, 1989.

Ronald Kessler. *Inside the CIA. Revealing the Secrets of the World's Most Powerful Spy Agency.* New York: Pocket Books, 1992.

Mark Lane. *Plausible Denial. Was the CIA Involved in the Assassination of JFK?* New York: Thunder's Mouth Press, 1991.

Walter C. Langer. *The Mind of Adolph Hitler. The Secret Wartime Report.* New York: New American Library, 1972.

Lincoln Lawrence. *Were we controlled?* New York: University Books, 1967.

Robert J. Lifton. *Thought Reform and the Psychology of Totalism: A Study of "Brainwashing" in China.* New York: W.W. Norton, 1961.

Robert Jay Lifton. *The Nazi Doctors. Medical Killing and the Psychology of Genocide.* New York: Basic Books, 1986.

Michael Meiers. *Was Jonestown a CIA Medical Experiment?* Lewiston: Edwin Mellen Press, 1988.

Fletcher Prouty. *JFK. The CIA, Vietnam, and the Plot to Assassinate John F. Kennedy.* New York: Birch Lane Press, 1992.

Nelson Rockefeller. *The Nelson Rockefeller Report to the President by the Commission on CIA Activities.* New York: Manor Books, 1975.

Christopher Simpson. *The Splendid Blonde Beast. Money, Law, and Genocide in the Twentieth Century.* New York: Grove Press, 1993.

Christopher Simpson. *Blowback. The First Full Account of America's Recruitment of Nazis, and Its Disastrous Effect on Our Domestic and Foreign Policy.* New York: Weidenfeld & Nicholson, 1988.

Richard Harris Smith. *OSS. The Secret History of America's First Central Intelligence Agency.* Berkeley: University of California Press, 1972.

Russell Jack Smith. *The Unknown CIA. My Three Decades With the Agency.* New York: Berkeley Books, 1989.

William Turner and Jonn Christian. *The Assassination of Robert F. Kennedy. The Conspiracy and the Coverup.* New York: Thunder's Mouth Press, 1993.

Dougls Valentine. *The Phoenix Program.* New York: Avon Books, 1990.

Jonathan Vankin. *Conspiracies, Crimes, and Coverups. Political Manipulation and Mind Control in America.* New York: Paragon House, 1991.

Ernest Volkman and Blaine Baggett. *Secret Intelligence. The Inside Story of America's Espionage Empire*. New York: Berkeley Books, 1989.

Alan J. Weberman and Michael Canfield. *Coup D'Etat in America. The CIA and the Assassination of John F. Kennedy*. San Francisco: Quick American Archives, 1992.

Denise Winn. *The Manipulated Mind*. London: The Octagon Press, 1983.

Movies

Altered States

Closetland

Heaven and Earth

Jacob's Ladder

La Femme Nikita

Lawnmower Man

The Manchurian Candidate

Point of No Return

A P P E N D I X   B

Exercises for Healing and Awakening Higher Consciousness

These are some of the gifts that came in the form of self-help tools during my journey. They are not intended to replace therapy. I found that once I reached a certain level of healing, my frequencies were enhanced and meditation and breathing became easier. I hope you find these helpful. I have kept the instructions simple on purpose. There is so much help available now—you know the old phrase, "Seek and you shall find." These are just a few suggestions; seek out the ones that resonate with you. Always consult your intuition as you work. If it feels right for you, proceed. No one carries an external key or secret to your healing and awakening. The path is different for everyone. Explore your path, your unique journey. Good luck, and remember to laugh a lot, have fun and take the time to enjoy the beauty of life, for that is the best medicine. May your journey bring you many blessings.

All of the exercises are best done by first centering your energy, taking some deep cleansing breaths and meditating. The exercises will be more effective when you are centered and relaxed.

1. Breathing Technique to Integrate Past, Present and Future

My housemate contributed this breathing exercise. She received it in a meditation. I use it to balance my energy, for protection and to integrate past, present and future.

During each inhale and exhale you will be silently saying from your heart center: "Kodoish, Kodoish, Kodoish, Adonai' Tsebayoth (Holy, Holy, Holy is the Lord God of Hosts)!" According to the book, *The Book of Knowledge: The Keys of Enoch*, the Ophanim messengers, the angelic orders of light and the elders of light sing the above praise before His throne of light. It is one of the highest protection prayers you can use. This is a mantra where the breath-giving capacity of the subject is wholly divine, absorbed in the person of the life-giving Lord.

It is important to say the above words in their ancient Hebrew tongue because they faithfully connect with the masters who are still administering wisdom to this program of intelligence. These are sounds of light, used in laying the foundation of the present program. These energy words are to be used to code your body directly into the light. They also provide the sound vibrations of greeting and protection in working with the Brotherhoods of Light and the Spiritual Hierarchy. To place these ancient energy words into English, modern Indo-European languages or some other language, would deprive consciousness of a direct experience with the power of the sacred language. Transposing these words would cause them to lose their energy pulse, which is similar to the symphonic song of a musical masterpiece transposed out of its original key into a strange cacophony. Therefore, the keys work through the vibrations of light and use these sacred expressions for the unfolding of the seals and the direct experience of God's higher mysteries.

I had to call a local Jewish synagogue to receive the correct pronunciation of the above mantra. I would advise everyone to do the same since these are sound and light frequencies and vibrations, and it is important for them to be spoken correctly.

Breathing Exercise

Sit and center yourself by taking a few deep breaths. When you are ready to begin, be conscious of opening your chakra/energy centers. During each inhalation you will bring the universal light energy down from above and into the crown of your head.

Step 1: Inhale and silently say from your heart center the mantra, "Kodoish, Kodoish, Kodoish, Adonai' Tsebayoth," bringing your breath down to your tailbone. Exhale from your tailbone, visualizing and allowing your breath to circle up behind you, going back to the crown of your head, while silently saying from your heart, "Kodoish, Kodoish, Kodoish, Adonai' Tsebayoth."

Step 2: Inhale again as above, saying the mantra from your heart, only this time take the breath down to your sexual center. Exhale from your sexual center while visualizing and allowing your breath to circle up in front of you, going back to the crown of your head, while repeating the mantra.

Step 3: Inhale again as above, saying the mantra and bringing your breath down to your sexual center. Exhale from your sexual center while visualizing and allowing your breath to go straight down into the core of Mother Earth.

Continue to repeat the above three steps a minimum of four times.

As you exhale and bring your breath around your back and then inhale again, you are integrating the past with the present. Once you exhale and bring your breath around to the front and then inhale again, you are integrating the future with the present. Upon your exhale into the core of Mother Earth, you are anchoring the light of past, present and future. In the beginning, you may find the technique to be a little slow; however, as you continue to do the breathing, it will become very smooth and easy. Imagine that you are working with the infinity symbol.

2. Maya Yoga

This exercise is done by breathing in through your nose and out through your mouth. It is useful for grounding and opening communication up to the higher realms.

Imagine that you extend your energy with your breath to the center of creation. Now, breathing in, visualize yourself drawing the power of creation in with your in-breath through your crown chakra (the top of your head) and down your spine, and while still on the in-breath, anchor it in the crystal core of Mother Earth. Then, as you exhale, send the energy back from the center of the Earth to the heart of creation.

3. Chanting

Chant using alternate *NNNN* sounds, placing your tongue on the roof of your mouth until you feel a vibration in your brain. An example is:

nnnaaaaannnaaaaaaaa, ommmmmmmm,
maaaaaaaaaaaaaa, nnnnnnnnnnnneeeeeeeeeeeee.

4. Relaxation Exercise

Sit in a comfortable position and relax. Visualize your hands floating as if attached to helium balloons. If you have any tension in your arms, consciously relax them until you feel they are floating. Visualize a ball of light floating between your hands. Tighten your right hand while you leave your left hand floating. Bring your right hand up to your right side while your left hand floats. If you feel tension in your left hand, focus until you relax it. Attempt to tighten the entire right side of your body while the left remains relaxed. Then allow the right hand to return to the floating position and reverse the process with the left tight and the right relaxed. Repeat the process several times. This exercise is very powerful to balance the right and left hemispheres of the brain.

5. Exercises for Protection

Psychic protection is very important. It is an act of empowerment and setting boundaries. I learned that my home was more peaceful and felt better when I did these things. As time passed, I learned to establish boundaries on a routine basis. Also, as my energy changed to a higher frequency because I did not have inner fear, I found that I no longer attracted negative energy. It is very challenging at first. When you become aware of negative energy, it can be frightening. But as you make the journey from fear to freedom, the process of protecting your energy space becomes easier. You may develop your own special techniques.

a. Visualize mirrors that reflect negativity back to the sender, and allow positive energy to enter and surround you.

b. Place yourself in a bubble of blue-green energy and cover it with the light of Christ. State that only things for the higher good can enter the energy field.

c. See yourself in the care of Jesus Christ. See him placing his hand over you to protect you.

d. Visualize yourself with Archangel Michael. Ask him to give you the sword of truth to slice away negativity and dispel illusion.

e. If you are receiving programmed messages, imagine them as coming from a radio. Visualize yourself plugging the cord into the Earth, and ask the Earth to transmute the negative messages.

f. Invoke the sapphire blue ray above, below and in all dimensions. Just say it and set the intent, and you will be protected.

g. To dispel illusion sent by negative forces, state that anything that is not in the light of Jesus Christ must leave, and it must.

h. Bless your house with olive oil you have prayed over. Place an infinity sign over the doors and windows saying that you place the Seal of Kabetza on your home.

i. Put a ring of sea salt around your home

j. Using sage to clear energy fields is important. Native Americans use sage; you can buy it at health food stores and metaphysical book-stores. Light one end and wave it around, using the smoke to smudge yourself and your home.

k. Call upon Archangel Michael and Archangel Gabriel for protection.

l. Open your doors and windows and clear your house with a feather or just your hands. Make sweeping motions and state that anything that is not for your higher good must leave your home. Then fill your home with the light of Christ.

Remember, Christ said that if you send one demon from your home, he will return with seven more, so continue to be vigilant. The fact is, you are only as safe as you feel. If you are deeply convinced that the negative forces have power over you, they do. Once you gain empowerment and feel protected, you are not as vulnerable to attack. However, there is a lot of negativity in the world, so it is wise to be lovingly protective of your energy field, your home and loved ones. It is possible to be free from the forces that have controlled our planet in fear; it is a journey, not an act of magic. The journey requires a change in your belief systems, an enhancement of your energy fields from a fear vibration to a love vibration and a great deal of willingness to face your inner shadow.

A P P E N D I X   C

Author's Bibliography

Bass, Ellen. *The Courage to Heal: A Guide for Women Survivors of Child Sexual Abuse.* New York: HarperPerennial, 1994.

Beattie, Melody. *Codependent No More: How to Stop Controlling Others and Start Caring for Yourself.* New York: Harper & Row, 1987.

Black Elk. *Black Elk Speaks: Being the Life Story of a Holy Man of the Oglala Sioux.* As told through John G. Neihardt. Lincoln: University of Nebraska Press, 1979.

Braden, Gregg. *Awakening to Zero Point: The Collective Initiation.* Bellevue, WA: Radio Bookstore Press, 1997.

Buscaglia, Leo F. *Living, Loving and Learning.* Edited by Steven Short. New York: Fawcett Columbine, 1982.

Campbell, Joseph. *The Power of Myth.* With Bill Moyers. New York: Doubleday, 1988.

Cohen, Alan. *The Dragon Doesn't Live Here Anymore.* Farmingdale, NY: Coleman Publishing, 1981.

Hanh, Thich Nhat, and others. *For a Future To Be Possible: Commentaries on the Five Wonderful Precepts.* Berkeley, CA: Parallax Press, 1993.

Hassrick, Royal B. *The Sioux: Life and Customs of a Warrior Society.* In collaboration with Dorothy Maxwell and Cile M. Bach. Norman: University of Oklahoma Press, 1964.

Hurtak, J.J. *The Book of Knowledge: The Keys of Enoch.* Los Gatos, CA: Academy for Future Science, 1977.

Icke, David. *And the Truth Shall Set You Free.* Isle of Wight, UK: Bridge of Love Publications, 1998.

Icke, David, et al. *I Am Me I Am Free: The Robots' Guide to Freedom.* Isle of Wight, UK: Bridge of Love Publications, 1996.

Knowlton, Judith M. *Higher Powered: A Ninety Day Guide to Serenity and Self-Esteem.* Edited by Rebecca D. Chaitin. Photographs by Gayle Burns. New York: Continuum, 1991.

Lifton, Robert Jay. *The Nazi Doctors: Medical Killing and the Psychology of Genocide.* New York: Basic Books, 1988.

Miller, Alice. *For Your Own Good: Hidden Cruelty in Child-Rearing and the Roots of Violence.* Translated by Hildegarde and Hunter Hannum. New York: Farrar, Straus, Giroux, 1984.

O'Brien, Kathy. *Trance: Formation of America.* With Mark Phillips. Las Vegas: Reality Marketing, Inc., 1995.

Oksana, Chrystine. *Safe Passage to Healing: A Guide to Survivors of Ritual Abuse.* New York: HarperPerennial Library, 1994.

Peck, M. Scott. *People of the Lie: The Hope for Healing Human Evil.* New York: Simon and Schuster, 1983.

Redfield, James. *The Celestine Prophecy: An Experiential Guide.* New York: Warner Books, 1995.

Schaef, Anne Wilson. *When Society Becomes an Addict.* New York: Harper & Row, 1987.

Sitchin, Zecharia. *The 12th Planet.* New York: Avon Books, 1978.

Weiss, Brian L. *Through Time into Healing.* New York: Simon & Schuster, 1992.

Whitworth, Eugene E. *Nine Faces of Christ: Quest of the True Initiate.* Marina del Ray, CA: DeVorss and Company, 1994.

About the Cover Art

"No," replied the publisher, her voice crisply decisive as it came through the telephone. "I don't like that idea at all. The image of an angel carrying a child out of darkness would send the message that Judy did nothing to help herself. The truth is that Judith Moore is one of the strongest, most courageous women I know, so you'll just have to come up with another concept for the cover art for her book."

The new picture came to me even before I hung up the phone. The publisher's explanation had brought to mind some wise advice I had once received: If someone is calling for help from the bottom of a deep, dark hole, it's okay to drop a rope or a ladder to them so that they can climb up out of the blackness. It's *not* a good thing to go down into the hole with them, or to deplete your own personal power trying to pull them out. After all, healing is only authentic when we finally rescue ourselves.

Having crawled out of a few abysses myself, I found it no problem to visualize Judy Moore as she had made her way out of her own private hell. The lower portion of the cover depicts fiery darkness, filled with numerous beings expressing various emotions. Looking at them, one is unsure whether they have helped or hindered Judy's journey into the light. The denizens of the dark are indistinct and undefined, controlled by nebulous, free-floating fears about changing their personal realities. Not until Judy had resolved to do exactly that was she able to separate from the masses and be perceived, on every level, as a unique and actualized individual.

I chose to paint Judy wearing blue jeans, the traditional American work uniform. Her shirt is turquoise, symbolizing healing, truth and protection. The sleeves are rolled to her elbows, because changing one's life is hard work. Her feet are bare, showing her willingness to be vulnerable while on her spiritual journey. Judy's right hand, the masculine *doing* hand, is on the top rung of the ladder. *She will succeed in entering her new world!*

The garden is lushly abundant, filled with fruits ready to be harvested. There are flowers of every color. Rays of light stream down from above, separating into five strands. The light is the hand of the divine, the gift of consciousness that is always within our reach.

An angel with a flute hovers nearby, playing the song of love and freedom that Judy has always heard. The angel is actually Judy's higher self, with whom she is now consciously reuniting. It is readily apparent that there is more than one path in this garden of self to which Judy is returning; however, they all have at least one thing in common: No matter which one she chooses to travel next, it will be filled with heartfelt light and love and the desire to share her inspiring experiences with others. May we all be as blessed with strength of soul as is Judith Moore.

Namasté,

Rush Cole